THE FICTION OF GEOPOLITICS

The Fiction of Geopolitics

*Afterimages of Culture,
from Wilkie Collins to Alfred Hitchcock*

Christopher GoGwilt

*Stanford University Press
Stanford, California*
2000

Stanford University Press
Stanford, California

© 2000 by the Board of Trustees of the
Leland Stanford Junior University

Printed in the United States of America

Library of Congress Cataloging-in-Publication Data
GoGwilt, Christopher Lloyd.
   The fiction of geopolitics : afterimages of culture, from Wilkie Collins to Alfred Hitchcock / Christopher GoGwilt.
      p.   cm.
   Includes bibliographical references (p.   ) and index.
   ISBN 0-8047-3726-6 (alk. paper)—ISBN 0-8047-3731-2 (pbk. : alk. paper)
   1. Political fiction, English—History and criticism. 2. Politics and literature—Great Britain—History—19th century. 3. Politics and literature—Great Britain—History—20th century. 4. Cunninghame Graham, R. B. (Robert Bontine), 1852–1936—Political and social views. 5. Schreiner, Olive, 1855–1920—Political and social views. 6. Conrad, Joseph, 1857–1924. Secret agent. 7. Collins, Wilkie, 1824–1889. Moonstone. 8. World politics in literature. 9. Imperialism in literature. 10. Anarchism in literature. 11. Utopias in literature.   I. Title.

PR878.P6 G64 2000
823.009′358—dc21   00-055704

∞ This book is printed on acid-free, archival quality paper.

Original printing 2000
Last figure below indicates year of this printing:
09   08   07   06   05   04   03   02   01   00
Typeset by Robert C. Ehle in 11/14 Minion.

Part-opening illustration: Frantisek Kupka, "L'Homme est la nature prenant conscience d'elle même." Illustration from Reclus, *L'Homme et la Terre*, Vol. 1. Courtesy of the Harvard College Library.

*For my parents, George and Ann D. Gwilt
and for my grandmother, Marjory Gwilt*

Contents

Illustrations ix
Acknowledgments xi
Introduction 1

Part I. A Genealogy of Geopolitics

CHAPTER 1. The Geopolitical Image: Anarchism, Imperialism, and the Hypothesis of Culture in the Formation of Geopolitics 17

H. J. Mackinder, the Hypothesis of Culture, and the Formation of Geopolitics 20
Mackinder's Geopolitical Image of Britain 28
Ratzel's Anthropogeographical Image of Humankind 36
Reclus's Social Geography, the Image of the State, and the Hegemony of Europe 43
Imaginary Institutions of Geography 51

Part II. Culture and Nihilism: Prefiguring Geopolitics

CHAPTER 2. The Victorian Blot: Wilkie Collins, *The Moonstone*, and the Concept of Culture 57

The Plot of The Moonstone: *"The blot of the Diamond"* 60
Framing the Plot: Critical Perspectives on Imperialism 67
The Blot of Victorian Subjectivity: "On the unanswerable evidence of the paint-stain" 71
Victorian Cultural Capital and the Formalizing of Empire, 1858–1876 79

CHAPTER 3. Victorian Nihilism: Friedrich Nietzsche and Olive Schreiner   86

    Friedrich Nietzsche's "Sisters"   90

    Olive Schreiner's "Strangers"   106

    Aesthetic Form, European Nihilism, and Pathologies of Power   119

Part III. Utopia and Sabotage: Contesting Geopolitics

CHAPTER 4. Broadcasting News from Nowhere: Utopian Narrative and the Sketch-Artistry of R. B. Cunninghame Graham   127

    Afterimages of R. B. Cunninghame Graham   129

    The News of "Bloody Sunday": Lessons in Working-Class Consciousness   135

    News from Overseas: The Ipané *and Edward Garnett's Overseas Library*   141

    News of Death: "Heather Jock" and Cunninghame Graham's Utopian Sense of Community   150

    News of War: Cunninghame Graham's "Victory" and the Spanish-American War of 1898   156

CHAPTER 5. The Geopolitics of Screenplay: Sabotage from Joseph Conrad to Alfred Hitchcock   160

    The Meaning of Sabotage   162

    Anarcho-Syndicalist Origins   167

    The Anarchist Premises of The Secret Agent: *From Agency to Secret Agency*   173

    Mass Media, Cinematic Narrative, and the Subject of Geopolitics   184

    Sabotage and the Geopolitics of Screenplay   190

    Coda   198

    Notes   201

    Bibliography   233

    Index   249

Illustrations

Part-Opening Illustration
Kupka, "L'Homme est la nature prenant conscience d'elle même"
1 Kupka, Study for *Amorpha, Fugue in Two Colours* (1911–1912)   9
2 Kupka, Illustration for Reclus, *L'Homme et la Terre*   10
3 The Natural Seats of Power   21
4a Thirteenth-Century Map   30
4b Mackinder's Key to Figure 4a   30
5a The World according to Eratosthenes   31
5b The World according to Ptolemy   31
6 The Land Hemisphere   32
7 Photograph of a globe   32
8 Classificatory Chart of Humankind   38
9 Kupka, "L'Angleterre et son cortège"   44
10 Wilkie, *Sir David Baird Discovering the Body of the Sultan Tippoo Sahib* (1839)   61
11 Detail from Wilkie, *Sir David Baird Discovering the Body of the Sultan Tippoo Sahib* (1839)   81
12 Lavery, Portrait of Cunninghame Graham (1893)   131
13 Scottish Labour Party ticket   132
14 Lavery, Portrait of Cunninghame Graham and Horse "Pampa"   133
15 Still from Hitchcock's *Sabotage* (1936)   185

Acknowledgments

Research for this book began with a summer faculty fellowship from Fordham University, granted in 1989 and delayed until 1990. I thank Fordham for allowing me to defer the fellowship to attend to my first newborn, Cai; and I thank Cai—and then Keir, who arrived in 1991—for helping extend, delay, and enrich the experience of working toward the completion of the present book. I thank Fordham, too, for the semester's leave granted in 1994 to work on the first chapter; and for a course reduction in the spring of 1998 to complete the last chapter while directing Fordham's Literary Studies Program.

Chapter 4 appeared in an earlier version as an essay in Maria DiBattista and Lucy McDiarmid's *High and Low Moderns: Literature and Culture, 1889-1939*. I thank Oxford University Press for granting permission to publish it here in a revised and altered form. A condensed version of Chapter 1 appeared in *Modernism/modernity* in Fall 1998. I would like to thank Lady Polwarth for allowing me access to her Cunninghame Graham papers at Harden; and for permission to quote from those and the papers deposited in the National Library of Scotland. I owe thanks to members of the staff at the National Library of Scotland (including the Map Library), at the New York Public Library, at the Harvard College Library, at the British Library, and at Fordham's libraries at Lincoln Center and Rose Hill, for all their assistance.

It would not be possible to thank all the many individuals who have, directly or indirectly, helped realize the studies that make up this book. I thank Ian Duncan, and another, anonymous reader for their sympathetic comments and for their invaluable suggestions which encouraged me to make this a stronger, clearer book. I am indebted to Helen Tartar for having supported this project from the very start. I am grateful to her for her advice, her editorial eye, and her friendship. I thank, too, my editor Kate Warne and my copy editor Ruth Steinberg for their care and expertise in seeing the book through to its final form.

John Archer patiently read a number of chapters in draft form, as did Fraser Easton. Their comments, criticisms, encouragements, and friendship have been invaluable. I am indebted to another good friend and colleague, Fawzia Mustafa, for her advice, support, and clairvoyant understanding of the risks and rewards of interdisciplinary work. For support and encouragement on various aspects of this book, I'd like to thank Laurence Davies, Maria DiBattista, and Mary Poovey.

Among those whose comments and advice have shaped and reshaped my thinking on a host of issues connected with this book, I'd like to thank Madeleine Brainerd, Robert Caserio, Yvette Christiansë, Chris Chyba, Arnaldo Cruz-Malavé, Jane Davis, Mary Erler, Susan Greenfield, Kim Hall, Stephen Henighan, Anne Hoffman, Leslie Katz, T. Kaori Kitao, Siobhán Kilfeather, Holt V. Meyer, Dorothea von Mücke, Gerry O'Sullivan, Philip Sicker, and Jean Walton. For his appreciation of Wilkie Collins as well as for the inspiration of his cello playing, I would like to thank Steven Isserlis.

I owe a very special debt to all my students: to those on whom I have inflicted the peculiar question "Which way did the turn of the last century turn?"; and to those who are already at work in turning the twentieth century into something else. I also want to thank all those who participated in the events at Fordham organized by the symposium on the Diaspora of Cultural Studies; and all those who continue to participate in the seminars, lectures, and discussion groups that make learning possible here and elsewhere. My thoughts have been decisively shaped by these ongoing dialogues; and I owe a special debt to everyone who has contributed to the extraordinary discussions of the May colloquia organized by Fordham's Literary Studies Program.

I would also like to thank Indonesian novelist Pramoedya Ananta Toer, whose novels and stories I discovered during the writing of this book. Although I do not discuss them here, they have probably influenced my thoughts more than I can say (and any reader of this book who has read Pramoedya's "Buru" quartet of novels might keep this in mind).

ACKNOWLEDGMENTS

This could not have been written without the support of an extended family complex of Gwilts, Gos, and GoGwilts. Siu Li, Cai, and Keir have been, and continue to be, my greatest companions, friends, and inspiration, and I thank them for all their patience. I also owe a special debt of gratitude to my father-in-law, Go Tie Siem; to Soesilowati; and to May Li. Much of the book was conceived, researched, and written in Edinburgh—on a semester's leave and during Scottish summer months. I owe a great debt of gratitude to my parents for welcoming a New Yorker back home to do this. I dedicate the book to them, and to my grandmother, for having insisted on the freedom and the spirit of thinking as one will.

C.G.

THE FICTION OF GEOPOLITICS

Introduction

Geopolitics, I argue in the following pages, is neither a science nor a sociology but a fiction. A powerful fiction that has dominated the twentieth century, it constitutes a complex, unresolved legacy from the nineteenth century. The subject of this book is the intertwined fate of nineteenth-century conceptions of culture and twentieth-century discourses of geopolitics. In a variety of different ways I argue that the fiction of geopolitics took shape around the turn of the century through a breakdown and reconfiguration of nineteenth-century European ideas of culture. This is an argument, in part, about the way European conceptions of culture get displaced with the emergence of geopolitics. It is also, however, an argument about the way geopolitical imperatives remain shaped by unresolved problems of culture.

A twentieth-century invention, the word "geopolitics" (together with its various cognates) has come to apply to a wide range of international social, political, and historical phenomena. Often used simply as a synonym for international political relations, and (a little less simply) to imply the global structure of such relations, contemporary usage is drawn from the early-twentieth-century term for a pseudo-science of political geography. The term's currency has been usefully clarified in a set of recent surveys and anthologies by political geographers.[1] As John Agnew puts it:

> The term geopolitics has long been used to refer to the study of the geographical representations and practices that underpin world politics. The

word 'geopolitics' has in fact undergone something of a revival in recent years. The term is now used freely to refer to such phenomena as international boundary disputes, the structure of global finance, and geographical patterns of election results.²

Agnew goes on to offer his own, "more specific" definition: "examination of the geographical assumptions, designations, and understandings that enter into the making of world politics." This definition is useful because it applies both to the imperialist geographers of the early twentieth century who first elaborated the term and to the work of recent anti-imperialist geographers who have sought to develop what Gearóid O Tuathail calls "critical geopolitics."

What that definition misses, however, is the way in which early-twentieth-century geographers, politicians, and historians created a term for something that could not be established as a field of study. "Geopolitics" failed to define the political science imagined by Rudolf Kjellén and others; but the word succeeded in naming something other than an academic field of study or a government's practice of foreign policy. The discursive effect of the word geopolitics, indeed, is all the more powerful for that failure, shaping the way the term can be applied to a variety of different concerns about the relation of geography to politics. Geopolitics ambiguously implies both that the relation between geography and world politics is determined and that such a relation has yet to be determined. Furthermore, geopolitics may mean either the study of or the practice of world politics, or both together. These ambiguities reinforce the imperative to understand what "geopolitics" failed to construct as its object of scientific study at the beginning of the century. That imperative—to imagine an organized set of determined relations between geography and politics—is what I consider here as the fiction of geopolitics.

The failure to establish a science of geopolitics for the twentieth century is integrally linked to a range of unresolved intellectual and political debates from the nineteenth century about Europe's place in the world and in world history. This range of debates may be grouped together under what I call, throughout the book, the hypothesis of culture: the hypothesis that Europe's social, political, and historical development may be connected with a universal, world historical development. By the turn of the century this hypothesis gets eclipsed, most notably with anthropology, in the shift from a singular idea of human culture to a relativist idea of separate cultures; and also, as I have elsewhere argued, with the displacement of the idea of Europe with that of "the West," and the crystallization of an idea of "Western" culture distinct and separate from human history as a whole.[3] The discursive formation of geopolitics, as I argue in Chapter 1, is premised on the eclipse of this European hypothesis of culture. The rest of the book considers the consequences of this both for the cosmopolitical claims of nineteenth-century ideas of culture and for the geopolitical claims that condense and displace them in the twentieth century.

This focus on the relation between twentieth-century paradigms of geopolitics and nineteenth-century culture concepts informs the organization of the book around the meaning of four words: culture, nihilism, utopia, and sabotage. These keywords offer a way to delineate the transformation of nineteenth- to twentieth-century paradigms of culture which takes place across the discursive formation of geopolitics. Each rubric outlines a set of different issues organized in historical sequence from the novels of Wilkie Collins to the films of Alfred Hitchcock. Thus, Chapter 2 focuses on Victorian concepts of culture in the 1860s; Chapter 3 considers the combined social and philosophical significance of nihilism in the 1880s; Chapter 4 examines the utopian imperative of socialist geography and politics in the 1890s; and Chapter 5 traces the concept of sabotage to its anarcho-syndicalist origins in the 1900s.

The basic premise of the set of studies to follow is outlined in the genealogy of geopolitics offered in Part I. Tracing discourses of geopolitics to a crisis in the discipline of geography and, more generally, in the human sciences, this opening section examines the work of three geographers: Elisée Reclus (1830–1905), the French anarchist geographer; Friedrich Ratzel (1844–1904), the German geographer whose theory of "Lebensraum" is often considered a touchstone of geopolitics; and Halford J. Mackinder (1861–1947), the British geographer who championed the "new geography" in schools and universities in Britain over the turn of the century. Two guiding features of the section's genealogy of geopolitics are important, both for introducing the chapters that follow and for distinguishing the book's contribution to recent critical debates about and studies of geopolitics. In the first instance, the work of Elisée Reclus forms the basis for my claim that the discursive formation of geopolitics has its roots in an appropriation of anarchist geography and of the utopian imperative of nineteenth-century socialism. The other guiding feature of this genealogy is its claim that twentieth-century geopolitics emerges from an abandonment of the nineteenth-century hypothesis that European culture belongs to a universal history of cultural development.

In the two chapters of Part II, concerned for the most part with the genre of the novel, I consider the mid- to late-Victorian shape of this culture hypothesis. There is, of course, no one conception of culture that might adequately cover the plurality of senses of culture proliferating throughout the nineteenth century. What I call the European hypothesis of culture is, rather, a set of unresolved questions and debates that characterize a wide range of discourses and that typically cluster around the word "culture." As I discuss in Chapter 2, part of the tenacity of Matthew Arnold's famous elaboration of the term culture in *Culture and Anarchy* (1869) lies in the success with which it combines in a single word a number of different questions—of education, of aesthetics, and concerning the nation-state. Depending on which of these are emphasized, the idea of culture may yield sharply different meanings. Indeed, in this chapter I deliberately juxtapose the Arnoldian concept of culture with the very different texture of Wilkie Collins's novels to explore Victorian conceptions of respectability and middle-class values. It is through such a perspective, and following the work of Raymond Williams, Edward Said, and Gauri Viswanathan (among others), that I examine governing colonial distortions of culture that shape twentieth-century geopolitical discourses.

Chapter 3 sets the European hypothesis of culture within a rather different kind of colonial perspective. In a number of respects Nietzsche's philosophy remains studiously distant from the cultural and political questions of colonialism reshaping nineteenth-century Europe. Set next to the work of the South African novelist Olive Schreiner, however, Nietzsche's philosophy can be read in terms of characteristically Victorian preoccupations. Biographically, the pairing is a study both in opposites—feminist novelist and anti-feminist philosopher—and in shared concerns: two cosmopolitan thinkers caught between the conflicting demands of an older European ideal of culture and of the newer imperatives of what Benedict Anderson describes as "official nationalism."[4] Nietzsche and Schreiner usefully illuminate the older ideal of culture: by looking back to the German idealist notion of education associated with Wilhelm von Humboldt, "Bildung," translated into English as "human development" by

J. S. Mill and "culture" by Matthew Arnold, each presents nineteenth-century European humanism as, in its origins, nihilist. What emerges in Schreiner's *The Story of an African Farm* and Nietzsche's late work is not only a critique of the narrowness of European middle-class ideals, but also a novelistic and philosophical grasp of the simultaneous globalization and disappearance of European cultural ideas. Each holds on to the cosmopolitan imperative of an older European humanist ideal in the moment before its eclipse by the geopolitical imperative of two of the most violent "official nationalisms" of the twentieth century: the national socialism of Friedrich Nietzsche's sister, and the Afrikaaner nationalism taking shape in Olive Schreiner's South Africa.

To characterize the European hypothesis of culture as cosmopolitan, or cosmopolitical, is one way to characterize the overall concerns of Part II of the book.[5] Conceived in terms of the educational ideal of "Bildung," with its cosmopolitan narrative imperative to unfold the individual's story in harmony with the development of human history as a whole, the eclipse of the European hypothesis of culture may be explained in terms of the failure to resolve all those abiding middle-class questions that, politically, are usually grouped under the heading of liberalism. In Part II, then, it is this question of middle-class consciousness that concerns me: first, in considering the blurring of mid-Victorian conceptions of culture that occurs during the formalization of the British Empire between 1857 and 1877; and then, in considering in what ways Nietzsche's diagnosis of nihilism constitutes, rather than an assault on middle-class ideals, a rigorous working-out of the hypothesis of culture.

Part III of the book emphasizes another side of this same European question of culture: the problem of working-class consciousness. E. J. Hobsbawm usefully poses the problem confronting international socialism at the turn of the century when he points out that "what, from one point of view, looked like a concentration of men and women in a single 'working-class,' could be seen from another as a gigantic scattering of the fragments of societies, a diaspora of old and new communities."[6] In Chapter 4 I consider the significance of utopian socialism and socialist utopias from the perspective of the unusual double-vision of Cunninghame Graham's sketch-artistry, as it seeks to grasp simultaneously the immense scattering and fragmentation of social formations and the concentration of populations into an industrial workforce. The representative idiosyncrasies of Cunninghame Graham—Scottish nationalist aristocrat, travel adventurer, and socialist agitator—call attention to the problematic geography of political consciousness informing socialist movements and literary modernism in the 1890s.

If the German notion of "Bildung" signals the riddle of European middle-class consciousness, the riddle of working-class consciousness is signaled by the concept of "hegemony," whose emergence as a key concept in theories of working-class leadership Ernesto Laclau and Chantal Mouffe have traced to the turn-of-the-century crisis of Second International Marxism.[7] The word "hegemony" is itself bound up with the discursive formation of geopolitics. Associated with the politics of German unification, and with the "Kulturkampf" (cultural struggle or culture war) against perceived Vatican interference in Bismarck's "hegemony-politics," the resonance of the word emerges from the new configurations of political power reshaping Europe, particularly after 1870.[8] By analogy to the way in which the concept of "Bildung" marks the limits of a cosmopolitan bourgeois consciousness, "hegemony" as a concept marks the limits to that awakening of an international working-class consciousness and solidarity so strongly imagined in the nineteenth century and so fiercely afterthought in the twentieth century.[9] It marks these limits in terms of the problem of leadership faced by the emergence of new mass political movements. In Chapter 5 I consider how the ideological containment of the syndicalist tactic of "sabotage" serves to reformulate the nineteenth-century socialist imperative for international working-class solidarity into the geopolitical imperative of national security against the threat of sabotage in time of world war. This chapter's study of Conrad's *The Secret Agent* and Hitchcock's *Sabotage* considers these changing imperatives in relation to the emergence of the new media whose dominant coordinating form will become, by the 1940s, American cinema.

The historical scope of the book's study of the long turn of the century, from 1860 to 1940, is also guided by attention to the significance of novel form for the nineteenth century and to the significance of film for the twentieth century. This generic concern for the ways in which Hitchcock's cinematic narrative reconceives Victorian novel conventions lies at the heart of the claim that geopolitics is neither a science nor a sociology but a fiction. But the argument cuts both ways, back and forth across the turn of the century. It is not simply a matter of cinema taking over from the novel as the dominant medium. Narrative cinema, as an effort to coordinate different media, is in many respects not so different from the novel, itself a coordination of different media. There is a dialectical relation between the classic aura of Hollywood narrative cinema and continuing fascination with the Victorian novel. One of the concerns of the current book is to examine the formal structure of this relation. The underlying claim is that the aura and fascination, in both cases, is that of the fiction of geopolitics.

Rather than political theory, then, it is the changing nature of fictional form over the turn from the nineteenth to the twentieth centuries that provides the methodological framework for the book's various studies. In large part this is because, as the book argues, discourses of geopolitics are constituted and sustained through essentially fictive forms. The changing nature of these fictive forms can be explained from a number of methodological perspectives. Jean-François Lyotard's celebrated analysis of the postmodern condition describes the legitimation crisis of nineteenth-century humanism in terms of a breakdown of narrative form,[10] and this argument provides a useful way of tracing the emergence of geopolitical thinking to the collapse of those characteristically grand narrative accounts of nineteenth-century European geographers. From another perspective, Friedrich Kittler's analysis of the "discourse networks" of 1900 provides a basis for examining the breakdown of a discourse of "Bildung" with the emergence of the new, as yet uncoordinated media systems of the typewriter, phonograph, and cinema.[11]

At the heart of the overall argument of the book is a question of perspective, which is a matter of both political and aesthetic form. The terminology I use throughout tends to emphasize the visual image—hence, the "geopolitical image" is constituted around "afterimages" of nineteenth-century culture. By underlining this emphasis I aim to do something more than critique what O Tuathail calls the "Cartesian perspectivalism" of geopolitics.[12] "Visualisation," in the terms of H. J. Mackinder's political geography, does indeed provide a distorted perspective of the world. If that distorted, partial perspective provides the opportunity for alternative perspectives—such as those O Tuathail and other geographers are now offering in the form of a "critical geopolitics"—it also provides the opportunity for reexamination of the long "ocularcentric" tradition of European enlightenment thinking.[13]

Such a reexamination is what Jonathan Crary opens up in his *Techniques of the Observer*, which traces to the beginning of the nineteenth century the emergence of a new kind of subject produced through and disciplined by a variety of physiological technologies of vision. This argument's focus on institutional practices or disciplinary techniques is very different in scope and accent from my emphasis on fictional form. Crary demonstrates, however, that the retinal afterimage was a guiding physiological principle in the development of nineteenth-century optical techniques. This has important implications for my own work, which pays increasing attention to turn-of-the-century formulations of the afterimage from Nietzsche to Bergson, more generally, in the developments of photomontage and cinematography, and perhaps most importantly of all with Walter Benjamin's efforts to theorize the simultaneously revolutionary and reactionary transformations in nineteenth-century European cultural forms.

The ambiguity of the "geopolitical image," as discussed in Chapter 1, is usefully set in context by Crary's attempt to reconceive the "rupture" in modernist forms of representation ascribed to the turn of the century. Abstract artistic forms of representation—in a variety of different media, and in various coordinations of those different media—are constituted, so Crary's argument suggests, around peculiarly Victorian optical concerns. To illustrate this visual point and to indicate its significance for the emergence of geopolitics, one might consider one of the very first examples of modernist abstract art: *Amorpha, Fugue in Two Colours* (1912), by the Czech émigré to France Frantisek Kupka (see Figure 1). Exhibited in Paris in 1912 along with the related *Amorpha, Warm Chromatics*, the painting baffled and intrigued viewers and critics, and created something of a sensation when Gaumont newsreels filmed the paintings and showed them all over Europe and America.[14] Like his *Disks of Newton* (1911–1912), the painting grew from extensive experiments in the effects of optical distortion, chromatic form, and consecutive images. Margit Rowell traces the evolution of *Amorpha* from Kupka's sketches of a child playing with a ball to studies that "transcend the notion of bodily movement to suggest cosmic motion in time and space."[15] Drawing inspiration both from the latest developments in chrono-photography and from much older nineteenth-century optical theories (most notably Goethe's color theory), the painting forms part of a matrix of turn-of-the-century interests in optical

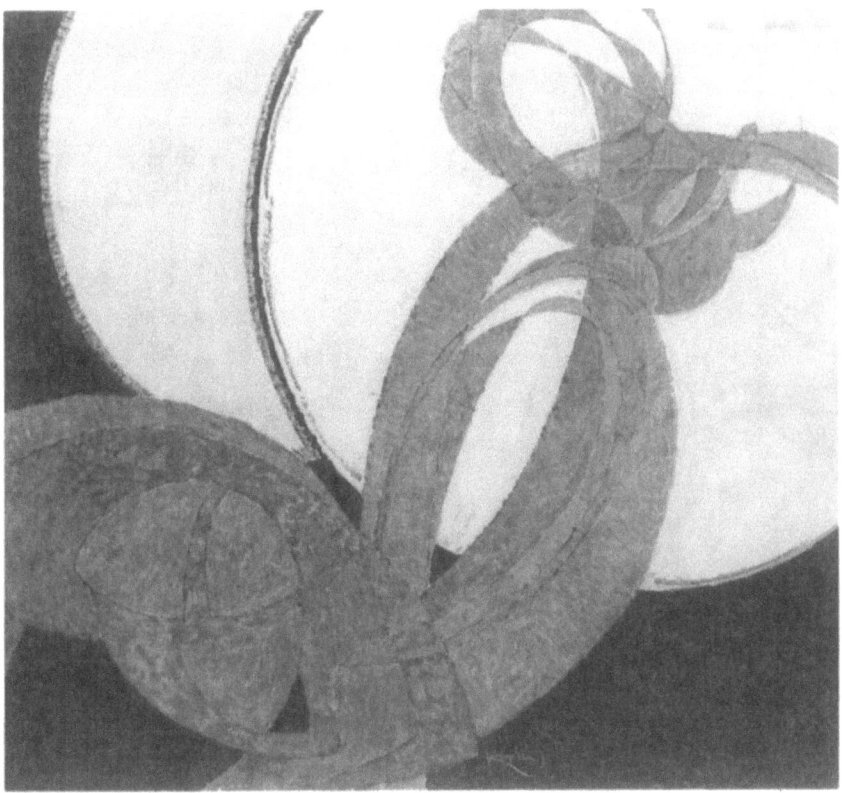

FIGURE 1. Frantisek Kupka, *Amorpha: Fugue in Two Colours* (1912). Gouache and brush and ink, 16 ⅜ in. x 18 ⅝ in. (41.6 cm x 47.3 cm). Courtesy of the Museum of Modern Art, New York.

experiments generally and the retinal afterimage in particular. In Crary's sense, then, the painting may be considered a continuation rather than a "rupture" in nineteenth-century visuality.

Kupka's painting is also interesting once set next to his illustration work for the anarchist geographer Elisée Reclus's *L'Homme et la Terre* (1905–1908). Two characteristic examples include Kupka's illustration of the geographer (see Figure 2) and the illustration of a pair of hands holding a globe, which decorated each of the six volumes of Reclus's final work (see part-opening illustration). A third example, Kupka's sketch of "England and its Cortège," is offered in Chapter 1 to illustrate Reclus's critique of British imperialism. If one is struck, at first, by the immense difference between the abstract formalism of the painting and the realist populism of the set of illustrations, it is for the connection between the two that I

FIGURE 2. Frantisek Kupka, illustration of "The Geographer" for Elisée Reclus, *L'Homme et la Terre*, vol. 1 (1905). Courtesy of the General Research Division, the New York Public Library, Astor, Lenox and Tilden Foundations.

invite the reader to consider them as illustrations of my general argument that the ambiguity of the geopolitical image is shaped by Victorian "afterimages."

Where Crary traces, in the "new disciplinary techniques" of physiological optics, the emergence of a subject that becomes "*visible*,"[16] however, my interest is rather in examining distortions of this emerging norm. Side by side with the nineteenth-century disciplinary techniques of the observer exist a range of other forms of "discipline"—for example, "culture," in its distinctive nineteenth-century formulations. The hypothesis of a universal, cosmopolitan reading, viewing, and consuming human subject posits an invisible, indeed perhaps unimaginable, unlocatable subject—and for that very reason it is a hypothesis that disturbs the kind of optics Crary suggests become dominant in the nineteenth century.

It is in order to examine nineteenth-century ideas of culture from the point of view of their *failure* to consolidate a disciplinary subjectivity that I turn to the notion of anamorphosis—a deformed figure that appears in proper proportion once correctly viewed. If Kupka's title "Amorpha," meaning lack of form, suggests this principle, it is notably ambiguous as to whether there can be a perspective—visual or auditory—from which the form can "correctly" be apprehended. In emphasizing a relation of continuity between the abstract modernism of Kupka's *Amorpha* and the Victorian perspective of his illustrations for Reclus's anarchist geography, I wish to draw attention to the ways in which each might form the anamorphotic point of perspective for viewing the other. This double movement—looking back and forth from the Victorian nineteenth century to the modernist twentieth century—is the premise for each chapter of the book.

The theoretical use of anamorphosis to which I refer is one borrowed from Jacques Lacan by Slavoj Žižek to explain Hitchcock's cinematic technique: what Žižek calls "the Hitchcockian blot."[17] The effect produced by Hitchcock's characteristic tracking shot allows Žižek to explain, by way of examples from Hitchcock's films, Lacan's psychoanalytic argument about the illusory structure of the ego-ideal. Although I draw on psychoanalytic models only tangentially in this book, Žižek's Lacan provides a helpful way to analyze how Hitchcock reconstitutes Victorian optical and narrative forms to produce an imaginary coherence of organized world political relations.

In Chapter 2, I reformulate Žižek's "Hitchcockian blot," and pictorial anamorphosis in general, in terms of a specifically Victorian "blot"—following Wilkie Collins's own pun on "plot," as well as his lifelong preoccupation with painting. While the "Hitchcockian blot" describes a cinematic visual effect, this Victorian blot concerns a narrative, reading effect particularly evident in the so-called sensational novels of the 1860s. Such sensational narrative distortions implicate one of the most characteristic of Victorian practices (novel writing and reading) in another set of characteristic Victorian social practices—the practices of colonial governance. Within the historical context of the formalization of the British Empire, from 1857 to 1877, Collins's sensational novel-writing techniques provide a fictional measure for examining the unmanageable form of the simultaneously European and extra-European modern imperial nation-state and the reciprocal distortions of collective ethnic and national imaginings that underpin it.

There are numerous points of connection between the imperial imaginings of the British Empire after 1857 and the consolidation of American geopolitical hegemony during the Second World War. One such point of connection is provided by Hitchcock's own explanation for the so-called MacGuffin, the plot "device" or "gimmick" around which to make a movie. As he explained it to Truffaut in 1955, the MacGuffin has its origins in Kipling's "spy stories."[18] This is revealing, first, because Hitchcock specifies the politics of colonial and anti-colonial struggle in what Kipling called the Great Game ("the fighting between the natives and the British forces on the Afghanistan border").[19] It is also revealing in that the fictional formula involves a deliberate displacement of that political context: the stolen "plans, documents, or secrets" that concern such spy plots must seem of inordinate significance to the characters; but "to me, the narrator, they're of no importance whatever." This *displacement* of a real political reference is an essential feature of the fiction of geopolitics. Its fictive structure emerges in the second account he offers immediately following the reference to Kipling:

> You may be wondering where the term originated. It might be a Scottish name, taken from a story about two men in a train. One man says, "What's that package up there in the baggage rack?" And the other answers, "Oh, that's a MacGuffin." The first one asks, "What's a MacGuffin?" "Well," the other man says, "it's an apparatus for trapping lions in the Scottish Highlands." The first man says, "But there are no lions in the Scottish Highlands," and the other one answers, "Well then, that's no MacGuffin!"[20]

The name MacGuffin here serves to signify a place and setting for the train journey (a train on its way to the Scottish Highlands) in a little joke. But particularly in its anecdotal presentation ("It *might* be a Scottish name . . ."), its wit turns on an exaggerated metonymic displacement of nationality—a joke that works by suggesting an exaggerated deflection of some ethnic slur (Scottish, or perhaps Irish). What one presumes to be a

Scottish name is then applied to a far-fetched contraption that could not possibly be imagined in Scotland. This joke-work of vanishing ethnic and national identity points to an essentially unstable element of racial and ethnic identification motivating Hitchcock's transatlantic films and the hallucination of white racial identity they produce.

The fiction of geopolitics, as I trace it here, is not so much the product of one ideological system or another (what Thomas Richards traces, for instance, as the "imperial archive" produced in the late-Victorian British imperial moment;[21] or what Alan Nadel traces as the "containment culture" of postwar American cinema[22]). In this respect, the premise of these studies is also crucially different from that of Fredric Jameson's set of important and influential studies of narrative form (in *The Political Unconscious*), postmodern culture (in *Postmodernism, or the Cultural Logic of Late Capitalism*), and postwar cinema (in *The Geopolitical Aesthetic*). While this book clearly builds on Jameson's arguments, what I have called the fiction of geopolitics, by contrast to what Jameson defines as "the geopolitical aesthetic," is not the product only of the post–World War I "world system." Rather, the fiction of geopolitics is the product of those distortions of effect that attend the dissolution, on the one hand, of European novel form and, on the other hand, the formation of dominant Hollywood cinema.

The study of the reciprocal, distorting effects of aesthetic form and political identification demands something of a theoretical and methodological shift in the paradigm of the "world-system" argument that underpins much of Jameson's work.[23] In the following studies, I write about the nineteenth-century culture-concept in terms of an amalgam of different "culture systems": systems of education, of colonization, of entertainment, of consumption and production. These overlapping, contested, and discrepant "culture systems" constitute part of the complexity condensed and displaced in the discursive formation of geopolitics. To the extent that "world-system" theories, too, remain bound to the unresolved questions of the nineteenth-century European hypothesis of culture, my formulation "culture systems" is deliberately meant to blur the conceptual clarity of that model in order to underscore how analysis of, say, the entrepreneurial capitalist "world system" of the mid–nineteenth century might yet more fully be grasped in terms of the discrepant "culture systems" that constitute the premise both for that "world system" itself (e.g., pre-nineteenth-century plantation systems, labor systems, educational systems, communication systems) and for the present standpoint from which we view that "world system." I do not pretend to offer here a revision of world-systems analysis. Nonetheless, these studies are intended as a modest, experimental step toward re-thinking, re-reading, and re-imagining "world culture systems."

This study's preoccupation with geopolitics has its roots in research conducted before 1989—the year of the Tiananmen Square massacre, as well as the year in which the Berlin Wall came down. Each of the chapters has gestated slowly through the decade of the 1990s, which might be characterized as the decade of geopolitical deadlines: from the crossed deadline that precipitated the Persian Gulf war to the pattern of deadlines that have marked the deadlocked dialectic of genocide and bombing in the Balkans. Although the study has surely been shaped by my responses, conscious and unconscious, to these events, I have not attempted to offer any sort of direct commentary on world politics in our time—whether on the geopolitics of war, or on the decade's realignment of national and international imaginings, or on the emergence and emergencies of new democracy movements. In that sense, this is emphatically not a study of contemporary geopolitics. It is, rather, an attempt to bring critical attention to the formation, from 1860 to 1940, of a powerfully distorting network of discourses, which I have called the fiction of geopolitics.

PART I

A GENEALOGY OF GEOPOLITICS

1 The Geopolitical Image
Anarchism, Imperialism, and the Hypothesis of Culture in the Formation of Geopolitics

> "A geography text should aim at literary form. It should present a standard of knowledge, a method, and a perspective. Supplementary ideas ought to be built round the map, not the printed page, for only so can we cultivate the visualizing habit of mind."
> —H. J. Mackinder, *Lands Beyond the Channel*, 1908

> "A philosophy of the history of the human race, worthy of its name, must begin with the heavens and descend to the earth, must be charged with the conviction that all existence is one—a single conception sustained from beginning to end upon one identical law."
> —Friedrich Ratzel, quoted by H. G. Wells as the epigraph to *The Outline of History*, 1920

> "If you knew the threefold sorrow with which my life is barred, like those well-fortified cities one sees in Elisée Reclus's Northern Europe volume, you would forgive me."
> —Marcel Proust, letter to Suzette Lemaire, 1 November 1894

Early in Joyce's *A Portrait of the Artist as a Young Man* the reader encounters an auditory image of the infantile artist's first experimentation with language:

> O, the wild rose blossoms
> On the little green place.
> He sang that song. That was his song.
> O, the green wothe botheth.[1]

This prototypically modernist linguistic play—"the green wothe botheth"—establishes a problem of imagining to which the young Stephen will return, although as a problem that cannot be resolved: "You could not have a green rose. But perhaps somewhere in the world you could."[2] In its encoded contestation of national and poetic imagery (the Irish green, the poetic rose), Stephen's "green wothe" is an exemplary geopolitical image. It posits a form of cultural and political identification whose difficulty

Stephen later finds inscribed in and around the "picture of the earth on the first page of his geography."[3]

The meaning of "geopolitics," as a common word that has come to be used to describe a variety of global political problems, is by no means easy to pinpoint. It is a charged term. Associated with Nazi Germany's policies of military expansion and genocide, it has since acquired a resonance less specific to German Geopolitik, evoking, generally, a complex interrelation of global and regional politics. To theorize that complexity, Fredric Jameson has formulated the idea of a "geopolitical aesthetic," applied not to the early-twentieth-century modernism of Joyce's *A Portrait of the Artist* but to the postwar "world system" of the late twentieth century. Increasing use of the term as a critical watchword here and elsewhere in contemporary cultural studies calls for reflection on the freighted history of the term and its associations. The genealogy I offer here is complemented by a number of recent surveys of geopolitics that trace the formation of what Gearóid O Tuathail calls "classical geopolitics" back to the turn of the last century.[4] What distinguishes my account from those, and provides the organizing argument for the set of studies to follow, is my focus on two defining features in the discursive formation of geopolitics: the suppressed significance of socialist anarchism for imperialist geopolitics, and the fate of nineteenth-century ideas of "culture" in the construction of twentieth-century geopolitical paradigms.

The history of geopolitics may briefly be described in terms of the failure to constitute "geopolitics" as a scientific study, a failure on which the very success and persistence of reactionary geopolitical paradigms are premised. Most of my examples in this chapter are drawn from the work of geographers, anthropologists, and social scientists, and something I attempt to emphasize is the way geopolitical paradigms took shape around disciplinary boundary crossings within the academy, not unlike the interdisciplinarity that characterizes cultural studies today.[5] At issue is not only the fate of an academic field of study, but also the ensemble of residual problems and questions that come to mark the wider sense of "geopolitics." Stephen's problem of imagining a "green rose" is exemplary of this ensemble of questions, because it offers not a definition but a problem—"It pained him that he did not know well what politics meant and that he did not know where the universe ended."[6]

A geography textbook, in Joyce's novel, precipitates Stephen's problem of identification, and it is to geography books that I turn to examine the emergence of what I call the geopolitical image. In particular, I am interested in the work of three geographers: Elisée Reclus (1830–1905), the French anarchist geographer; Friedrich Ratzel (1844–1904), the German geographer whose theory of "Lebensraum" and political geography generally set the terms for the later development of "Geopolitik"; and Halford J. Mackinder (1861–1947), the British geographer who championed the "new geography" in schools and universities in Britain, and whose political geography exercised considerable influence, not least on the Nazi geopoliticians of the 1930s.

Mackinder is given special prominence, not only for the central place he occupies in genealogies of geopolitics,[7] but also because his geography illustrates a formalist logic at work in the formation of geopolitics—a logic reminiscent both of the strategies of literary modernism and of the Freudian dream-work of condensation and displacement. The significance of Mackinder's geography, I propose, lies in its ability to synthesize the radically different political implications of Ratzel and Reclus into a single geopolitical image, and most notably, the geopolitical image of Britain in his *Britain and the British Seas* (1902). In that image are constellated not only the political contradictions of European geography over the turn of the century, but also the distinctive features of the breakdown of nineteenth-century European ideas of culture.

Stephen's "green wothe" articulates, in miniature, this reconfiguration of the culture-concept into a geopolitical image. If the attempt to imagine a "green rose" "somewhere in the world" figures a contestation of political identity and identification, it is premised on a collapse of nineteenth-century assumptions about the coordination of natural, individual, national, human, and ultimately universal processes of development. The German idealist notion of "Bildung" as a process of individual development, aesthetic education, and national culture is perhaps the most important touchstone for what might generally be called the European hypothesis of culture. Wilhelm Humboldt's educational theories, Herder's theories of national development and world history, the aesthetic theories of Schiller and Goethe, as well as the paradigmatic example of Goethe's "Bildungsroman" *Wilhelm Meisters Lehrjahre*—all form points of reference for the variety of different variations and inflections of "Bildung" throughout Europe in the nineteenth century.[8] In a far-reaching translation-effect—

by which, for example, Matthew Arnold translates the German idealist notion of "Bildung" as "culture"—"Bildung" forms part of the same culture-complex that Raymond Williams has shown to accrue around the English keyword, "culture."[9] Stephen's "green rose" constitutes a complex afterimage of these notions of culture, articulating a problem of identity formation, a splitting of national cultures (English and Irish), and a disjuncture between these national histories and human history as a whole, inscribed then in the picture of the earth in his geography textbook.

H. J. Mackinder, the Hypothesis of Culture, and the Formation of Geopolitics

It is chiefly for his famous Heartland thesis that Halford Mackinder is remembered as an important figure in the development of geopolitical thinking. First formulated in "The Geographical Pivot of History," a paper delivered in January 1904 to the Royal Geographical Society, Mackinder's thesis projects global political power as naturally pivoting around Central Asia, the "heartland" of land-based power in what Mackinder sees as the fundamental strategic and historical interplay of land and sea. The thesis is concisely abbreviated, first in the form of the map of "The Natural Seats of Power" (see Figure 3), which accompanied the 1904 paper, and then in the set of maxims Mackinder wrote in *Democratic Ideals and Reality* (1919):

> Who rules East Europe commands the Heartland
> Who rules the Heartland commands the World-Island
> Who rules the World-Island commands the World.[10]

The key features of this rhetoric and iconography of geopolitics may be seen in formation as early as 1887 with Mackinder's influential address to the Royal Geographic Society, "On the Scope and Methods of Geography." Assuming leadership of the "new geography" movement, Mackinder took up the "educational battle" over the place of geography in British schools and universities. Mackinder argues not only for the unity of geography as a discipline, but also for its central place in general education. The "continuous argument"[11] of geography—from physical geography to political geography—makes it the discipline able to bridge the gap between the natural and the human sciences: "One of the greatest of all gaps lies between the natural sciences and the study of humanity. It is the duty of

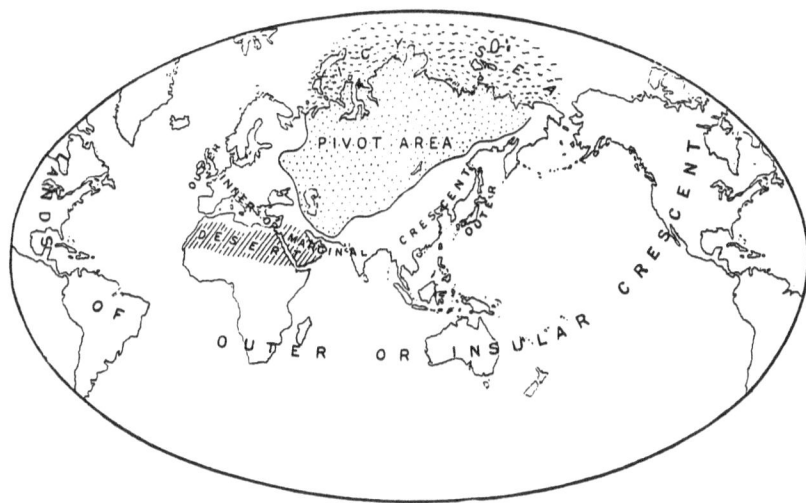

FIGURE 3. The Natural Seats of Power (pivot area: wholly continental; outer crescent: wholly oceanic; inner crescent: partly continental, partly oceanic), from H. J. Mackinder, "The Geographical Pivot of History."

the geographer to build one bridge over an abyss which in the opinion of many is upsetting the equilibrium of our culture."[12]

In all of these claims, and perhaps most particularly the gesture toward resolving a general crisis of "culture," Mackinder condenses and displaces the range of debates giving shape to the formation of geopolitics.

One thing Mackinder finesses is the fragmentation of the discipline of geography, from which was to emerge the pseudo-science of "geopolitics." By framing discussion around "physical geography" and "political geography," Mackinder contains the proliferating terminology then eroding the unity of geography as a discipline. Mackinder's "political geography," in particular, displaces a variety of contending ways of classifying the second "stage" in his "continuous argument," for example, "historical geography," "social geography," "human geography," "anthropogeography," or "cultural geography," to name a few.[13]

Mackinder's claim for what connects "physical geography" to "political geography" abbreviates a great many important debates in geography and surrounding disciplines—most notably the theoretical debates in Germany, and above all those raised in Friedrich Ratzel's *Anthropogeographie* (1882–1891). The opening sections of the first volume of *Anthropogeogra-*

phie offer a comprehensive classification of the different branches of the science of geography as a whole, which Ratzel divides into "Physikalische Geographie" (physical geography) and "Anthropogeographie" (Ratzel's coinage for "human geography"). As his title indicates, Ratzel is most concerned with the second of these branches of geography, whose systematization as a science was the project of the two volumes of *Anthropogeographie*. His definition of "anthropogeography" asserts, first, that priority should be given to human geography, since the human being ("der Mensch") is the main object of study for every science.[14] He then goes on to insist, however, that anthropogeography is intimately connected to the natural sciences. It is this connection between the natural and the human sciences that gives geography—or, rather, *anthropogeography*—its distinctive object of study, namely "the geographical diffusion of humankind across the earth's surface."[15]

This core claim of Ratzel's—what Woodruff Smith has dubbed the "diffusionist revolt" against dominant liberal patterns of academic thinking in nineteenth-century Germany—has a great many implications for the disciplines of geography and anthropology. Its innovative construction of what each discipline takes for its object of study belongs, moreover, to the interesting story of the late-nineteenth-century attempt to unify the so-called cultural sciences, "Kulturwissenschaften."[16] The significance of "culture" as the shared object of study is suggested by the fact that Ratzel's classification of the branches of geography renders "Kulturgeographie" as a synonym for "Anthropogeographie." Neither "culture" nor "humanity" survives, however, as the principle of coherence around which Ratzel is able to construct geography as a science. By the late 1890s, "biogeography" displaces "anthropogeography"—eclipsing both "culture" and "humankind" as the proper object of geographic study—to produce a geography in the service of an expansionist, imperialist politics.

The logic of the formation of geopolitics may be traced, in large part, in the changing focus of Ratzel's works from *Anthropogeographie* (1882–1891) to *Politische Geographie* (1897) and *Der Lebensraum* (1901). The same logic, at once disciplinary and political, simultaneously informs Mackinder's "new geography"—a formulation (Mackinder's) aptly reminiscent of the "new imperialism." It is hardly a surprise that the formation of geopolitics coincides with the rise of the "new imperialism" in Europe in the late nineteenth century, although the full scope and importance of this for the foundations and legitimation of the modern discipline of geography has only recently been addressed.[17] What Mackinder's work helps illustrate is the wider cultural crisis within which geopolitics takes shape: the logic by which nineteenth-century notions of culture are reconfigured by the formation of geopolitics.

In his *Democratic Ideals and Reality* (1919), Mackinder looked back with revealing ambivalence on the success of German geography: "Judged from the standpoint of Berlin, it was a wonderful thing to have impressed Kultur, or *Strategical mentality*, on the educated class of a whole people, but from the standpoint of civilisation at large it was a fatal momentum to have given to a nation."[18] In abbreviated form, Mackinder's phrase "Kultur, or Strategical mentality" encapsulates the conceptual knot twinning the definitional confusion of "culture"—in translation across a variety of languages—and the formation of geopolitics. Among the many things condensed in Mackinder's use of the German term "Kultur" is the logical culmination of Ratzel's attempt—and failure—to unify a science of cultural studies ("Kulturwissenschaft") around geography.

Mackinder's diagnosis of the "fatal momentum" of "Kultur" is attended, of course, by a barely concealed admiration for the "wonderful success" in making geography the teaching of "strategical mentality." Part of Mackinder's ambivalence comes clearly from the fact that this was what he had been advocating since the 1880s. If the difference for Mackinder lies in the distinction between German "Kultur" and "civilisation at large," this only makes all the more visible the key role of the "culture" concept in the formation of geopolitics. It also conceals the extent to which Mackinder's own "educational battle" in the 1880s to bring geography into schools and universities formed part of a complex collaboration and competition amongst geographers from different European countries who, together, were shaping their disciplines to legitimate, and be legitimized by, official nationalism.[19]

One immediate source for Mackinder's arguments, J. Scott Keltie's influential 1885 report on geographical education throughout Europe, is particularly interesting for the emphasis placed on the value of German models of geography education.[20] In an appendix, Keltie's report translates the curriculum statement for the military academy of the University of Berlin.[21] This "'Instruction' as to the scope and method of studies to be observed at the Kriegs-Akademie, Berlin"—a title echoed in Mackinder's

"On the Scope and Methods of Geography"—has strong affinities with Mackinder's claim for the "continuous argument" of geography: "The circle of sciences, comprehended generally under the name of geography, forms the transition and concatenating link between the natural and historical sciences."[22] The imperialist "scope and methods" of each educational program is suggested in the final section, with its significant emphasis on the term "culture":

> A systematic scientific conception of geography will take the whole earth's surface as the subject of its comparative studies, and all the more when at the present time European culture is pressing forward on every hand with rapid progress. In consideration, however, of the historical task devolving on Europe, to become the representative and leader of this worldwide culture, the student in his historico-geographical studies will specially apply his mind to the appreciation of the physical configuration of Europe, and how it exercised such influence on its inhabitants as to qualify them for such a mission.[23]

Here, perhaps, is registered the birth of geopolitics. If so, it is more than an embryonic version of German "Geopolitik," the draft plan of Haushofer's program to make the man in the street "think geopolitically" and to train the nation's leaders to "act geopolitically."[24] Translated for an English evaluation of the place of geography in education throughout Europe, which in turn served an international readership, it is a document that registers the moment in which a discourse of geopolitics takes shape in translation. In its formulation of "European culture," most importantly, it registers the roots of geopolitics in a knotted entanglement of geography and culture, anticipating the later terms of Mackinder's equation between "Kultur" and "strategical mentality."

It is not only, however, from the new imperialist and militarist discourse of post-1870 Europe that Mackinder's "political geography" draws its rhetorical strength. The generalist vision of his 1887 address also looks back to the mainstream of nineteenth-century European geography and its encyclopedic ambition to provide an inclusive description of the earth and its inhabitants. This had been Alexander Humboldt's ambition, in his travel writings and his *Kosmos*; it had been Carl Ritter's, too, in his *Erdkunde*. Perhaps the fullest, most ambitious attempt to realize the grand narrative claims of nineteenth-century geography was the nineteen-volume *La Nouvelle Géographie Universelle* by Elisée Reclus. Reclus's work provided a monumental precedent for Mackinder's vision of a geography that sought to follow the "continuous argument" from "physical geography" to "political geography." From his first major work on physical geography, *La Terre* (1868–1869), through the *Nouvelle Géographie Universelle* (1876–1894), up to his final, six-volume work of "social geography," *L'Homme et la Terre* (1905–1908), Reclus had followed just such an argument.

For Reclus, however, the argument of geography was a matter of human emancipation. Writing in the second volume of *La Terre*, Reclus articulated the connection between the work of geography and the work of political emancipation:

> Human beings, these "reasonable beings" who love so much to boast about their free will, nonetheless cannot make themselves independent of the climates and of the physical conditions of the country they inhabit. Our liberty, in our relations to the Earth, consists in understanding the laws of these relations to confirm the liberty of our existence.[25]

Liberty was a theme Reclus would never abandon. The experience of imprisonment as a Communard a few years later only helped confirm that theme more clearly with the simultaneous formulation of his anarchist position and his project to write the *Universal Geography*.[26]

Liberty, of course, was also the great theme of nineteenth-century liberalism, and in its effort to realize the full emancipatory impulse of the grand-narrative ambitions of the nineteenth century, Reclus's *Universal Geography* underscores the role of geography in helping shape the principles of both freedom and science in what Lyotard calls "the narrative of legitimation" of knowledge in the nineteenth century.[27] The central place of emancipatory principles in nineteenth-century geography shows through even in the "new imperialist" rhetoric with which the Berlin Instruction characterizes Europe's "mission" as "representative and leader of this world-wide culture." The same terms—with a different inflection from that given in Keltie's translation—belong to the emancipatory claims with which Reclus conditions the narrative of his *Universal Geography*. Reclus, in his introduction of 1876, writes that Europe's "inhabitants, whatever their failings and vices, or their state of barbarism in some respects, still impel the rest of mankind as regards material and mental progress."[28]

"Progress" for Reclus, of course, has a different political significance than for the curricular Instruction (or its likely English readers). That very difference, however, draws attention to the importance for geography of the definitional confusion over the term "culture" in the formulations "European culture" and "world-wide culture." For Reclus, "first place" is accorded to Europe, the historical and geographical formation of whose "material and mental progress" is made the narrative condition for a "universal" geography. This Eurocentric imperative also informs the Berlin Instruction—both in its explanation for why special curricular emphasis is to be placed on the physical geography of Europe, and in the implied synonymy of "European culture" and "this world-wide culture."

What gets blurred in the Berlin Instruction's use of the term "culture," however, is a hypothesis on which Reclus's "universal" descriptive geography depends: that the "progress"—or "laws of liberty"—of Europe's historical development may be linked to the universal history of humankind. This hypothesis of culture in the broadest sense might be said to be the founding ideal of European historical geography. Herder's *Ideen zur Philosophie der Geschichte der Menschheit* (1784–1791) is a crucial antecedent, because, while attacking the presumptive superiority of European culture, it made European geography the condition for imagining what principle of development or culture ("Bildung") connects European culture with the history of all humankind. The connection between the two remains a hypothesis for a whole range of nineteenth-century formulations of culture, including Immanuel Kant's idea for "a universal history with a cosmopolitan purpose." Although Kant's idea of a "cosmopolitan right" contrasts with Herder's concern for natural laws of development, both constituted attempts to hypothesize a relation between natural and human laws. Each frames a different side of the same hypothesis of cultural development: Herder, in deriving universal human rights from natural laws; Kant, in postulating nature's plan according to a universal idea of human right.

At the heart of this hypothesis lies a central, ambiguous question about the place of Europe in world history. If, as Williams points out, Herder calls into question the superiority of European culture ("The very thought of a superior European culture is a blatant insult to the majesty of Nature"[29]), elsewhere Herder's book claims that European culture is in fact superior ("How then did Europe come by its culture and the rank this has given it above other peoples?"[30]). This is an ambiguity rather than a contradiction, because it constitutes a question about European culture to which Herder repeatedly returns throughout the *Ideas*—how it came to seem superior, whether it will continue to seem so, where it stands in relation to the cultural development of humankind considered as a whole.

Herder's ambiguous question of European culture is particularly interesting for the later formation of geopolitics because of its concern for the relation between natural laws of development and the cultural development of humankind. Both senses of development (natural and human) inflect Herder's conception of culture as "Bildung." Early in the first book, Herder asks: "Why does Europe stand out as the place with the most national diversity, the place with the greatest multiplicity of arts and customs, and above all as the most powerful of all parts of the world?"[31] His answer hinges on the geographical situation of "the unique Mediterranean sea," about which he writes "how much has it become the determinant of all Europe":

> Were one to change the borders of these lands [Spain, France, England, Greece], take away a channel here, close up a waterway there; then the development [Bildung] and the destruction [Verwüstung] of the world, the fate of whole peoples and parts of the world through centuries takes a different course.[32]

The geographical condition of Herder's hypothesis of culture, and of Europe's relation to the general development of humankind, has a crucial influence on the notion of "Bildung" which, together with Goethe's poetics and Humboldt's educational theories, as well as Kant's cosmopolitical conception of culture, shaped nineteenth-century European ideas of culture.[33] The specifically geographical formulation of Eurocentrism in this hypothesis of culture conditions many of the most ambitious nineteenth-century narratives—Hegel's *Philosophy of History*, Buckle's *History of Civilization*, and Marx's *Capital* are some of the more influential.[34]

The rhetoric of Mackinder's call for a "new geography" is shaped around the ambiguous legacy of this older geography: hence the "duty" of the geographer to make a "bridge" over the "abyss" that is "upsetting the equilibrium of our culture." What makes Mackinder so revealing a figure in the crisis of legitimation at the turn of the century is the manner in which he attempts to remodel the old into the new imperialist vision. His talent as a synthesizer of knowledge is perhaps the key thing. If this enabled him to reproduce the theoretical arguments of Friedrich Ratzel while masking their real consequences for the discipline of geography, it also enabled him to abbreviate the emancipatory narrative claims of that earlier "universal" geography embodied in the work of Elisée Reclus.[35]

Mackinder's Geopolitical Image of Britain

Outlining his "geographical philosophy" in 1908, Mackinder wrote:

> When you have got your myriad facts, registered by the labour of all the generations which have gradually built up the map of the world in its infinite detail, you have then got to play with them. You have to acquire such facility in this respect that you are able to see with the mind's eye, not the mere map of Italy with the boot at the end of it, but the blue sky, and the blue sea, and the brilliant sun. . . . You must be able to see this image, and then to prolong it by an effort of imagination beyond the horizon. Thus to be able to visualize is of the very essence of geographical power.[36]

Confirming the rhetorical power of synthesis in Mackinder's "new geography," this characteristic statement underscores the central place of visualization in that rhetoric. "Visualization," as Derek Gregory argues, is at the foundation of the modern discipline of geography; its "Cartesian perspectivalism" defines what O Tuathail, following Gregory, argues is the key feature of Mackinder's "geopolitical gaze."[37] In his series of geography textbooks, which reflect an ambitious attempt to reshape all aspects of education from kindergarten to university,[38] Mackinder sought to provide a solution for the problem Joyce formulates in Stephen's encounter with his geography textbook.

For Stephen the geography textbook reveals a contestation of political perspectives through the colors green and maroon, which his school-mate Fleming has used to illustrate the picture of the world, and which Stephen associates with the colors of Davitt and Parnell: "He turned over the flyleaf and looked wearily at the green round earth in the middle of the maroon clouds. He wondered which was right, to be for the green or for the maroon, because Dante had ripped the green velvet back off the brush that was for Parnell one day with her scissors and had told him that Parnell was a bad man."[39] If for Mackinder the geography textbook ought to resolve such contradictions, simultaneously instructing the pupil "what politics meant" and "where the universe ended," Mackinder's emphasis on the formative imaginative experience of the child's "varying at will the pattern seen"⁴⁰ nonetheless draws attention to a process of "play" in visualization reminiscent of the auditory, verbal, and visual play inaugurated by Stephen's "green wothe."

Some of the founding ambiguities of Mackinder's "geographical philosophy" emerge in his most important geography textbook, *Britain and the British Seas* (1902). The influential first chapter, "The Position of Britain," provides a revealing illustration of how he uses the visual aid of the map. In the process, he abbreviates almost subliminally a whole history of geographic representation from classical antiquity to the present, in which the position of Britain shifts from the periphery to the center of the world:

> Before the great geographical discoveries of the fifteenth and sixteenth centuries, the known lands lay almost wholly in the Northern Hemisphere and spread in a single continent from the shores of Spain to those of Cathay. Britain was then at the end of the world—almost out of the world. . . . During two thousand years Britain was at the margin, not in the centre, of the theatre of politics, and for most practical purposes her position was accurately shown in the maps of the Greek geographers and in the fantastic charts of the medieval monks.⁴¹

Mackinder's emphasis on Britain's peripheral position is illustrated by two pairs of historical maps—the thirteenth-century Mappa Mundi together with an explanatory key (see Figures 4a–b), and the Greek maps according to Eratosthenes and Ptolemy (see Figures 5a–b).⁴²

The maps serve more than an illustrative purpose, however, as becomes clearer in Mackinder's second paragraph: "The historical meaning of the Columbian discoveries can best be realised by turning a terrestrial globe so that Britain may be at the point nearest to the eye" (see Figure 6).⁴³ As "the eye" of the reader turns from the ancient to the contemporary world maps, the gradually emerging contours of a familiar Mediterranean yield suddenly (with a turn of the page, as it happens) to the global projection. All the while illustrating the text's argument about the position of Britain, this sequencing of maps abbreviates, diagrams, and illustrates a history of geographical exploration as a history of the world. The text sustains the

FIGURE 4a. Thirteenth-Century Map, preserved in Hereford Cathedral, showing the terminal position of Britain in the known world, from H. J. Mackinder, *Britain and the British Seas*.

FIGURE 4b. Mackinder's Key to Figure 4a, from H. J. Mackinder, *Britain and the British Seas*.

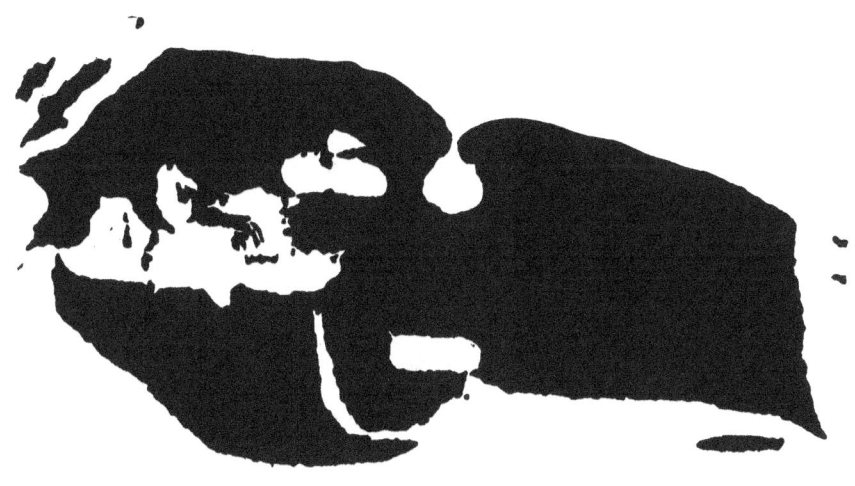

FIGURE 5a. The World according to Eratosthenes, showing the terminal position of Britain [—after Bunbury], from H. J. Mackinder, *Britain and the British Seas*.

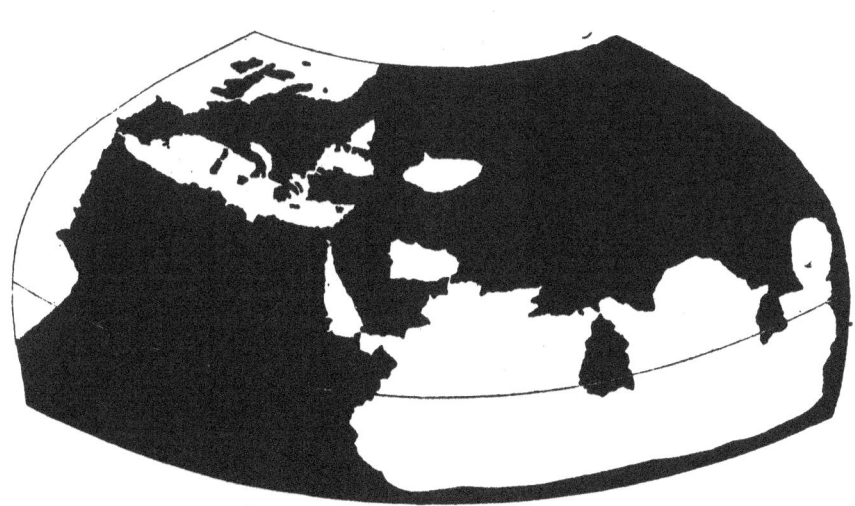

FIGURE 5b. The World according to Ptolemy, showing separate Eastern and Western Oceans [—after Bunbury], from H. J. Mackinder, *Britain and the British Seas*.

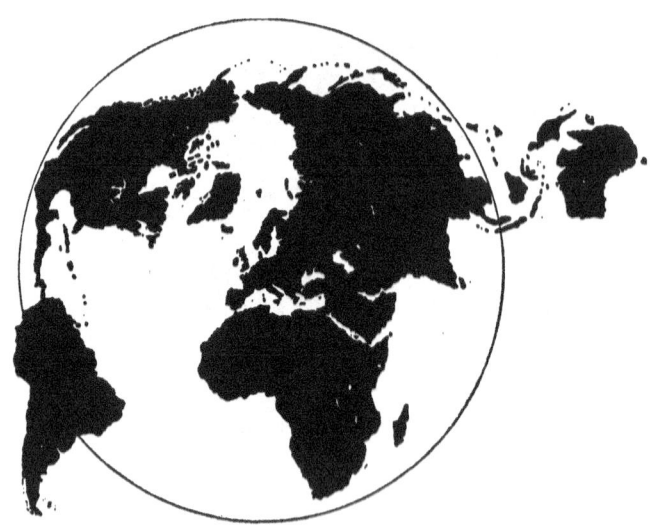

FIGURE 6. The Land Hemisphere, showing the Mediterranean Ocean and the central position of Britain, from H. J. Mackinder, *Britain and the British Seas*.

FIGURE 7. Photograph of a globe showing the true form of the North Atlantic, from H. J. Mackinder, *Britain and the British Seas*.

argument about the position of Britain, although it has modulated into an argument about how the "globe-wide" world may best be viewed, geographically and historically, from the point of view of Britain.[44] This modulation becomes complete when the text ends the sequence of figures by reference to a "Photograph of a globe showing the true form of the North Atlantic" (see Figure 7):[45]

> Europe, Asia, Africa, and the two Americas are thus included within the visible hemisphere; but the chief feature even of the land-half of the globe is a great arm of mediterranean ocean, Atlantic and Arctic, winding northward.... No flat chart can give a correct impression of the form of the North Atlantic. Only a globe can suggest its vast bulging centre, and the relative insignificance of its Arctic, Mediterranean, and Caribbean recesses.... For most purposes, therefore, the North Atlantic is a rounded basin, with eastward, northward, and westward gulfs, and a southern exit. But the five historic parts of the world are accessible from its waters, and for the generations that followed Columbus history centred increasingly round its shores. Thus Britain gradually became the central, rather than the terminal land of the world.[46]

The effect of this series of images is to produce an argument independent of the text—a field of visual play whose medium owes something, perhaps, to early developments in the technology of the moving picture. Certainly Mackinder's educational program involved close attention to turn-of-the-century developments in multimedia—as indicated by his work for the Visual Instruction Committee of the Colonial Office, set up in 1902.[47] If, as O Tuathail argues, Mackinder's was a "conscious reaction" to "new technological developments like cinema"—a "modernism of reaction"—the reactionary formalism that results is founded on a thoroughgoing ambiguity, displacing geography's "Cartesian perspectivalism" within a discursive frame of reference that includes the simultaneous emergence of high modernism and mass culture.[48]

Much of Mackinder's political geography, and geopolitics generally, may be derived from the striking juxtaposition of the Ancient map of the world, with the Mediterranean in the center, and the world map as organized with an "eye" on Britain. The formalist logic of this play on the visual image is most evident in the middle two maps (Figures 5a–b and Figure 6) of the four-part sequence. Here, without the distraction of the details on the Medieval map or the claim to realism in the photograph of a globe, there is a stark contrast of black against white. The black and white spaces of the Ancient map effect, indeed, a momentary confusion while the eye sorts out the relation of black, corresponding to land, and white, corresponding to water—a correspondence confirmed as one turns to the continents and oceans of the global vision. This play of figure against ground is reminiscent of the perceptual experiments in literary and artistic modernism discussed by Fredric Jameson in *The Political Unconscious* and Rosalind Krauss in *The Optical Unconscious*. If the formalist play of figure and ground results in what Jameson calls the modernist "declaration of independence of the image as such," the modernist logic of this "optical unconscious," in Krauss's terms, is as applicable to Mackinder's political geography as it is to what Jameson traces in the "perceptual vocation" of Conrad's "sensorium" and to what Krauss traces to the origins of abstract art.[49] It is according to such a logic that Mackinder establishes a central aspect of his political geography, the interplay of sea-power and land-power.

The reversal of figure against ground is by no means incidental to the overall argument. In Figure 4a it is the *land* that is white, and the sea black, something that surely contributes to the initial confusion, looking across to the blank spaces of the sea and the blackened land masses of Figure 5a. Similarly, the curious effect of the photograph of a globe is, in part, produced by the visual contrast of white continents and black seas, juxtaposed with the white seas and black continents of the preceding image of the Land Hemisphere. This alternating pattern produces a sort of formalist ambiguity of figure against ground, and not only in the sense that what stands out as figure in the one map—the shape of continents—becomes ground in another map. There is also the sense that on any one map figure and ground might be reversed: land and sea must both be grasped as potentially figure or ground.

Mackinder's visual contrast is reminiscent of Joseph Conrad's notoriously ambiguous use of the high-colonialist trope of the "blank space" on the map of Africa: "a white patch for a boy to dream gloriously over," it "had become a place of darkness."[50] Mackinder's visual contrast of black against white is, of course, more abstractly technical and scientific. It is no less implicated, however, in the exploitative assumptions and racial identifications that shape the core problem of political imagining in *Heart of Darkness*. The political use to which Mackinder puts this simplified formalism emerges in the first of his "elementary studies" for school children, *Our Own Islands* (1906). In its concluding chapter on "Area," the image of the British Isles is used to illustrate the technical question of geographical measurement. In a series of figures representing the areas of Canada, South Africa, India, Australia, and New Zealand, all of these maps are presented as black land masses, with a white insert of the British Isles (except in the case of New Zealand, where the two are presented side by side). The exercises in the measurement of "area" are revealed to have been part of an ideological argument when the chapter concludes with an appeal that serves in retrospect as a caption for the series of maps: "Those who can find work to-day in Britain should stay . . . , but those who have not work should cross the ocean to make new homes for themselves in Canada, or Australia, or New Zealand, or South Africa. In all these lands they will remain the subjects of our King, Edward VII; the same flag will be theirs, and they will not be among foreigners."[51]

In *Britain and the British Seas*, the visual trick of what might be called an unconscious optical geopolitics[52] establishes the image of Britain in world-historical relation to the educational and formalist imperative of the child's "varying at will the pattern seen." Concluding the argument of his first chapter, Mackinder writes:

> Seen thus in relation to earlier and to later history, Britain is possessed of two geographical qualities, complementary rather than antagonistic: insularity and universality. Before Columbus, the insularity was more evident than the universality. . . . After Columbus, value began to attach to the ocean-highway, which is in its nature universal.[53]

There is good reason to recognize in this, if not the central paradigm of geopolitics, at least one of its most characteristic abbreviations of world history. It constitutes the rhetorical power of the opening to Mackinder's 1904 address to the Royal Geographical Society, "The Geographical Pivot of History," in the argument that "from the present time forth, in the post-Columbian age, we shall again have to deal with a closed political system, and none the less that it will be one of world-wide scope."[54]

Virtually the same abbreviation of world history accompanies perhaps the first use of the word "geo-political" in the English language. In the same year that *Britain and the British Seas* was published, Emil Reich, the Hungarian-born historian who settled in England in the 1890s, introduces the term with special emphasis in his review of the monumental *Cambridge Modern History*.⁵⁵ Nor is Reich's formulation of the term "geo-political" merely an idiosyncratic, isolated, or accidental coinage. It recurs in his noted *Foundations of Modern Europe* (1904), and again in the two-volume *Handbook of Geography* published in 1908, itself a testament to Reich's sense of the importance of "what [the author] has ventured to call geopolitics, or the combined influence of geographical with political facts."⁵⁶ The *Handbook* has a revealing relation, too, to Mackinder's *Britain and the British Seas*, since its opening chapter, "The British Isles," follows the general shape of Mackinder's own argument in his opening chapter. Reich reiterates Mackinder's central point about the "position of Britain" in the concise argument that "English history falls, from the geo-political point of view, naturally into two divisions, prae-Columbian history and post-Columbian history."⁵⁷

Reproducing this paradigmatic abbreviation of world history, Reich codifies Mackinder's "position of Britain" as a specifically "geo-political" image.⁵⁸

Ratzel's Anthropogeographical Image of Humankind

The invention of the word "geopolitics" is usually credited to Rudolf Kjellén, the Swedish political scientist, who indeed credits himself with coining the term. It is Kjellén, too, who established Friedrich Ratzel's prominence as the father figure of his pseudo-political science. In his 1920 *Grundriss zu einem System der Politik*, Kjellén wrote, "The word was first coined in a public lecture in April 1899, which later appeared in the series 'Inledning till Sverigen geografi' (1900); where it was originally meant to signify the same as Ratzel's 'political geography' and partly also his Anthropogeography."⁵⁹

Emil Reich's formulation of "geo-politics" also emphasizes the importance of Ratzel, but his account is in many respects more revealing about the tradition within which Ratzel stands, as well as about what links Ratzel's to Mackinder's political geography, and what makes each significant for the discursive formation of geopolitics. In his 1902 account of the "geo-political" study of history, Emil Reich names Alexander von Humboldt, Karl Ritter, and Elisée Reclus, "and other geographers," as those "who held that the abiding and most determinative cause of the broad events of History is the configuration and physiology of the planet on which we live."⁶⁰ Laying particular emphasis on the work of Friedrich Ratzel, he offers the following account of Ratzel's contributions, providing (at the end of this long quotation) an interesting echo of the famous passage from Herder's *Ideen* cited above:

> At present the greatest exponent of Anthropogeography, as he calls it, is Professor Frederick Ratzel, of Leipsic. In various works, especially in his "Politische Geographie" (1897), [Ratzel] has thrown out an astounding number of suggestions and thoughts pointing out the correlation between Geography and History. Nor can it be doubted that the irregularly varying ordinates in History, that is, the events, cannot be reasonably supposed to be comprehensible without assuming the existence of regularly variable *abscissae* in the form of geographical, or rather geo-political, influences of an abiding character. Let the Dogger Bank be a large island such as Ireland, or widen the Channel at Dover to the extent of its width at the Lizard, and the whole history of England is different from what it has actually been. Suppose the Danube, instead of flowing into the Euxine, to fall into the Greek Sea, and the history of the Balkan peoples assumes dimensions totally different from what it has taken these three thousand years. *Est locus in rebus.*⁶¹

This interesting transposition of Herder's determinants of European geography is also revealing in adjusting the concerns of Ratzel's "anthropogeography" to the optical formalism of Mackinder's maps. Although Ratzel was indeed interested in the "strategy of situation" that makes for the power of Mackinder's maps, Ratzel's geographical picture of the world (see Figure 8) is far less able to formulate what Reich calls the "power of localities."⁶² In certain crucial respects, the unconscious optical logic of Mackinder's map of "the (globe-wide) world" emerges from a reversal of Ratzel's geographical picture of the world.

Mackinder's opening chapter draws attention to this in citing Ratzel as an authority for explaining the term "OEcumene." As part of the geographical justification for the perspectival shift which puts Britain at the center of the world stage, Mackinder appends a "Note on the word 'world,'" explaining, with reference to Ratzel, the "technical sense" of "OEcumene," or "Mundus," meaning not "the entire globe-world" but the "Habitable World."⁶³ The reference is to the second volume of Ratzel's *Anthropogeographie* (1891), where the notion of "OEcumene" plays a key role in the work's ambitious attempt to establish a science of human geog-

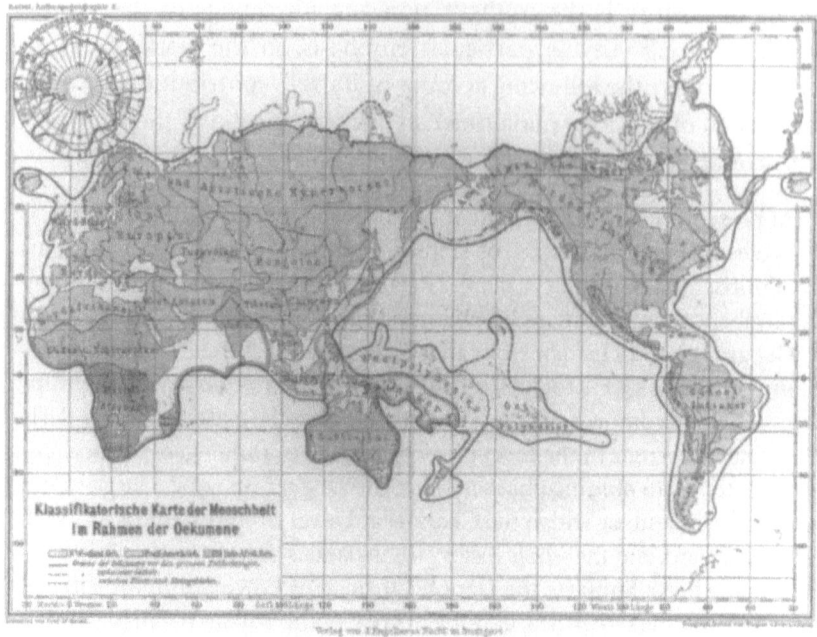

FIGURE 8. Classificatory Chart of Humankind in the Frame of the Oecumene, from Friedrich Ratzel, *Anthropogeographie* II. Courtesy of the Harvard College Library.

raphy. Mackinder, however, in his characteristic abbreviation of debates and theories of geography, circumvents Ratzel's theoretical grounds for establishing what constitutes the object of study for human geography. Undeterred by Ratzel's complications in articulating that object of study ("Kultur"), Mackinder himself makes the map the medium of "strategical thinking." It is the political and strategic significance—what Reich evokes in his paraphrase of Horace, "Est *locus* in rebus" (i.e., there is a "power of localities" in things)—that interests Mackinder in considering the globe from the point of view of human habitation.[64] The anthropological object of geographical study that was the foundation of Ratzel's work as a geographer gets condensed and displaced, as the riddling leftover "rebus," as it were, of Reich's "power of localities."

Ratzel's concept of the "OEcumene" provides a useful frame of reference for examining this displacement of culture in the shift from Ratzel's "anthropogeography" to Mackinder's "political geography." Though not made explicit until volume 2 of his *Anthropogeographie* (1891), the concept of the "OEcumene" defines the book's central focus on "the geographical diffusion of humankind." Developed from the natural sciences of zoology and botany, Ratzel has made this aspect of "anthropo-geography," by the end of volume 1, the fundamental principle for realizing a universal history of humankind. Taking up this principle in the succeeding volume, Ratzel uses the concept of the "OEcumene" to represent the distribution of the human species throughout the habitable world.

The "OEcumene" provides a technical term for the "anthropogeographical picture of humankind" with which volume 1 concluded (as the "necessary end result of our observations"). Volume 2 takes this up as the "geographical picture of humankind." At the end of volume 2, this "picture" or "image" (Bild) of humankind is represented by a "classificatory map of humankind in the framework of the Oecumene" (see Figure 8). Ratzel's map seeks to provide the most comprehensive image of the history of humankind, condensing into a single "picture" (Bild) the spread of different peoples throughout history over the surface of the earth.

Ratzel's world map is, indeed, hardly a map in Mackinder's sense at all, and it is worth noting that Ratzel's *Anthropogeographie* makes remarkably little use of maps. Volume 1 has no maps; and the maps in volume 2 are sometimes no more than "schemae." If for Mackinder "visualisation" involves a sort of diagrammatic formalism, Ratzel invokes a very different model—that of realist pictorial perspective in the visual arts. Analogies to the three-dimensional perspective of painting, landscape painting in particular, abound in Ratzel's work. One example occurs in the concluding sections of *Anthropogeographie* II, where Ratzel repeatedly emphasizes the difficulty of representing, without distortion in this or that way, the true geographical "picture," or "image" (Bild) of humankind. So, for example:

> To the geographical image/picture of humankind belong, besides the horizontal distribution, that we determine through the depiction of the boundaries of the OEcumene, and the shadings of distribution density—to these belong also the distances, in which the various parts of humankind are ordered one behind the other according to historical age, and the heights to which better-positioned or culturally better-equipped peoples have risen.[65]

It is a telling image. As an embellished metaphor for the scope and methods of Ratzel's anthropogeography, the extended analogy to the visual tricks of pictorial realism aestheticizes the scientific claims for a systematic organization of the human sciences. As a description of the ethnographic chart of the OEcumene, it is not only presented as more pleasing to the eye, it explains what the chart can only indicate in abbreviated form—that is, the problem of perspective necessary for appreciating the nuances of population density, historical stages, or levels of cultural development. The metaphor of aesthetic perspective underscores the extent to which the full "scope and method" of anthropogeography remains an imaginary projection.

Ratzel's imaginary picture, moreover, illustrates the problem of human perspective which must vanish in the production of Mackinder's geopolitical image. As one moves from Ratzel to Mackinder, the question of anthropology disappears so that the geopolitical image constitutes the riddling afterimage of all those attempts to systematize and explain human history which characterized nineteenth-century European humanism in the broadest sense—and most notably, in the ensemble of concerns constellated around the concept of culture.

In *Anthropogeographie* I, where "anthropogeography" is rendered by the bracketed synonym "Kulturgeographie," the term "Kultur" seems to haunt the text, as if it embodied a dream once believed in, now abandoned. Meant to connect with the cultural development of all humankind, it repeatedly fragments into pieces: different levels of culture ("Kulturhöhe"); different circles of culture ("Kulturkreisen"); and, perhaps most important of all, the idea of "Halbkultur"—semi-culture, or half-culture—about which Ratzel himself comments, "that somewhat obscure idea of semi-culture" (einigermassen dunklen Begriff, den der Halbkultur).[66] All of these formulations register that crisis of nineteenth-century anthropological views, from which would emerge, in James Clifford's words, a "new ethnographic conception of culture."[67]

In *Anthropogeographie* Ratzel's anthropological arguments must resist pluralizing the notion of culture, since its entire scheme rests on viewing the *unity* of humankind in its historical development and diffusion throughout the world. The conceptual strain this imperative places on the concept of culture emerges at the end of volume 1, in Ratzel's grand summation of "the anthropogeographical image/picture of humankind." Arguing (as Ratzel always did) that differences of racial origin should not be exaggerated, he goes on to evoke a grand process of human development to which "one people after another" contribute as "carriers" of its "own phase in the unfolding" of "culture." And he concludes: "So that the racially highest of contemporary humankind are not only the carriers of culture ["Kulturträger"] because they are so highly developed; but also on the other hand are so highly developed because they are the carriers of culture."[68]

The tautology of this definitional confusion of culture, people, and race signals a particularly ambiguous moment in the scientific legitimation of racism, the defining moment of crisis in that general European hypothesis of culture conceived in relation to a single unfolding development of humankind.[69] The place of anthropology in Ratzel's *Anthropogeographie*, intended to correct the historiographic bias of Eurocentric views of culture, in fact reveals the logic of Ratzel's increasing abandonment of this very hypothesis that one might yet understand Europe's position in a single unfolding cultural development of humankind. Ratzel's most extensive attempt to sort out the contradictions involved in defining "culture" is to be found in *Völkerkunde* (1885–1888), his influential work of anthropology written between volumes 1 and 2 of *Anthropogeographie*. The book's first definition enacts in miniature a fragmentation of nineteenth-century culture concepts:

> With the word "culture" we usually designate the *sum of all the spiritual and mental (geistigen) achievements of an epoch*. Yet this is obviously not a simple or firm one. We speak of levels of culture, of higher or lower culture, of semi-culture, and above all we set in opposition peoples with culture and peoples without culture (Kultur- und Naturvölker).[70]

In seeking a solution to this problem, Ratzel reiterates an apparent critique of Eurocentrism elaborated in *Anthropogeographie* which echoes the seminal terms of Herder's *Ideen*. Drawing, in passing, first on a plural notion of culture ("different cultures") and then on a relativism of cultural perspectives, Ratzel writes:

> It follows from this that we apply a certain measure for evaluating the different cultures that we find among the peoples of the earth, and that we obviously take this measure from the level of culture that we ourselves have reached. Our culture is for us *the* culture. Assuming that in fact the highest and richest development of this idea is to be found with us, so it appears most important, in order to gain an understanding of the matter itself, to trace the flowering of this blossom back to its seed. We can only

succeed in gaining an insight into the essence of culture, if we understand the driving force which has developed, from the first small beginnings, everything that we call, simply, culture.[71]

This almost definitive hypothesis of culture for Ratzel cannot, however, be sustained by the terms of his *Völkerkunde*. The concept of "Halbkultur" is developed to hold in place the fragmenting senses of culture. "Halbkultur," designates, he argues, those cultural levels that lie between the extremes of the most integrated collective social groups and the loosest of social aggregates. Described as a "Halbwegsbegriff" (literally, "half-way idea"), it emerges as a stopgap measure for sustaining the hypothesis of culture.[72] In *Anthropogeographie* II, Ratzel no longer writes of "Halbkultur." Instead, the contrast between lower and higher, or between weaker and stronger cultures becomes more pronounced, as Ratzel develops the idea of the "struggle for space." With his adoption of the term "Lebensraum" (the title of his 1901 book and one of the keywords of German geopolitics), Ratzel abandons altogether the hypothesis of a single unfolding culture.

In the shift from *Anthropogeographie* to the *Politische Geographie*, what in *Völkerkunde* emerged as the breakdown of the singular unfolding culture of all humankind into different levels of culture leads from the problem of "Kultur" as an object of anthropological study to the problem of "Kultur" as an object of military power, political strategy, and territorial control—in short, the geopolitics of Reich's "Est locus in rebus" and Mackinder's maps. In Ratzel's *Politische Geographie*, the definitional confusion over "Kultur" produces a set of terms that fuse ethnographic and territorial designations: "Kulturkräfte" (cultural powers), "Kulturkreise" (cultural circles), "Kulturgebiete" (cultural regions).[73]

The development of this ethnographic and strategic idea of "Kultur" is prefigured in 1886 in a commemorative essay on Herder's *Ideen zur Philosophie der Geschichte der Menschheit* entitled "Das geographische Bild der Menschheit" (The Geographical Picture/Image of Humankind). Highly nationalistic and patriotic, the essay reveals the political logic informing the anthropogeographical picture of humankind in *Anthropogeographie*. Opening with an address to "this Germany, for whose education to humanity [an dessen Bildung zur Humanität] [Herder] had worked his whole life," the essay ends with the argument that, a hundred years after Herder's great work, "Science no longer depends on deceptive pictures [Täuschungsbildern]."⁷⁴ Herder's idealist project of grounding science in the unfolding development of physical nature and human history is characterized as having been realized. The project of "Bildung" over (for Germany, as Ratzel here clearly specifies), geographical science has arrived at the true picture ("Bild") of humankind—and can be put to the service of the new German state: "From the narrow perspective of the history of European states, Germany has stepped out into the wide open prospect of world history."⁷⁵ Where Ratzel's *Anthropogeographie* was conceived as laying the scientific foundations for unifying the cultural sciences, its actual project turned out to be the systematic dismantling and delegitimation of the human sciences.

In the process, Ratzel reconfigures the relation between "Kultur" and "Bildung" governing the contrast between Herder's nationalism and Kant's cosmopolitanism. Herder had speculated on those organic laws of natural and human development ("Bildung") that would explain the common basis for the claims of enlightenment reason ("Aufklärung") and culture ("Kultur").⁷⁶ For Ratzel, those natural laws have been mastered, "the image/picture of humankind" almost conquered. What remains is for culture ("Kultur"—not "Bildung") to "bring together people into humanity" (Die Kultur, welche die Menschen zur Menschheit zusammenschloss): "However different humanity once might have been, it *must* come to terms with its amalgation into one and with accelerating steps. The earth is small, humankind old, history long."⁷⁷ This ominous imperative for an accelerated amalgamation of different peoples brought together by a dominant "Kultur" signals the transfiguration of nineteenth-century culture concepts into the classic geopolitical stereotype of German "Kultur" as a means toward world power and domination. As Mackinder so concisely formulates it: "Kultur, or *Strategical mentality*."

Reclus's Social Geography, the Image of the State, and the Hegemony of Europe

Even as Emil Reich was codifying the "strategical mentality" of Mackinder's geography as "geo-political," an alternative reading of Mackinder's argument was being advanced by Elisée Reclus, in his last monumental work, *L'Homme et la Terre*. As Reclus argued in the final volume's analysis of contemporary history, Britain occupies a unique position because "each movement of the British Isles, which little England symbol-

FIGURE 9. Frantisek Kupka, "L'Angleterre et son cortège" [England and its cortège], from Reclus, *L'Homme et la Terre*, vol. 6 (1908). Courtesy of the Harvard College Library.

izes, has its repercussions throughout the entire world."[78] In a chapter entitled "England and Its Cortège," and illustrated with a Kupka sketch of an Englishman in plus fours trampling dead bodies underfoot (see Figure 9),[79] Reclus's analysis of British imperialism emphasizes the contradiction around which Mackinder's geopolitical image of Britain is shaped: "The life of the nation finds itself thus split and determined, in certain respects, by a contradictory politics, since it must act all at once to safeguard the ferocious insularity of the homeland, and ever more actively to maintain its relation to its colonies in order to assure the means of conquest and domination over tributaries spread in all parts of the earth."[80] Reclus's alternative reading of the "position of Britain"—based, indeed, on a rereading of the opening chapter of *Britain and the British Seas*[81]—calls attention to the fundamental ambiguity of Mackinder's geopolitical image.

Of all the prominent European geographers from the turn of the century, Reclus was perhaps the best positioned to illuminate in what sense it was around the blindspot of the nation-state that the narrower sense of "geopolitics" as a putative science took shape. The centrality of the State is made clear in the classic definition of the "science" of geopolitics by Rudolf Kjellén:

> Geopolitics is the teaching of the State as a geographical organism or as a spatial phenomenon: thus the State as country, territory, region or, at its most pronounced, as sovereign-state. As political science, it keeps constantly in view the unity of the state; while political geography studies the earth as the habitat for human existence in relation to the other characteristics of the earth.[82]

This distinction between geopolitics and political geography tells what happens once "analytical geopolitics" crystallizes around the idea of the State. Geopolitics can become a "science" only by renouncing the shared ambition of turn-of-the-century geographers (Mackinder, Ratzel, and Reclus) to unify the discipline of geography. Carrying to its logical conclusion Ratzel's efforts to systematize the various branches of geography, Kjellén in fact systematically dismantles the discipline. For Ratzel, the "State" becomes the focal point for attempting to imagine the "form" in which the contradiction between "anthropogeography" and "biogeography" is to be worked out. The blindspot of Ratzel's geography becomes the central principle for Kjellén's "system of politics," and "geopolitics" is baptized under the sign of a hyperformalism of the State.

Reclus, by contrast to just about all geographers after 1870, rejects the nation-state as the legitimate and legitimizing focus either for politics or for geography. The implications of this radical difference are suggested by the very different ways in which Ratzel and Reclus carry forward the nineteenth-century German geographical tradition. In the first volume of *Anthropogeographie*, Ratzel elaborates on an image attributed to Carl Ritter. Discussing "natural determinants," Ratzel refers to Ritter's "image" for the State: "We recall Carl Ritter's expression, which is more than an image: The State bound to the natural conditions of the land."[83] It is an image that presents the most rudimentary of geopolitical claims: social forms are contingent on geographical factors. Yet the image means very different things for Ratzel and for Reclus. For Ratzel, the State is the natural form produced by the interplay of humankind and environment.[84] For Reclus, precisely insofar as it depends on the interplay of humankind and environment, the form of the State is open to change, both evolutionary and revolutionary.

Ritter's image of the state concisely presents a crucial ambiguity in the formation of geopolitics: whereas imperialist geopolitics makes the state the fixed position for geopolitical analysis, anarchist geopolitics recognizes the state as only part of a larger, more complex interaction of nature and humankind.[85] It is just this ambiguity that may be seen to shape the formalist play of figure against ground in Mackinder's geopolitical image of Britain. If that image seems singularly fixed on the British nation-state, what makes for the very fascination with its fixed position on the world map is not the Britishness of the image at all, but rather the potential global rearrangement of the world and of world history that it makes imaginable. To be sure, Mackinder's *Britain and the British Seas* is fairly explicitly premised on projecting the political unity of the British state and its empire—thus the "geographical qualities" of "insularity" and "universality" are said to be "complementary." Yet the very terms in which Mackinder attempts to resolve the split imperatives of national sovereignty and imperial power call attention all the more clearly both to that very contradiction and its attendant political instability. Mackinder's imperialist geopolitical image is not only haunted by Reclus's anarchist geopolitics, its very power depends on the anarchist thesis that the nation-state is a contingent form of social organization,[86] a thesis which geopolitics articulates in the ambiguous imperialism and anarchism of its own image.

The anarchy in international relations presupposed by imperialist geopolitics is nonetheless to be distinguished from the anarchist principles with which Reclus analyzes international relations. Indeed, what enables Reclus to analyze the "contradictory politics" of the imperial nation-state is the manner in which he holds onto the prior terms of debate about the state that Ratzel and Mackinder have abandoned along with the nineteenth-century hypothesis of culture.

Reclus's geographical work had always been based on a critique of territorial state-based arguments about "the so-called 'balance of European powers.'"[87] In *L'Homme et la Terre*, this critique forms the theoretical basis for his "social geography." "The equilibrium of societies," he writes in the preface, "is unstable only because of the constraint imposed on individuals in their free expansion. The freedom of society is established by the liberty supplied in the full development of each individual human person, the first fundamental unit which then aggregates and forms associations according to its own preference with other units of changing humanity."[88] Reclus's emphasis on the "full development of each individual human person"—and not the state—as the fundamental unit of analysis in social geography recalls the kind of libertarian argument in Herder's notion of "Bildung" that Immanuel Kant had criticized at the end of the eighteenth century. Kant's counterargument—that there need to be limitations imposed on Herder's "self-determining power"[89]—laid the basis for a contrast between Kant's enlightenment cosmopolitanism and Herder's nationalism which gets played out in the odd reversals and contrasts we have already seen in Ratzel and Mackinder—between "Bildung" and "Kultur" and between "Kultur" and "civilization."

The significance of Kant's position is that it placed the question of state power within an international, cosmopolitical context: civil freedom, Kant argued, depended as much on "external" relations as on the development of a state's "internal culture."[90] As he argued in "Perpetual Peace: A Philosophical Sketch":

> The peoples of the earth have thus entered in varying degrees into a universal community, and it has developed to the point where a violation of rights in *one* part of the world is felt *everywhere*. The idea of a cosmopolitan right is therefore not fantastic and overstrained; it is a necessary complement to the unwritten code of political and international right, transforming it into a universal right of humanity. Only under this condition can we flatter ourselves that we are continually advancing towards a perpetual peace.[91]

This Kantian, cosmopolitical feature of the nineteenth-century hypothesis of culture set the terms for later debates about the limits of state power and about the role of education and culture ("Bildung") in setting those limits. Wilhelm von Humboldt and Matthew Arnold are notable examples, Arnold drawing directly from Humboldt's *The Limits of the State* to elaborate the notion of "culture" in *Culture and Anarchy*. Hegel and Marx also provide important touchstones, incidentally showing how their opposing idealist and materialist conceptions of culture are nonetheless both premised on the same cosmopolitical hypothesis. For Hegel, state sovereignty is premised on an idea of education ("Bildung") as what gives universality to the formation of citizens serving the state, its relation to other states, and to the process of world history as a whole.[92] For Marx, Hegel's "Doctrine of the State" depends on a bureaucratic notion of culture as the education of civil servants, a "formalism of the state" that misrecognizes the "true agents" (family and civil society) of state-formation.[93] These debates about social agency, education, and the role of the state in the development of a universal human community form a crucial part of the nineteenth-century hypothesis of culture.[94] Their unresolved legacy surfaces in the failure of imperialist geopolitics to rationalize the political basis for the state's relation to other states.

Reclus does not reject this cosmopolitical framework, but rather radicalizes its implications for international political relations through the socialist critique of the extent to which international commerce has developed a "universal community," "to the point where a violation of rights in *one* part of the world is felt *everywhere*." Reclus holds onto both sides of the European hypothesis of culture—the Herderian organicist "Bildung" and the Kantian cosmopolitical "Kultur"—that Ratzel and Mackinder abandon in their attempt to turn the one against the other.

The principles of "social geography," which enable Reclus to redirect Mackinder's geopolitical image toward a critical analysis of conquest and domination, have a striking resemblance to later Marxist theories, particularly from Lenin on, of imperialism, uneven development, and the global reach of capital. It is in this radical socialist sense that, as Lacoste argues, *L'Homme et la Terre* anticipates twentieth-century critiques of imperialism.[95] As Reclus outlines these principles in his introduction to *L'Homme et la Terre*: "'Class struggle,' the quest for equilibrium, and the sovereignty of the individual's self-determination ["la décision souveraine de l'individu"], these are three types of phenomena that are revealed to us in the study of *social geography* and which, in the chaos of things, prove sufficiently constant for us to be able to give them the name of 'laws.'"[96] Among the many striking points to emerge from these "laws" is the way "class struggle" and "the search for equilibrium" both follow from the splitting of all human collectivities as the result of "an unequal development."[97]

The anarchist politics informing all these laws explains, however, not only the "repression" of Reclus in the formation of academic geography,[98] but also his rejection by Marxists, for whom "the sovereignty of the individual," for example, would have been suspect in its utopian refusal to engage in a politics of wresting control of the state.[99] Consigned to the utopian nowhere of nineteenth-century anarchism, Reclus's geography nonetheless illuminates the persistence with which the ambiguities of nineteenth-century ideas of progress, evolution, and culture shape the formation of twentieth-century geopolitical paradigms.

Significant, too, is the insistence with which Reclus sustains the Eurocentric imperative for hypothesizing the connection between European culture and the cultural development of human history as a whole. The narrative condition of the *Universal Geography*'s emphasis on Europe's "moral ascendancy and industrial preponderance" had depended on the hypothetical, utopian future condition that "equality will obtain in the end" and "what we call civilisation will have 'its centre everywhere, its periphery nowhere.'"[100] Between the completion of the *Universal Geography* and work on *L'Homme et la Terre*, Reclus reformulated the terms of this future "equilibrium" to argue, in an essay entitled "The Hegemony of Europe" (1894), that Europe had become "the centre of equilibrium between the forces of the human race."[101]

Reclus's notion of "hegemony" is premised on a Eurocentric articulation of the accelerated unification of the world under the forces of global capital. Such forces involve a process of "Europeanisation"; all parts of the world, he writes in *L'Homme et la Terre*, are being drawn into "the atmosphere of a general culture, of a predominantly European type."[102] The ambiguities with which Reclus formulates the connection between European culture and the global strategies of domination and conquest come close to the leverage Gramsci gives his key concept of "hegemony"—in the outline, for instance, of his "Hegemony of Western Culture over the whole World Culture."[103] The affinities are interesting to note since Gramsci's concept of "hegemony" has played a particularly important role in current cultural studies, opening nineteenth-century formulations of "culture" to anticolonial contestations of Eurocentric assumptions.[104]

Reclus's is necessarily a Eurocentric perspective on that contestation, but its relevance for his analysis of the means of imperial conquest and domination sheds light on the conceptual riddle of culture that haunts the imperialist formation of geopolitics. Mackinder's ambiguous evaluation of the success and "fatal momentum" of "Kultur, or Strategical mentality"—anticipating later repudiations of Nazi "Geopolitik"—now suggests that Mackinder's political geography is constructed to condense and displace the connection between European culture and policies of colonial governance and imperialist war strategy. This is necessary for Mackinder's imperial geography, because what for Reclus is only implicit in the formulation of "Europe's hegemony"—anticolonial contestation of European culture—is what imperialism seeks to make unconscious. It is in this sense that the geopolitical image might be considered the shared dream-work—"Europe's hegemony"—of both anarchism and imperialism.

Something of the spirit of Reclus's conception of Europe's hegemony shows through in his remarks on the effects of "Europeanisation" on the "citizen of the world":

> In spite of his aversion to the foreigner, in spite of the tariff which protects him against outside business, in spite of the cannon facing the two sides of the tabooed line, he eats bread which comes from India, drinks coffee which is harvested by the Negroes or the Malaysians, dresses himself in material made from American fibre, uses devices which are the product of the combined work of a thousand inventors of every time and race, experiences the sentiments and the thoughts which millions of men experience with him from one end of the world to the other.[105]

In what sense the "sentiments" and "thoughts" of this cosmopolitan "he" might be "experienced" by millions of other men and women remains, of course, open. Addressed not only to the kind of complacent European bourgeois "world citizen" caricatured in the sketch, Reclus opens the question of this cosmopolitan nexus of consumption and production to the awakening political consciousness Reclus always sought to address both in his encyclopedic geographies and in his anarchist propaganda.

This is precisely the sort of question Mackinder's geopolitical image of Britain seeks to foreclose through formalist abstraction. Nonetheless, *Britain and the British Seas*—whose "idea," Mackinder notes, "was first suggested to me by the needs of some foreign students visiting Britain"[106]—

can only ever reiterate the "play" of the pupil's imaginative "varying at will the pattern seen." For all the "ocularcentrism" of Mackinder's geography—and geopolitics generally—the geopolitical image is always open to the fullest kind of contested cultural play. The place of Reclus in the formation of geopolitics provides a reminder of this contest of political consciousness—one that not only haunts, but that determines any reading of the geopolitical image.

Conrad's "blank space" on the map, Joyce's "green rose," and Proust's incidental reference in a personal letter to the image of "those well-fortified cities one sees in Elisée Reclus's Northern European volume"[107] [from the *Nouvelle Géographie Universelle*]—each of these, in their own way, might be read as enacting the same unresolved ambiguous fiction of geopolitics. In the chapters that follow, I take up the unresolved ambiguities of this fiction by looking, in Part II, more closely at the nineteenth-century complex of culture concepts (or "Bildung"), and in Part III, by examining their contested twentieth-century afterimages (or "hegemony").

Imaginary Institutions of Geography

The formation of "geopolitics" over the turn of the century is not a history of geographical institutions. It is, rather, the story of imaginary institutions of geography. Indeed, the foundation in 1923 of Haushofer's famous Institut für Geopolitik turns out, as O Tuathail describes, to be a fiction, an "imaginary" embellishment on German geopolitical theories, that reveals more about the "unconscious fears and fantasies" of U.S. political discourse than it does about the role of Geopolitik in shaping Nazi policy.[108] Far from suggesting that geopolitical theories have no effect on the real world, what this underscores is the fact that the influence of geopolitics persists long after its failed institution as a "science."

The history of geopolitics I have traced here is a genealogy of an imaginary institution of geopolitics whose contours and legacies are defined not only be the reactionary politics of European imperialism, but also by the emancipatory politics of European socialism and anarchism. Perhaps no image captures the political ambiguity of the moment in which geopolitics took shape better than the Great Globe proposed by Elisée Reclus for the World Exhibition of 1900. Exceeding both the scale and exhibitionary spectacle of previous globes, such as the one built for the Great Exhibition in 1851, Reclus's "dream monument," as he called it himself, sought to achieve a scientific precision in geographic measurement, description, and representation, after the pattern of Enlightenment ideals, rationalism, and scientific inquiry.[109] In the elaborate scaffolding of galleries, ladders, and elevators necessary for its exhibition, it offers a striking illustration of Timothy Mitchell's thesis that the apparatus of nineteenth-century representation and its "metaphysic of modernity" constructs "the world-as-exhibition."[110] It illustrates the role of geography in the imperialist project of European enlightenment, the "conquest of the world as picture" in the Heideggerian terms of Mitchell's formulation.[111] Reclus's Great Globe is also, though, a perfect example of those ambiguous "dream images" of the nineteenth century discussed in Benjamin's "Paris, Capital of the Nineteenth Century," from which Mitchell draws to reformulate the terms of Martin Heidegger's conception of the "age of the world picture."

The Reclusian Great Globe might thus be seen, in Benjamin's terms, as the "dialectical image" of that historical moment between Ratzel's "anthropogeographical" world picture and Mackinder's globe-wide world organized with an "eye" on the position of Britain. In representational terms, the Reclusian Great Globe encapsulates the ambiguity with which geopolitics is formed all at once by the rejection and incorporation of nineteenth-century forms of representation. In presenting his project at the Sixth International Geographical Congress in London in 1895, Reclus suggested the accuracy of relief might make the Globe a model for the photographic reproduction of maps, possibly creating "a complete revolution in the cartographic industry."[112] Mackinder's photograph of a globe, the last in the sequence of images demonstrating the position of Britain, is an interesting modification of Reclus's ideal. Combining a nineteenth-century fascination for the modern photographic image with a twentieth-century "visualisation" of earth from space,[113] it illustrates the curiously Victorian optical illusion around which the geopolitical image constitutes its modernist perspective.

If Ratzel's, Mackinder's, and Reclus's "world pictures" each share the dream Heidegger characterizes as "the conquest of the world as picture/image [Bild]," the utopian form of Reclus's Globe best locates the imaginary place and ambiguous politics of that claim to representational conquest. Imagined for display at the World Exhibition of 1900, in Paris, capital of the nineteenth century, the Great Globe could hardly seem more European, more bourgeois, more an assertion of Europe's worldwide hegemony.[114] In this respect, however, its utopian form confronts what Ratzel's and Mackinder's world pictures seek to render unconscious. It projects the work of geography in the center of those extraordinary exhibits of cultural objects, people, and whole villages and parts of cities, from all over the world, which Mitchell has in mind when he reformulates Heidegger's argument that "the fundamental event of the modern age is the conquest of the world as a picture [Bild]."[115] As Mitchell formulates the riddle of European culture and hegemony, here explaining the effect of the world-as-exhibition on non-Europeans visiting Europe: "Non-Europeans encountered in Europe what one might call, echoing a phrase from Heidegger, the age of the world exhibition, or rather, the world-as-exhibition. World exhibition here refers not to an exhibition of the world but to the world conceived and grasped as though it were an exhibition."[116] Recalling both Ratzel's "anthropogeographical" world picture and Mackinder's formalist reconfiguration of that world picture around the geopolitical image of Britain, the "dream monument" of Reclus's Great Globe poses an unresolved question of perspective: For whom is this world-as-exhibition? This radically open question haunts still the geopolitical image.

PART II

CULTURE AND NIHILISM

Prefiguring Geopolitics

2   The Victorian Blot
Wilkie Collins, The Moonstone, *and the Concept of Culture*

> Blot . . . , *sb.*[1] . . . [Appears first in 14th c.: no corresponding form is known outside English, and the word may be really connected with PLOT, or may unite a notion of *spot* with some words in *bl-*. . . .]
> 1. A spot or stain of ink, mud, or other discolouring matter; a disfiguring spot or mark.
>   *c.* . . . 1876 E. JENKINS *Blot on the Queen's Head* 31 The ruthless hand had painted in an ugly black crown, which . . . only looked like a great blot.   b. An obliteration by way of correction. . . .
> 2. *fig.* A moral stain; a disgrace, fault, blemish.
>   *c.* . . . 1790 BURKE *Fr. Rev.* Wks. V. 61 Do these theorists . . . mean . . . to stain the throne of England with the blot of a continual usurpation? . . .   b. Imputation of disgrace; defamation . . .
> <div align="right">—<i>Oxford English Dictionary</i></div>

The mid-Victorian elaboration of nineteenth-century notions of culture produces a blot. In a word, this is the thought I want to develop in the following chapter. The Arnoldian idea of culture—the study of "the best that has been thought and known in the world"[1]—is perhaps the best-known mid-Victorian formulation of culture, one that continues to shape the terms for some of the most important programs of literary and cultural study. Such influential critics as Raymond Williams and Edward Said have pointed out the abstraction and confusion inherent in Arnold's formulations of "culture"; yet it is Arnold's *Culture and Anarchy* we hear echoed not only in the titles but also in the critical interventions of Williams's *Culture and Society* (1958) and Said's *Culture and Imperialism* (1993).

What makes Arnold's notion of culture perhaps most interesting is its distortion of other usages of the term: we see the differing things to which it refers—education, national heritage, artistic production—being blurred in a single word. In this sense, Arnold's mid-Victorian articulation of "culture" persists not despite but because of its confusions. In abstracting "culture" from the forces of industrialization and democracy, as Williams notes, Arnold blurs a number of notions of culture: in particular, culture as a spiritual process of learning and the notion of culture as the material works of art produced by a specific historical development.

Appropriating and translating earlier ideas of culture, Arnold adapted these to suit the peculiarities of the mid-Victorian English social moment as he saw it. In the process, European notions of culture get inflected by distinctive concerns about English middle-class values and power. Most prominent—and what concerns me here—are those mid-Victorian concerns whose aftereffects still shape Williams's *Culture and Society* and Said's *Culture and Imperialism*: the concerns for democratic reform (precipitated around the 1867 Reform Act) and for colonial governance (precipitated by the Indian Mutiny of 1857–1858 and Morant Bay rising in Jamaica in 1865). As many studies have now begun to show, *Culture and Anarchy* took shape around the particular mid-Victorian urgencies and imperatives to reform democracy and to formalize Empire.[2] As a result, the Arnoldian formulation of "culture" accentuates as a question what we have already characterized as the underlying hypothesis informing almost all nineteenth-century formulations of culture: the hypothesis that particular cultural developments might be linked to a single unfolding universal human culture.

The argument of *Culture and Anarchy* emphasizes the ambiguity of this underlying hypothesis. If, as Robert Young succinctly points out, Arnold's central claim is "that culture in England is lacking,"[3] his advocacy of culture implies that England's particular cultural development does not yet, and *might not* ultimately belong to what Arnold called "general human culture."[4] The threat of anarchy in Arnold's title, against which "culture" is recommended as the "great help," serves all the more to emphasize what has yet to be achieved, in Arnold's view, before the English way of life can become a part of the main current of human development in the largest and most universal sense. The future tense in which Arnold formulates this hoped-for "culture" is thus highly ambiguous. Shaped around the related predicaments of democracy and Empire, *Culture and Anarchy* looks all at once back on the cosmopolitan European hypothesis of culture and forward to its eclipse with geopolitics.

The Arnoldian confusion is not, however, Arnold's own, nor one of his own making. It belongs to the mid-Victorian moment; and to examine this moment I examine the dynamics of Victorian novelistic plotting through the lens of that master of plot, Wilkie Collins. With the Collins novel one encounters a form in transition, a genre whose early-nineteenth-century coordinates (Austen's family plots, say) are being reoriented to shape the plots of thrillers and detective fiction. In this, Collins's novels are all the more representative and significant for what the Victorian novel draws from the past and what claims it lays on the future. The Victorian plot as improvised by Wilkie Collins in the 1860s calls attention to a problem of form, at once political and narrative, which lies at the heart of mid-Victorian formulations of culture. It is this formal problem I call the Victorian blot.

The *Oxford English Dictionary* cites precedents for linking the word "blot" not only to "plot" (a pun on which Collins plays, as we shall see), but also to a problem of English political sovereignty. Their citation from Edmund Burke presents, as an example of the figurative use of the word "blot" as "moral stain," a classic revolutionary threat to sovereignty. Burke's "blot of a continual usurpation" is the core problem of formal democracy, according to Claude Lefort, as rendered by Slavoj Žižek: "*Everyone* who occupies the locus of Power is by definition a usurper."[5] Formulated in response to the Second Reform Bill of 1867, the Arnoldian concept of culture is the attempt to revisit Burke's question of democracy—explicitly; indeed, "culture" is the attempt to "resist" "Jacobinism."[6] The citation from Edward Jenkins's *Blot on the Queen's Head* is then offered to illustrate the literal meaning of "blot" as, "A spot or stain of ink, mud, or other discolouring matter; a disfiguring spot or mark." Here, too, the "blot" refers to English sovereignty: Jenkins's book was a satirical attack on the Royal Titles Act of 1876, whose passage made Queen Victoria not only queen of Great Britain and Ireland but also empress of India.

Thus the word "blot" seems already to designate a problem of formal democracy and of formalizing Empire. The Arnoldian attempt to resolve such questions of political form with the idea of "culture" belongs to what Williams characterizes as Arnold's "confusion of attachment" to social institutions, and what Said characterizes as the Arnoldian sense of culture as "a sort of theater where various political and ideological causes engage one another."[7] The sensational novel of the 1860s, with its eagerness to engage an ever wider "unknown public" (as Collins phrased it[8]), is a particularly relevant place to turn to track mid-Victorian formulations of culture. Collins practiced the sensations of mid-Victorian plotting in the same pages (and for the same "unknown public") to which Arnold brought his appeal for "culture" as the "great help out of our present difficulties."[9] Even more than Arnold's *Culture and Anarchy*, Collins's art of measuring respectability, perversity, and power in middle-class perspective opens his novels to the split claims and imperatives of an older cosmopolitanism and an emerging geopolitics. Looking back to decades of debate on democratic challenges to the British constitution, and looking forward to decades of debate on the consolidation of the British Empire, the 1860s represent a turning-point in the formalization of democratic institutions and the formalization of Empire. In the form of the novel— and particularly in *The Moonstone*, the last of the great sequence of Collins's sensational novels of the 1860s (*The Woman in White* [1860], *No Name* [1862], *Armadale* [1866], and *The Moonstone* [1868])—we see how this turning-point constitutes the specifically Victorian blot.

The Plot of *The Moonstone*: "The blot of the Diamond"

Like so many Wilkie Collins novels, *The Moonstone* makes use of a standard feature of Victorian novel plotting, the family legacy. This family legacy, the diamond of the novel's title, is also loot from a British military campaign in India, as the prologue already specifies in its account of "The Storming of Seringapatam (1799)." The fame of that campaign, together with the notoriety of the looting that accompanied it, is illustrated by a work of historical portraiture completed at the inauguration of Queen Victoria's reign (see Figure 10). Executed by the celebrated master of genre painting, Sir David Wilkie, the novelist's godfather after whom Collins was christened, the painting constitutes an important source for *The Moonstone*'s representation of the relation between Britain and India.[10] I return later to examine how the painting frames my reading of the novel. Here, the early Victorian historical portrait can stand as a revealing contrast to the way in which Collins's mid-Victorian novel depicts the scene of conquest and looting as *mise en scène* for a rather different grasp of the relation between world history and everyday middle-class concerns.

When Rachel Verinder inherits the moonstone on her eighteenth birthday, the questionable terms of the inheritance promise a story premised both on a family and an international scandal. Both are implicated in

FIGURE 10. Sir David Wilkie, *Sir David Baird Discovering the Body of the Sultan Tippoo Sahib, after having captured Seringapatam, on the 4th of May, 1799* (1839). Courtesy of the National Gallery of Scotland, Edinburgh.

what the house steward of the Verinder estate and first narrator of the novel, Gabriel Betteredge, calls "the blot of the Diamond."[11] Referring to the moral taint attached to the moonstone with its arrival in Yorkshire as the legacy of the "wicked" uncle, Colonel Herncastle, the novel's own figurative use of "blot" grafts a problem of family genealogy onto world history.

The thrill of scandal is what the sensational novel seeks most of all to exploit, and most often through the blot on the family name. *The Moonstone*'s plot seems designed to disrupt all the proprieties—political, familial, sexual—of Victorian social order. With the loss of the moonstone the night Rachel Verinder inherits it, suspicion is cast on a widening range of characters: on the disguised Brahmin priests who have come to England in search of the moonstone; on the servant with a guilty past, Rosanna Spearman; on the hero Franklin Blake and the villain Godfrey Ablewhite, rivals for the attention of Rachel Verinder. Most of all, suspicion is cast on Rachel Verinder herself.

A measure of *The Moonstone*'s economy of plotting is its ability to turn a "public" and "private" disgrace into a single plot, organized around that well-nigh foundational problem of domestic fiction, compromised feminine virtue. The mysterious disappearance of the diamond from Rachel's bedroom suite is too closely bound to the most intensely supervised site of sexuality—the young lady's "boudoir"—for readers to miss the possibility of sexual scandal.[12] The blot thus cast on Rachel's character, and confirmed by Sergeant Cuff's (erroneous) deduction that "Miss Verinder has been in possession of the Moonstone from first to last" (*Moonstone*, 173), enables the narrative to manipulate the melodramatic distress of the heroine for virtually the entire novel. This dimension of plotting is particularly significant for what *The Moonstone* shows about the mid-Victorian turn of narrative form, and its construction of the domestic, hystericized space of subjectivity.

As with Collins's other novels of the 1860s, the social space of the English country house provides a prime location for plotting troubled family legacies. *The Moonstone* adjusts the country-house settings of *The Woman in White* (Limmeridge Hall), *No Name* (Combe-Raven) and *Armadale* (the Armadale estate), to provide, in the "quiet English house" of the Verinder estate, what seems the very image of Victorian stability, order, and propriety. That image, however, rather than projecting a secure social (or literary) space in a stable Victorian world order, constitutes a fundamentally unstable, ambiguous perspective, as suggested in Betteredge's concluding ruminations on the "blot of the Diamond":

> Here was our quiet English house suddenly invaded by a devilish Indian Diamond—bringing after it a conspiracy of living rogues, set loose on us by the vengeance of a dead man. . . . Who ever heard the like of it—in the nineteenth century, mind; in an age of progress, and in a country which rejoices in the blessings of the British constitution? (*Moonstone*, 67)

The fantasy of social order consolidated in the concluding set of metonymic associations ("the nineteenth century," "an age of progress," "the blessings of the British constitution") is a fantasy, not of a stable Victorian world order, but of an uneasy sense of isolation from the world and from world history.

The fundamental instability of perspective at the kernel of this fantasy is explained in part by the argument of Raymond Williams's *The Country and the City*, which traces to the mid-Victorian moment the emergence of a "new and weak form" of the English novel, "the country house not of land but of capital."[13] Organizing the inheritance plot around the "blot of the Diamond" rather than that of the landed estate, *The Moonstone* seems to embody this shift from land to capital, with the diamond itself objectifying the intrusion of capital into the landed estate. It is no coincidence that this mid-Victorian moment is also the moment of Karl Marx's *Capital*, volume 1 (1867).[14] The novel's melodrama of class rivalry tells a very different story from *Capital*, but the problem of values is, at root, the same: the riddling value of the moonstone; the workings of what Marx called "surplus-value"; and, in Williams's words, "Money from elsewhere."[15]

This riddle of value shapes the middle-class distortion of social realities that makes Williams diagnose the mid-Victorian country-house novel as a "decadent form." As he argues, as if with *The Moonstone* in mind, "the true fate of the country-house novel was its evolution into the middle-class detective story."[16] If what interests Williams are those rural and then working-class perspectives that get "excluded and blurred" by literary form, it is precisely the "blurred" middle-class perspective that interests us here; for *The Moonstone*'s distorted class perspective shows how the country house of English fiction figures not the location, but the *dislocation*, of middle-class social values.[17]

This is, moreover, what the "decadent" form of the country-house novel shares with the Arnoldian abstraction of "culture": an abstracted sense of cultivating the landed estate. Arnold's "culture" embodies an ideal of learning attached to educational institutions, while the country house of the mid-Victorian novel is a place where, to quote Williams, "people bargain, exploit and use each other."[18] It is just those forms of middle-class entitlement acquired through "bargaining" and "exploiting" that concern all of Collins's novels, where the country estate foregrounds the legacy of reputation and distinction, not landed entitlement.

The typical Collins novel illustrates generally what connects Arnold's idea of "culture" and the Victorian novel's preoccupation with respectability: namely, the concern for education ("cultivation," or Bildung) built into the genre of the novel.[19] However, whereas Arnold sought to recommend "culture" as "the great help out of our present difficulties,"[20] Collins's novels typically elaborate the various practices of "cultivation" as the great gamble of bourgeois respectability. On the one hand, this simply provides the useful point of reference for what may be seen, retrospectively, as the moral purpose of the English novel since at least Jane Austen. Yet the case of Wilkie Collins clarifies the point that "culture" is best viewed not as the *success*, but rather as the *failure* to articulate a stable world-view. The idea that literature and the arts constitute the measure of social respectability—a crucial component of Arnold's gamble on "culture" to fend off "anarchy"—remains for Collins, from beginning to end, the problem requiring solution.

From the earliest novels in the 1850s up until the posthumous novel *Blind Love* (1890), the dynamic of the Wilkie Collins plot—the blot on the family name—always hinges on the difficulty of that notion of elevation and refinement recommended by Arnold as "the great help out of our present difficulties."[21] This is what unites the series of great novels from the 1860s—*The Woman in White* (1860), *No Name* (1862), *Armadale* (1866), and *The Moonstone* (1868). Whether read as the unmasking or the masking of middle-class Victorian codes of respectability—and critical response remains divided over this very question[22]—the sensation of each novel turns on the plotting of individuals' attempts to sustain, or acquire, social respectability, as in the plot to rescue a reputation (*No Name*) or to secure a reputation by evil means (Lydia Gwilt's method in *Armadale*). Education and middle-class refinements, in each case, do indeed constitute a "great help" out of present difficulties; but all the signs of "culture" in Wilkie Collins are marked by a thoroughgoing ambiguity. This is particularly evident when Collins, improvising on novelistic tropes for female middle-class accomplishments like family theatricals or the accomplishment of piano playing, makes the first into the urgency of Magdalen Vanstone's having to survive as actress (in *No Name*) and sensationalizes the latter as an obscene sign of Lydia Gwilt's self-indulgent evil (in *Armadale*).[23]

As the titles of these middle two novels of the sequence foreground, the Victorian blot of middle-class respectability is characteristically plotted, for Collins, around what Ian Watt notes as a foundational feature of novelistic "formal realism," the use of "ordinary contemporary proper names."[24] The name Gwilt, from *Armadale*, registers what Collins's novels of the 1860s rehearse as the ambiguity of the Victorian blot of and on middle-class respectability. Not only does the name, by association with the word "guilt," signal a blot that must be erased (Lydia Gwilt's villainy), but through the use of a somewhat unusual Welsh surname, an "ordinary contemporary proper name," it also signals the elusiveness of guilt attached to the middle-class formation of individual identity. Thus, Gwilt—the name that is all at once (following the earlier novel's formula) "no name," a notorious name, and an ordinary contemporary proper name—conveniently condenses the ambiguity of perspective formulated by the plots of Wilkie Collins and by what we are calling the Victorian blot.

The "blurred" perspective of middle-class social values condensed in the name of Gwilt involves, however, a further distortion—the distortion of *colonial* perspective, which, as Edward Said and Gauri Viswanathan have argued, fundamentally shapes both the novel as a literary form and the Arnoldian abstraction of "culture" from society. Thus the "blot of the Diamond" brings dishonor to the family from an uncle who has made his name, title, and fortune outside the landowning order of entitlement and inheritance; indeed, his very name—"Honourable John" (to which Betteredge adds, "one of the greatest blackguards that ever lived" [*Moonstone*, 63])—signals a specifically colonial question of middle-class entitlement through service to the East India Company. "Honourable John" condenses into a single title the familial, social, and political dimensions of the novel's "blot": "honourable" was used as a title for members of the East India Company; "John Company" was slang for the East India Company.

"Honourable John," signifying the East India Company, thus names the ambiguous social status of colonial officer. The ambiguity of class entitlement signaled in this one instance is characteristic of the way "blurred" subaltern colonial perspectives constitute the very core of middle-class melodrama.[25]

The plot of *The Moonstone* hinges on the way both working-class and subaltern perspectives are coordinated as blurred perspectives. There is, first, a "blurring" of rural and urban working-class perspectives in the two physically deformed characters of the rural Limping Lucy and the urban Rosanna Spearman, whose petty-criminal past is essential for inaugurating the plotting of suspense. Those very distortions of class perspective are effective precisely insofar as they are coordinated with the "blurring" of a set of colonial, or subaltern, perspectives: those of the Brahmin priests disguised as traveling gipsies at the beginning of the novel; and the figure of Ezra Jennings, of mixed racial background from "one of our colonies" (*Moonstone*, 420), who resolves the plot of suspense in the end of the novel.

The ambiguity of middle-class perspective is, according to the established patterns of novel form, founded on a dislocation not only of country and city, but also of metropole and colony. The example of Austen's *Mansfield Park*—a central example for Said's *Culture and Imperialism*—illustrates how, behind every English estate there is likely to be, screened from view, a colonial plantation. Collins's plots offer numerous variations on this theme: the opening to *No Name* is a virtual rewriting of *Mansfield Park* in this respect; the prologue to *Armadale* offers a sort of hyperbolic proliferation of West Indian entanglements, suggesting in what ways the West Indian colonial estate provided something like a standard novelistic trope for the Victorian family plot.

In *The Moonstone*, screened from the Verinder estate by a "plantation of firs," are the Shivering Sands, the novel's primal scene of sensational mystery, whose topographical deformity is metonymically linked to Rosanna's vision of "hundreds of suffocating people":

> I looked where she pointed. The tide was on the turn, and the horrid sand began to shiver. The broad brown face of it heaved slowly, and then dimpled and quivered all over. "Do you know what it looks like to *me*?" says Rosanna, catching me by the shoulder again. "It looks as if it had hun-

dreds of suffocating people under it—all struggling to get to the surface, and all sinking lower and lower in the dreadful deeps!" (*Moonstone*, 58)

What intensifies the mystery of suspense produced by this hysterical evocation of collective trauma is its ambiguity of reference. It could evoke the historical memory of the Black Hole of Calcutta (1756), the Cawnpore Massacre (1856) of the Indian Mutiny—or indeed both, welded together as each had become in the aftermath of responses to the events of the Mutiny. Or it might evoke the more recent memory of the Morant Bay massacre in Jamaica three years before.[26]

Jaya Mehta argues that this ambiguity of historical reference may be explained in terms of the organizing displacement of the memory of the Indian Mutiny: "The Mutiny, simultaneously absent and present, inhabits *The Moonstone* as a powerful yet invisible undertow, featureless like the quicksand in the novel, yet drawing all into it."[27] One in an increasing number of recent critical attempts to explain the problem of historical perspective in *The Moonstone*, Mehta's essay is especially interesting in emphasizing the indeterminacy of temporal and geographical coordinates by which the narrative produces what Mehta suggestively calls its "nesting structure."[28] Although this indeterminacy by no means makes the novel oppositional to or subversive of imperialism according to Mehta's reading, it does radically open the novel to contested readings of its recollection and revision of history. The topos of the Shivering Sands produces an ambiguity of historical perspective that lies at the kernel of the fantasy-image of *The Moonstone*'s "quiet English house" and its afterimage in detective fiction. Rather than some fixed geopolitical system of Victorian English social hierarchies and cultural coordinates, I propose that it is this unstable point of reference in Victorian fiction that solicits repeated attempts to evaluate the geopolitical image of a "quiet English house."

Framing the Plot: Critical Perspectives on Imperialism

Attempting to weigh the importance of this ambiguity of perspective brings me a step closer to a reading of the relation between Collins's mid-Victorian novel and his godfather's early Victorian portrait. As a number of critics have debated, the novel's historical frame of reference is set up by the prologue's description of a well-known military campaign in the British conquest of India. What made the storming of Seringapatam so famous for the first half of the nineteenth century was the scandal of looting and plunder that marked the success of the campaign. Still visible throughout Britain are the aftereffects of what might be called a Tipu Sultan cult, since, as Denys Forrest writes, "Scattered up and down the British Isles to this day, in extraordinary profusion, is the loot of Tipu's storehouses and armouries."[29] In addition to the loot itself, there are numerous depictions of the military victory, ranging from staged melodrama to commissioned paintings[30]—and including, notably, the painting by Collins's godfather, Sir David Wilkie, entitled "Sir David Baird Discovering the Body of the Sultan Tippoo Sahib, after having captured Seringapatam, on the 4th of May, 1799" (see Figure 10). Commissioned by the widow Lady Baird and painted between 1835 and 1838, at the inauguration of Queen Victoria's reign, the portrait was certainly known to Wilkie Collins.[31] Jaya Mehta, whose discussion of the English Tipu cult calls particular attention to the significance of Wilkie's painting, claims: "Tipu's defeat would have been indelibly imprinted on Collins's imagination by the painting."[32] That influence is significant, according to Mehta, because Collins's displacement of the memory of the Mutiny depends on the prologue's framing historical reference: "In substituting the Storming of Seringapatam for the Mutiny, Collins chooses the event most sensationalized before the 1857 revolt; yet an event more distant, more equivocal, and hence more susceptible to revisionism than the more recent event."[33]

The precise significance of the prologue's Indian frame of reference for the story of the diamond's disappearance in England remains a matter of disagreement among critics of the novel. John R. Reed, offering the first of recent accounts of the novel as a critique of Britain's colonial involvement in India, argues that the prologue emphasizes the "historical significance" of the story's references to England's conquest of India.[34] For D. A. Miller's reading of *The Moonstone*, however, the historical reference of the prologue proves ultimately irrelevant, since the "crime" of imperialism abroad is much less important than the forms of policing and surveillance enabled and enacted at home by the sensational novel form itself.[35]

An account of a "great public event" (*Moonstone*, 33), the decisive defeat of the Sultan of Mysore that assured English domination of the subcontinent, the prologue, "Extracted from a Family Paper," is also the record of a family member "for the information of the family only" (*Moonstone*, 37). Read as a family paper, it frames world-historical questions in terms of the problems of domestic surveillance and policing that guide Miller's account of *The Moonstone*. Read as a retelling of the world-historical defeat of Tipu Sultan, however, it sets the family plot in counterpoint to that history of British imperial conquests to which Reed sees the story as a continuous reference.

Two other, more recent critical readings of *The Moonstone* suggest how the novel and its readers must remain divided on the question of its critical perspective on imperialism. Ashish Roy, arguing against Reed, claims that *The Moonstone* "produces a *mythos* entirely consonant with arguments for empire."[36] The references to Britain's colonial involvement in India inaugurate what Roy calls an "imperialist semiotic" emerging with the genre of detective fiction and running through both the text and its critical reception. More recently still, rejecting Roy's claim that the novel amounts to a "justification" of imperialism, Ian Duncan reads *The Moonstone* as articulating the "imperialist panic" of the decade following the Indian Mutiny of 1857.[37]

What both these last critics call attention to, even in their disagreements, is the abiding problem of evaluating the novel's own complicity in imperialism. It is just this question that is raised by Jaya Mehta's argument that the historical reference to Seringapatam displaces the memory of the Mutiny. The "revisionism" Mehta finds at work here is explained on the basis of a changing aesthetic response to the topic of Tipu's defeat, as registered by Wilkie's painting: "Public opinion about the defeat of Mysore was more ambivalent in 1839 than in previous decades, and some viewers sympathized not with the triumphant Baird, but with the dead Tipu in Wilkie's scene."[38] This shift of sympathies is itself a matter of considerable interest, although arguably public opinion was always more divided on the circumstances surrounding Tipu's defeat than Mehta suggests. Yet it is not the image of Tipu Sultan that Collins takes from Wilkie. What *The Moonstone* takes from Wilkie's historical portrait is, rather, the questionable image of English respectability in the face of looting and plunder.

Besides placing Baird at the site of victory, Wilkie's portrait also seeks to tell the story of Baird's efforts to police the looting and plunder. This point is illustrated by Wilkie Collins's version of this story in the prologue, where it is used to consolidate the family story of two cousins:

> It was only at dusk, when the place was ours, and after General Baird himself had found the dead body of Tippoo under a heap of the slain, that Herncastle and I met.
> We were each attached to a party sent out by the general's orders to prevent the plunder and confusion which followed our conquest. (*Moonstone*, 36)

As the details of Wilkie's painting suggest, the imposing, somewhat awkwardly gesturing figure in the middle of the foreground seems intended to portray a General Baird giving just such orders. Wilkie's painting attempts simultaneously to emphasize Baird's role in Tipu's defeat and to save his reputation from the controversial issue of looting. Both issues are related since, as Forrest notes, "the 'rapacity' of the senior commanders in 1799 was felt to contrast sharply with the behaviour" of commanders in the earlier campaigns against Tipu Sultan.[39]

Most important, in considering what Collins's novel takes over from Wilkie's painting, is the aesthetic failure of the painting's effort to combine historical painting with the genre painting on which Wilkie's reputation had been built. Wilkie's painting was, indeed, considered the notable failure of the 1839 Royal Academy's Exhibition. One critic noted, "In parts it is undoubtedly admirable, but as a whole it is A DISAPPOINTMENT."[40] Another critic, attributing the "disappointment" to Wilkie's experiments in the grand historical style, noted that "in his *Grace Before Meat*, Sir David is himself (or David without the *Sir*) again."[41] William Thackeray, in his persona as the art critic Michael Angelo Titmarsh, Esq., judged:

> The artists say there is very fine painting, too, in Sir David Wilkie's great "Sir David Baird"; for my part, I think very little. You see a great quantity of brown paint; in this is a great flashing of torches, feathers, and bayonets. You see in the foreground, huddled up in a rich heap of corpses and drapery, Tippoo Sahib; and swaggering over him on a step, waving a sword for no earthly purpose, and wearing a red jacket and buckskins, the figure of Sir David Baird.[42]

Thackeray's comments draw attention to the awkward disproportion of the painting's iconography of military conquest—the standing figure of

Baird as victor over the prostrate figure of Tipu Sultan, vanquished.[43] This might suggest, at least in part, why "some viewers," as Mehta claims, "sympathized not with the triumphant Baird, but with the dead Tipu." Simply put, Wilkie failed to paint a convincing portrait of Baird's claim to honorable fame. The failure, however, gives perspective to Collins's aesthetic representation of the same problem: the problem of English middle-class entitlement and respectability in world-historical perspective. What Wilkie's experiment in historical and genre painting so awkwardly frames, Collins's masterpiece of sensational fiction reworks to make the dynamic point of plot construction.

The Blot of Victorian Subjectivity: "On the unanswerable evidence of the paint-stain"

By contrast to the iconography of military conquest in Wilkie's painting, the sensational effects on which Collins's novel depends might be described in terms of what Nancy Armstrong has called "an iconography of subjectivity":

> Narratives tend to turn into pictures . . . , forming hypostatic images in which the materials of narrative—as the genre paintings and monuments that also characterize Victorian culture—are already interpreted. That is to say, these visual images control the response to materials contained within them by shaping those materials into conventional figures that express various emotions—a careworn governess, a young woman cast out of her father's house, a dog in mourning beside his dead master's shoes, Ophelia drowned.[44]

Such "art," Armstrong suggestively argues, "developed an iconography of subjectivity that could be transported from one text to another and extended across media."[45]

The "hypostatic images" around which the Collins narrative typically freezes to produce such effects are those of the female hysteric. The plot of *The Moonstone* generates a series of such images, beginning with Rosanna Spearman, whose "fainting fits" and vision of "hundreds of suffocating people" (*Moonstone*, 53, 58) at the Shivering Sands make her the first character on whom suspicion is cast. Her hysterical behavior provides mysterious indications even before there is a mystery to solve. Foreshadowing the clue of the paint-stain from the newly painted door of Rachel's boudoir, Rosanna's conversation with Betteredge about "stains" establishes an unstable metonymy of "stain"—referring all at once to a grease stain on Betteredge's clothing and, more mysteriously, to Rosanna's own guilty past: "The stain is taken off... But the place shows, Mr Betteredge—the place shows" (*Moonstone*, 57).

With the disappearance of the diamond, Rachel Verinder's actions, too, become symptoms of hysteria. As Gabriel Betteredge puts it, on observing the effect of hearing that Franklin Blake had supplied Sergeant Cuff with the clue to the mystery: "There seemed to be some strange disturbance in her mind. She coloured up, and then she turned pale again. With the paleness, there came a new look into her face—a look which it startled me to see" (*Moonstone*, 138).

The "truth of the diamond," the reader soon realizes, is somehow encoded in that series of images of hystericized subjectivity—Rosanna's trance-like behavior, then suicide; Rachel's refusal to speak and her sudden aversion to Franklin Blake. It is no accident that Rachel's "new look" forms in reaction to the discovery of the "clue" Blake provides by revealing the details of his new mechanism for drying paint: the metonymy of the "stain," established in Rosanna's behavior at the Shivering Sands, attaches ambiguity to the innocent circumstances of that "decorative painting" of Rachel's boudoir which had provided so obvious an image of happy lovers. The looks now exchanged between the two cast that humorously pre-Raphaelite image of interior decoration into a sinister, even obscene light. The hypothetical order of truth to which the reader is deferred by this suspicious metonymy of the "stain," "paint-stain," and "blot" suggests in what complex ways hysterical symptoms provide an anchor for that everyday sense of lived experience assigned to fictional interior spaces (Betteredge's "quiet English house"; Rachel's "boudoir").

The Moonstone's hystericized sense of subjectivity is sustained as the novel shifts from Betteredge's narrative to that of Miss Clack, moving from country estate to London house. Rachel Verinder, attempting to resist Godfrey Ablewhite's marriage proposal, comes close to confessing both her passion and her knowledge in "a form of hysterics that burst into words instead of tears" (*Moonstone*, 280). The formulation is that of Miss

Clack, who, "horror-struck" at the entire proceedings, has been spying on this unwholesome seduction scene: "I attribute my being still able to hold the curtain in the right position for looking and listening, entirely to suppressed hysterics. In suppressed hysterics, it is admitted, even by the doctors, that one must hold something" (*Moonstone*, 280).

It is a comic tableau in which the contending discourses of middle-class England—Miss Clack's evangelical zeal pitched against the medical profession—collaborate in depicting that "hysterization of the woman's body" Foucault classifies as one of the four great "unities" shaping the mechanisms of knowledge and power centered on sex.[46] This spying scene is instructive because the space of subjectivity produced by the novel emerges not merely from the disciplinary individualism of policing described by D. A. Miller, but also by a particular kind of controlled paranoia. Voyeurism is structured by the desire to discover what Rachel *knows*—and what will be revealed only much later, in the confrontation between her and Franklin Blake, when, in her "hysterical passion," she reveals "*I saw you take the Diamond with my own eyes*" (*Moonstone*, 393).

The sensational climax of the novel comes when this paranoid knowledge is shown to be fully justified. Franklin Blake *did* steal the diamond, and this is the truth to which all three women testify. It is a moment, significantly, of self-incrimination: Franklin Blake's surprise revelation when, "on the unanswerable evidence of the paint-stain, I had discovered Myself as the Thief" (*Moonstone*, 359). The scandal is not only, of course, that the upstanding Blake stands self-accused as Thief. Franklin Blake, editor of the family papers, is the one character in whom the reader has placed implicit trust—trust, that is, in providing a "record of the facts" that will clear "the characters of innocent people" from "suspicion" (*Moonstone*, 39). As the turning-point in the plot, the point of reference for all the other characters' testimonies, and the reason for the narrative structure of different testimonies, this moment of self-incrimination becomes the paradigmatic "blot" of the novel.

Its significance lies in the production of a perspective from which the "blot of the Diamond" gets reshaped into the form of middle-class respectability. As Tamar Heller points out, Blake will seem all the more respectable for having stolen the diamond, once he is shown not only to have stolen the diamond in his sleep, but to have done so, unconsciously, to protect Rachel.[47] Still more revealing, however, is Heller's larger argument about Collins's work as a whole, which she reads as a revision of "the female Gothic" into "the traditionally 'masculine' genre of detective fiction."[48] Besides adding the crucial axis of gender to Williams's genealogy of the country-house novel, this argument calls attention to a crisis of literary authority at the heart of mid-Victorian novel form.[49]

This moment of self-incrimination identifies, indeed, a sort of structural fault line in Victorian narrative as a whole, and, specifically, between the "two stories" Heller sees *The Moonstone* telling—"a masculine one about the triumph of male reason, and a feminine one about buried writing."[50] The "self" incriminated in this transitional moment from female Gothic to male detective work fits neither the story of women's "buried writing" nor that of "male reason": literally, this "Myself" emerges from the annihilation of each (Rosanna's suicide; Blake's oblivion). As the climactic effect of the novel's hysterization of female subjectivity, Blake's discovery of "Myself as Thief" produces what Ezra Jennings's detective work will show to be an impossibility of self-knowledge. If critical responses remain divided over whether Blake's theft figures a personal, social, or national disgrace, that is because the novel insists on a thoroughgoing ambiguity of perspective. Caught between hysteria and reason, this formal impossibility of subjective experience is the enabling scandal of narrative form.

It is an effect similar to that optical illusion, the anamorphotic blot, of a coherent individual subject as described in Lacanian psychoanalysis. Lacan refers to the *anamorphosis* of the distorted image of a skull at the bottom of Holbein's *Ambassadors* to illustrate the enabling distortion at the heart of the formation of a Renaissance construction of visual perspective and the Cartesian subject: "At the very heart of the period in which the subject emerged and geometral optics was an object of research, Holbein makes visible for us ... something that is simply the subject as annihilated."[51] As John M. Archer puts it, paraphrasing Lacan from an avowedly non-Lacanian perspective, "one is fascinated by the anamorphic shape ... because it signifies that only a second observer, someone or something who can gaze both upon the picture and its viewer, is in a position to understand the portrait's real, bleakly ironic relation to the viewer."[52]

Blake's reading of Rosanna's letter rehearses the Lacanian anamorphosis as a series of sensational reading-effects. In the culminating effect of that series of metonymies of the "stain," "paint-stain" and "blot," it is Rosanna Spearman's buried writing that produces the "self" that stands confessed; once this "stain" has been attached to Blake, the metonymic logic of narrative plotting is arrested around an effect of impossible self-(mis)recognition. What makes this a specifically Victorian blot is the organization of reading effects by which this "self" confession produces the mirage of respectable middle-class individuality. In a very Victorian, very Wilkie Collins twist to the plot, the reading of Rosanna's suicide letter stages the confession of *guilt* as a confession of *love* ("This confession can be made in three words. I love you." [*Moonstone*, 361]), made all the more Victorian for being the confession of a "disgraceful desire" ("It would be very disgraceful to me to tell you this, if I was a living woman when you read it." [*Moonstone*, 362]). Doubly entangled in sexual misconduct and theft, and knotted around the cryptic form of Rosanna's "disgraceful" desire, Blake's self-revelation constitutes an impossibility of "self" knowledge because he sees himself neither as a Thief nor as the object of Rosanna's desire.

The Moonstone here reiterates and at the same time reveals the secret to the basic formula of "blind love" that is the common feature of all Collins's novels from *Basil* (1851) to *Blind Love* (posthumously published in 1890): the quest to make of a socially unacceptable "blind love" the condition for middle-class respectability. Although Rosanna's "blind love" for Blake follows the conventional crossing of class divides that characterizes many other Collins plots—notably, in *Basil* and *The Woman in White*—that love, far from being confirmed either in conflict with or in victory over social codes and laws, is shown in fact to be groundless. The novel gives up the plot of "blind love" with Blake's refusal to see himself as the object of Rosanna's desire (and inability to complete reading her letter). Rather than proving an exception, *The Moonstone*'s reformulation of "blind love" reveals what is in fact at work in that root formulation: what seems, from one position to designate the organizing social drive, the most meaningful nexus of social codes, turns out to be the "blind" spot around which middle-class respectability and social power revolves.[53] This is the Foucauldian insight at the heart of *The Moonstone* and the Victorian novel generally—"sex," as the imaginary, "most speculative," "ideal point" in the deployment of sexuality, reveals how scandal *generates* middle-class respectability.[54]

The Moonstone's variation on the theme of "blind love" might seem a reversal of Collins's usual technique—in particular, it seems to turn inside out the *mise en scène* of *The Woman in White*, Walter Hartright's blindness in falling for Laura Fairlie, premised as that is on a failure to discipline desire:

> I should have remembered my position, and have put myself secretly on guard. I did so, but not till it was too late. All the discretion, all the experience, which had availed me with other women, and secured me against other temptations, failed me with her. . . . I should have looked into my own heart, and found this new growth springing up there, and plucked it out while it was still young. Why was this easiest, simplest work of self-culture always too much for me?[55]

In one sense, Hartright has what Blake lacks: with respect to Rosanna, there are no desires there to "pluck out." In another sense, though, Blake is the very model of what Hartright takes as the ideal: a self perfectly adjusted to ignore misdirected passions. Put together as two halves of the same riddle of "sex" or "blind love," Blake and Hartright each illuminate the idealized, abstracted "self" that is the mirage of middle-class respectability. The term "self-culture," moreover, gives the keyword—"culture"—for the process of discipline needed to produce that mirage.

"Self-culture," a revealing and unusual formulation in Collins's lexicon, is not so unusual elsewhere in mid-Victorian discourse. Its most representative and significant use is by Samuel Smiles, in the highly popular and influential *Self-Help* (1859). "Self-culture" is synonymous with "self-help" throughout; early in the book, Smiles reveals in what ways it is an appropriation of European ideas of culture:

> Schools, academies, and colleges, give but the merest beginnings of culture in comparison with [self-help]. Far more influential is the life-education daily given in our homes, in the streets, behind counters, in workshops, at the loom and the plough, in counting-houses and manufactories, and in the busy haunts of men. This is that finishing instruction as members of society, which Schiller designated "the education of the human race," consisting in action, conduct, self-culture, self-control—all that tends to discipline a man truly, and fit him for the proper performance

of the duties and business of life—a kind of education not to be learned from books, or acquired by any amount of mere literary training."[56]

Smiles offers something like the antithesis to the Arnoldian notion of culture, although both together provide a useful illustration of the mid-Victorian blurring of nineteenth-century European ideas of culture.[57]

The Moonstone is exemplary because it plots the respectable middle-class "self" as an effect of a whole range of *other* people's scandals. Thus scandal, as the characteristic form of middle-class distortion of real social experience, is the generating principle of sensational novel-plotting. In *The Moonstone*, the sensational incrimination of Blake's "self" is measured, most significantly, against the scandals attached to Rosanna Spearman and Ezra Jennings. The "slander" that follows Ezra Jennings is perhaps the most characteristically Victorian blot of the entire novel, although its contours are never made visible enough (as with Rosanna's "story") to assume the rudimentary features of a plot ("His story is a blank" [515]). As Jennings explains it, "The slander is as active as ever. But when it follows me here, it will come too late" (429). In its cryptic temporal form, this is the counterpart to Rosanna Spearman's suicide confession of "disgraceful" desire.

The perspective from which the "blot of the Diamond" reforms itself into the shape of middle-class respectability is provided, then, by the way in which the "dead secrets" of Rosanna's story, in the first part of the novel, and Ezra Jennings's story in the final part of the novel, are blurred.[58] Paraphrasing Slavoj Žižek's application of Lacan to the cinematic narrative effects of the "Hitchcockian blot," these stories—which respectively generate and resolve the plot—get blurred as part of the background, part of those "heterogeneous elements" that "must remain an inert, nonsensical 'blot' if the rest of the picture is to acquire the consistency of a symbolic reality."[59] Analogous to the anamorphosis of *The Ambassadors*, on the one hand, and the tracking shot of Žižek's "Hitchcockian blot" on the other, this narrative organization of subjectivity produces a Victorian subject-effect distinct both from the formation of Renaissance perspective around geometral optics and from the twentieth-century ego-ideal of montage and cinematic narrative.

The blurred contours of those working-class and rural, colonial and subaltern stories form part of an array of heterogeneous narrative elements, allusive references, or miniature "dead secrets"—like the metonymy of the "stain." In the range of such narrative elements, *The Moonstone* offers a virtual inventory of mid-Victorian notions of culture. Betteredge's comments on the cousins' occupations in "natural history" and "decorative painting"—occupations described as "torturing," "spoiling," and "staining" things in nasty ways—is itself rich in presenting a sampling of what Betteredge later calls "your cultivated modern taste" (*Moonstone*, 231). "Cultivated" is Betteredge's mildly derogatory term for the disruptive effects of the fads of the educated middle-classes. More serious an engagement with the debates of the 1860s are the comments on Blake's cosmopolitan Continental education, whose comic register nonetheless seems to allude to Arnold's efforts to recommend Continental methods of education to improve England's middle-classes: "After he had learnt what the institutions of Germany could teach him, he gave the French a turn next, and the Italians a turn after that. They made him among them a sort of universal genius" (*Moonstone*, 47–48).

If these gradations of senses of "culture" provide a general sense of the blurring of "culture" in the mid-Victorian moment—a blurring whose distinctive form, for the novel, is "your cultivated modern taste" rather than the Arnoldian recommendation of a taste for learning ("sweetness and light")—the mid-Victorian abstraction of culture is more clearly a formal part of plotting in the novel's examples of novel-reading, and specifically, Betteredge's attachment to *Robinson Crusoe* and Jennings's to *Confessions of an English Opium Eater*. These novels serve not only as part of *The Moonstone*'s oblique critical engagement with debates on the English novel and literature generally, but they also consolidate the significance for the plot of tobacco and opium respectively. Both are products of systems of cultivation, each with a very long and complex set of associations with colonial and imperial practices: tobacco, with the plantations of the New World and the Atlantic trading routes; opium, with the cultivation systems of India and the enforcement of "free trade" from the Near to the Far East. Not only does *The Moonstone* allusively connect the "composing influence of Standard Literature" (*Moonstone*, 470) with the narcotic influence of tobacco and opium, that connection is the crux of the plot: what makes Blake steal the diamond walking in his sleep is a dose of opium administered to counteract the withdrawal symptoms from having quit smoking tobacco. Thus the "self" incriminated in the sensational turning-point of plot is an effect of a wide variety of "cultivation"—or "culture"—systems.

Collins's novel writing as a whole constitutes an extended improvisation on such "culture" systems. *The Moonstone* grasps this in a formal novelistic sense by situating the country estate of the English novel in a range of global cultivation systems. In this, *The Moonstone* stands not only midway between the country house of Austen's novels and the country house of detective fiction; it also stands midway between the ideal, utopian New World plantation and such afterimages of the European hypothesis of culture as those tortuously extended, attenuated metaphors of estate-cultivation—the three worlds of West, East, and the Third World. This continuing confusion of culture is what *The Moonstone* plots for us in novel form.

Victorian Cultural Capital and the Formalizing of Empire, 1858–1876

"If a naked beggar is asked to hide the koh-i-noor, where does he conceal the jewel?"

Mahasweta Devi, *Imaginary Maps*

In the moonstone itself, Collins finds a fictional formula for objectifying the convergence of different "culture" systems in the mid-Victorian moment. As an image that stands both for India and for Britain's political relation to India, its complex figurative meanings constitute a riddle of cultural form that continues to shape the twentieth-century fiction of geopolitics.[60] According to Ian Duncan, "As its circulation drives the plot and maps the global imperial economy of modernity, the jewel is the vector of a universal history that cuts violently across societies and individuals."[61] This is not, however, to say that the moonstone provides an objective correlative for the disruption of "detached capital" and that *The Moonstone*—rather than Marx's *Capital*—constitutes the point of departure for an analysis of the geopolitical formation of the capitalist world system in the mid-Victorian moment. The variety of world "culture" systems converging on *The Moonstone* is coordinated in a fundamentally fictive form of geopolitics; and it is the fictive form of this coordination of culture systems that emerges around the Victorian confusion of culture I have been calling the Victorian blot.

As an object of loot and plunder, the moonstone provides a fictional formula for articulating the relation between culture and capital. Simultaneously objectifying economic and cultural values, the moonstone poses the problem of what Pierre Bourdieu calls symbolic, or cultural, capital.[62] The plot measures characters, readers, and critics alike by their ability to discriminate the various degrees of economic and cultural value they attach to the fictional object of the moonstone. Discussing the nineteenth-century art collector Eduard Fuchs, Walter Benjamin articulated this general problem of Victorian values in terms of what, for historical materialism, resists conceptualization—"the disintegration of culture into goods which become objects of possession for mankind."[63]

Wilkie Collins had long been concerned with the marketplace of art objects. The allusion to Sir David Wilkie's portrait of Baird is only one of many allusions to art, artists, and art collectors that run through his work, and that can be traced back through his own apprenticeship in portrait-painting, to his father's profession as a landscape painter, and to his grandfather's profession as an art dealer.[64] The rudimentary plot of *The Moonstone* itself recalls his grandfather's *Memoirs of a Picture* (1805), in which a Guido painting, stolen from the royal collections in France, circulates through many hands, becomes confused with its various copies, and enables the writer to mix comic satire with serious reflections on the state of art, art evaluation, and art dealing. In all of these concerns, the riddle of cultural capital, and "the disintegration of culture into goods," is articulated by a formal aesthetic question. This is the classical problem of *describing* objects of art, or *ekphrasis*. Narrowly defined as the "verbal representation of a visual representation," ekphrasis, as W. J. T. Mitchell has discussed, names a poetic genre that problematizes genre: "the genre in which texts encounter their own semiotic 'others,' those rival, alien modes of representation called the visual, graphic, plastic, or 'spatial' arts."[65]

The Moonstone has an interesting, double ekphrastic relation to Wilkie's portrait. If its prologue re-presents verbally the painting's visual representation of looting, the novel as a whole is organized around one particular object of looting, the moonstone of the title. This fictional object that Collins adds to the historical scene of looting condenses into a single image what might be called the painting's own ekphrasis: its difficulty in representing the objects looted from Seringapatam. The moonstone is, of course, Collins's own fanciful addition to the historical scene.

Insofar as it does not belong to the picture, however, it demonstrates all the more clearly the aesthetic problem of ekphrastic description common to both works of art—the problem, to paraphrase Walter Benjamin, of describing the disintegration of (Indian) culture into (British) goods.

Of particular significance for what Collins will do with the object of the moonstone is the painting's ekphrastic representation of objects looted from Seringapatam (see detail, Figure 11). Wilkie went to great lengths to find authentic objects on which to model his painting, most notably, in the amulet (*bottom left*), shield (*bottom center*), and scimitar (*directly above the shield*).[66] Wilkie's painting here provides a revealing illustration of the process of what the anthropologist and historian Bernard S. Cohn has described as "the cultural-symbolic constitution of British India,"[67] the process by which the English sought to represent and legitimize political authority in India during the Victorian era. It is a process whose starting-point Cohn has traced, in a more recent article, to the defeat of Tipu Sultan: "The capture of Seringapatam in 1799 and the final defeat of Tipu Sultan begins the direct involvement of the Company's government in a systematic effort to explore and document India's past."[68]

More difficult than gathering and documenting the Indian treasures depicted in the picture, however, is the difficulty in describing the missing

FIGURE 11. Detail from *Sir David Baird Discovering the Body of the Sultan*; [caption] "His turban, jacket, and sword-belt were gone!" (from Theodore Edward Hook, *The Life of General, the Right Honourable Sir David Baird, bart.*, vol. 1 [London: R. Bentley, 1832], 218; cited in the description that accompanied the first exhibition of Wilkie's painting at the Royal Academy in 1839).

objects. It is really in this that Wilkie's painting exhibits the classical problem of ekphrasis, using the portrait to narrate a particular moment in the story of looting. The moment Wilkie depicts is not only the discovery of the defeated Tipu Sultan, but also, and crucially, the discovery that his body has *already* been despoiled. Thus, despite the wealth of detail drawn from the Indian treasures depicted, the heightened narrative and dramatic effect of the scene is meant to be produced by the missing objects, as is underscored in an account cited in Hook's *The Life of Sir David Baird*, on which both Wilkie and Collins drew as a source for their respective works: "*His turban, jacket, and sword-belt were gone!*"[69]

This narrative detail is essential for the story of loot and plunder Wilkie's canvas seeks to depict. Following Hook's biography (commissioned, like Wilkie's portrait, to vindicate Baird's character), Wilkie's painting seeks to represent the story of an *unsanctioned* looting—the stealing of turban, jacket, and sword-belt—in order to show Baird's role in the official, *sanctioned* divestment of the sultan's body. Suspended between the moment of unauthorized looting and the authorized divestment of the king's body, Wilkie's portrait of Baird puts on display the "political paradox" Cohn ascribes to British rule in India before 1858: "The English could not be incorporated through symbolic acts to a foreign rule, and perhaps more importantly they could not incorporate Indians into their rulership through symbolic means."[70]

Sir David Baird's embarrassment is one all at once of formal rulership and of loot. As Cohn points out, East India Company officials found themselves compromised by the customary ritual acts of symbolic "incorporation" through the offering of *nazar* (gold coins) or *peshkash* (valuables) and the receipt of *khelats* ("sets of clothes, including a cloak, turban, shawls, various turban ornaments, a necklace and other jewels, arms and shields"[71]). Interpreted as "corruption" by the British, these ritual acts symbolically associated such corruption with the East India Company, whose status was constituted by the nominal authority of the Mughal Emperor.

In attempting to vindicate Baird's character, Wilkie needs to recast the stereotype of compromised respectability and mercantile opportunism associated with the worst excesses of the East India Company's mismanagement, fraud, and abuse of power.[72] The result is an uneasy portrait of middle-class entitlement to world power. That uneasiness is what Wilkie

Collins turns to virtuosic effect in the plotting of sensational novels in general, and *The Moonstone* in particular. The portrait's problem of entitlement is echoed in the naming of the wicked uncle who steals the moonstone from Tipu's treasury—"Honourable John," with its allusion to the slang name for the East India Company. It is in the sensational moment of Blake's self-incrimination, above all, that Collins provides the counterpoint to Baird's awkward world-historical posturing. Like Sir David Baird, Franklin Blake, the cosmopolitan "universal genius," also discovers himself, embarrassed, at the scene of a looting.

What makes for the parallel is less the comparison of the two main subjects of the novel and the portrait. The compromised position of this cosmopolitan middle-class "self" is produced, rather, by the object of most fascination for the gaze—the objects *missing* from each picture: the things stolen from the king's body, in the painting; and the moonstone, in *The Moonstone*. What Collins takes over from the Wilkie painting is, then, not only the questionable image of English respectability. He also borrows from the painting a fascination for missing loot, which he embellishes to sensational effect as the organizing absence around which the question of English respectability takes shape.

The cultural-symbolic value of Tipu's stolen objects is significantly different for each work of art. In its fascination for the symbolism of Indian objects (those on display *and* those scandalously missing), Wilkie's canvas exhibits an unresolved problem of sovereignty and middle-class power. This is the problem of formal Empire, whose political resolution begins with the disbanding of the East India Company in 1858 and concludes with the proclamation of Queen Victoria as Empress of India in 1877. While *The Moonstone* was written during this period, at the time of Wilkie's painting (to cite Cohn again), "The British crown was not the crown of India; the British in India were subjects of their own kings, but the Indians were not."[73] Sir David Wilkie's depiction of the dead king Tipu's body is here all the more significant. Reminiscent of the problem of sovereignty Ernst Kantorowicz designates in the phrase "the king's two bodies," the painting is interested both in the physical body of the dead sultan and also in that symbolic, sacred, immaterial body—the body of symbols (clothes, ornaments, etc.)—that invests him with sovereign power.[74]

This question of sovereignty is bound to the question of middle-class world citizenship not only in the contrast between the defeated Sultan and the victorious General Baird. Sovereignty and citizenship are also configured together in the body of Tipu Sultan. As John Barrell notes in his discussion of the influence of the Tipu Sultan cult on Thomas de Quincey's work, "A Jacobin club had been established at Seringapatam, and Tipu Sultan had become Citizen Tipu."[75] The Romantic image of Tipu, an ally of Napoleon's and Britain's most renowned and ferocious enemy in India, is a sort of sublime image of world history—a variation on the theme of Burke's "Indian sublime" as explained by Sara Suleri[76]— formed from the combined associations of despotic Oriental sultan and revolutionary Jacobin citizen. A fantasy resolution of the extremes of absolute monarchy and revolutionary republicanism, Tipu Sultan embodies the idealized nineteenth-century European dream-image of world citizenship. By contrast, Sir David Baird (whose cumbersome title mimics Sir David Wilkie's and the titling of the entire picture) foregrounds an embarrassment of entitlement, an anxious display of what Suleri calls "the rhetoric of English India," and an accidental stumbling onto the world-historical stage.

Wilkie Collins takes up in novel form the painting's problem of cultural-symbolic representation: Tipu's stolen objects represent a sovereignty, power, and political identity whose very loss constitutes cultural value. In the afterimage of those same missing objects, Collins reformulates the inaugural problem of Victorian sovereignty, citizenship, and world-historical power as the problem of Victorian cultural capital. Condensing and displacing the cultural-symbolic value of Tipu's stolen objects, the "blot of the Diamond" constitutes through fictional form what gets enacted and displayed between the disbanding of the East India Company and the proclamation of Queen Victoria as Empress of India.

Not only the object of Orientalist description and designation, the moonstone also signifies Britain's political sovereignty over India— obliquely, in the text's accumulating references to Queen Victoria; allusively and ambiguously, in the implicit association with Queen Victoria's "famous Koh-i-Noor" diamond, which Collins makes explicit in the 1868 preface when he describes it as one of the two "royal diamonds of Europe" on which the moonstone is, in part, modeled (*Moonstone*, 27). *The Moonstone*, moreover, reiterates the monumental exhibition and fabrication of Indian culture which characterized the period from 1860 to 1877. Looted from Seringapatam, Moslem India, the moonstone is returned to its "authentic" Hindu origins in "the sacred city of Somnauth" (*Moonstone*, 524). Although this conclusion has been read (by John Reed, for example) as part of the novel's critique of British intervention in India, it is important to note (as Ashish Roy does) that the designation of the Hindu temple as the moonstone's "proper home" (in Reed's words)[77] fits the ideological project of the British Raj, following the desacralization of the Moghul, to restore an idealized Hindu civilization from beneath the ravages of a demonized Islamic conquest.[78]

An afterimage of early-nineteenth-century questions of sovereignty and middle-class power, the fiction of the moonstone prefigures the late-nineteenth-century formation of geopolitics. Insofar as the novel enacts an imperative to locate culture politically and geographically, the moonstone, as a geopolitical image, conceptualizes "culture" as a problem of contested political form—the problematic relation between cultural traditions and sovereign state power. The contestation of cultural, political, and territorial form that makes the moonstone so compelling a fabricated image of Indian culture depends nonetheless on the cosmopolitan imperative of a universal cultural development, in which the objects of culture belong to a process of world-historical development. *The Moonstone* provides, in this sense, the split image of Victorian ideas of culture: the cosmopolitical hypothesis of a "general human culture"; and the geopolitical imperative to formalize the relation between culture and sovereign state power. That split image is the fascinating *in*coherence of the Victorian period that constitutes for us the Victorian blot. The form of this blot is of critical interest to the extent that it delineates the fiction of geopolitics by which our own contemporary cultural investments are organized.

3 Victorian Nihilism:
Friedrich Nietzsche and Olive Schreiner

> "Nihilism stands at the door: whence comes this uncanniest of all guests?" —from Friedrich Nietzsche, *The Will to Power*
>
> "'I was a stranger, and ye took me in,' he read." —from Olive Schreiner, *The Story of an African Farm*

"What does nihilism mean? *That the highest values devaluate themselves*. The aim is lacking; 'why?' finds no answer."[1] Nietzsche's celebrated diagnosis of nihilism finds corresponding echoes in many late-Victorian texts. Among the strongest, and strangest, echoes are those in Olive Schreiner's *The Story of an African Farm*, where the gist of Nietzsche's "the aim is lacking" is distilled into the epigraph that marks the division between the novel's two parts—"And it was all play, and no one could tell what it had lived and worked for. A striving, a striving, and an ending in nothing."[2] Schreiner's novel not only reflects the general mood of nihilism in the 1880s, it places nihilism at the very center of its experimental challenge to Victorian novel form. In what follows, I consider the shared concerns of these antithetical figures—Olive Schreiner, feminist novelist; Friedrich Nietzsche, anti-feminist philosopher—as each confronts the problem of what Nietzsche sought to diagnose as "European nihilism."

What makes Nietzsche's name virtually synonymous with nihilism is the fact that Nietzsche is himself a part of the "nihilism" he diagnoses—necessarily and problematically so, as the self-styled "first perfect nihilist of Europe."[3] Following a logic that Jean-Luc Nancy has traced from the beginning to the end of Nietzsche's career, Nietzsche's diagnosis of "European nihilism" remains, like his projected 1868 doctoral thesis on teleology, an incomplete thesis. Though everywhere implied in his writings through the 1880s, the work "On the History of European Nihilism," as it is projected toward the end of *On the Genealogy of Morals* (1887),[4] remains only a prospect—part of what Nancy calls "the last thesis . . . not to have taken place."[5] The claim to be the "first perfect nihilist of Europe," from the unfinished *Will to Power*, continues: "who, however, has even now lived through the whole of nihilism, to the end, leaving it behind himself, outside himself."[6] Did Nietzsche succeed in "leaving" nihilism "behind himself" or "outside himself"? The resonance of that question echoes throughout the proliferating literature on Nietzsche, leaving unresolved and incomplete, in Nancy's sense, Nietzsche's diagnosis of "European nihilism."

What makes Nietzsche's nihilist hypothesis relevant for analyzing the discursive formation of geopolitics is its close relation to the rhetoric of power, world politics, and global warfare that becomes increasingly strident in Nietzsche's later work. In the concluding chapter of *Ecce Homo* Nietzsche famously declares "I am no man, I am dynamite" and goes on to articulate one of the series of "declarations of war" that characterize his very last writings: "There will be wars the like of which have never yet been seen on earth. It is only beginning with me that the earth knows *great politics*."[7] The projected preface to *The Will to Power* insists, indeed, on a "logical," "psychological," and "necessary" connection between the meaning of nihilism and the gospel formulated in the title's "will to power."[8]

Anticipating discourses of geopolitics, *The Will to Power*, in particular, can easily confirm the popular misconception of Nietzsche as proto-Nazi ideologue: as, for example, in his description of the philosopher's use of "an ecstatic nihilism" as "a mighty pressure and hammer with which he breaks and removes degenerate and decaying races to make way for a new order of life."[9] The contemporary point of reference for this rhetoric of war is the militarization of Europe following the Franco–Prussian war of 1870 and the founding of the German Reich. If Nietzsche's polemic is consistently pitched against the militant German nationalism of his day, it is nonetheless difficult to ignore the disturbing affinities between the Nietzschean rhetoric of war and domination and later Nazi policies of the 1930s and 1940s.

The distorted afterimage of Nietzsche as Nazi ideologue—or precursor of German Geopolitik[10]—is one important consequence of the fragmentary, incomplete form of Nietzsche's philosophical work. After his mental breakdown in 1889, Nietzsche's work came under the control of his sister, Elisabeth Förster-Nietzsche, whose supervision over editing, publishing, and translation, notoriously recast unpublished and published work alike. This presents difficulties for critics attempting to distinguish Nietzsche's self-presentation from his sister's management of Nietzsche's public image and the official image of Nietzsche's life and work to emerge from the Third Reich. Given the problematic textual status and legacy of Nietzsche's work, his diagnosis of nihilism is unavoidably entangled in the increasingly polemicized meaning of nihilism over the extended turn of the century from 1860 to 1940.

In the introduction to his 1940 lectures on Nietzsche, Martin Heidegger offers a glimpse of this polemical history, even as he seeks to bracket it by specifying the philosophical prominence of Nietzsche's use of the term:

> The word "nihilism" is the term that the Russian Turgenev brought into currency, coined after the Latin nihil = nothing. It designates the view that only what can be perceived by the senses—that is, being as personally experienced—really is, and nothing else. Accordingly everything that is grounded in tradition and authority and other determined values is denied, negated. One mostly uses for this world-view the term "Positivism."[11]

By equating the ordinary sense of "nihilism" with "Positivism," Heidegger draws attention to a dominant nineteenth-century sense of "nihilism" that gets displaced over the turn of the century. This sense of nihilism, as positivist reliance on reason and enlightenment, is what Olive Schreiner characterizes in the fictional form of Waldo's "stranger."[12] The book he brings to the African farm is Herbert Spencer's *First Principles*, an embodiment of positivist nihilism, as important for Nietzsche's diagnosis of "European nihilism" as it was for Olive Schreiner's self-education as a freethinker.[13] This positivist nihilism plays an important part both in Schreiner's story and in the story of nihilism emerging from Nietzsche's nihilist hypothesis. As Heidegger's description already indicates, this shared story concerns a conceptual reversal in the meaning of "nihilism": once associated with a radical reliance on reason and enlightenment, "nihilism" comes to signify an attack on just those principles.

For Heidegger, the importance of this story is to show that what Nietzsche means by "nihilism" is "something fundamentally 'more'" than positivism.

> For Nietzsche however the name "nihilism" means something fundamentally "more." Nietzsche speaks of "European nihilism." He means by that not the positivism emerging around the middle of the nineteenth century and its geographical spread over Europe, but rather "European" has here a historical significance and is as much as to say "Western" (sagt soviel wie "abendländisch") in the sense of Western history.[14]

Heidegger's use of the term "Western" to explicate the charge of Nietzsche's "European" reveals, as I have elsewhere discussed,[15] the intervening formation of the geopolitical idea of "the West" between the 1880s and the 1940s. Despite its effort to extricate a philosophical definition of nihilism from the range of nineteenth-century uses, Heidegger's argument in fact underscores the importance of those polemical, "historical" meanings he seeks to winnow away—and perhaps most particularly Nietzsche's distinctive formulation of "European nihilism." What characterizes the increasing tempo of Nietzsche's attention to the question of nihilism through the 1880s is precisely the extent to which he makes use of the variety of differently accented senses of nihilism: from his satirical disdain for English thinkers ("One should recall what Huxley reproached Spencer with—his 'administrative nihilism'"[16]) to his disparaging references to the "nihilistic" Russian traits of "Petersburg metapolitics and Tolstoian 'pity.'"[17] It is just this heterogeneity of uses that gives the term polemical force, setting in perspective what Heidegger calls the "world-view" of positivism, which we might alternatively designate Victorian nihilism.

Both Nietzsche and Schreiner offer a peculiarly Victorian perspective on the changing meaning of nihilism in the decade of the 1880s. The problem of nihilism, for each, reformulates in a deliberately estranged form such familiar Victorian questions as the so-called Woman Question. Unlike the many women whose work contributed to the making of "Nietzsche" as one of the notable European phenomena of the turn of the century, Schreiner had no direct effect on Nietzsche's work—nor did Nietzsche on her work. Schreiner's distance from Nietzsche, however, sheds all the more light on the relevance of women writers and readers for Nietzsche's work. As a prominent "New Woman" and freethinker,

Schreiner's work articulates the challenges that occupied Nietzsche's most important interlocutors—those women who, for lack of a more fitting term (friends, colleagues, acquaintances, disciples, soul mates, fellow writers), one might call Nietzsche's sisters. Schreiner's work calls attention to the contradictory social and political significance of feminist struggle shaping both the wider social and political meaning of nihilism and the conceptual leverage of Nietzsche's diagnosis.

Where Schreiner's fiction seems furthest removed from Nietzsche's philosophy is in her response to colonialism. If Nietzsche's philosophy remains disengaged from the colonial questions of his day, Olive Schreiner provides a significant counterpoint. It is the colonial scene of Schreiner's fiction—the scene of the African farm on which the European "strangers" of Schreiner's novel appear—that will provide the revealing setting for understanding the Nietzschean thesis that "we are necessarily strangers to ourselves."[18] This thesis, closely bound to the incomplete thesis of European nihilism, suggests how it is the estrangement of European culture that constitutes the meaning of Victorian nihilism as the shared problem facing both Nietzsche and Schreiner.

Friedrich Nietzsche's "Sisters"

Nietzsche's critique of positivism, most fully embodied in *On the Genealogy of Morals* (1887), has its origins in the late 1870s and early 1880s, in work whose stylistic play and polemic is more sympathetic to the aims of positivism. There are a number of affinities between the Nietzsche of the early 1880s and the novelty of Olive Schreiner's first literary publication, *The Story of an African Farm*. Each responds to the philosophical challenges of a new scientific spirit of freethinking and positivism—as figured in the appearance of Spencer's *First Principles* in Schreiner's novel; and as formulated in Nietzsche's call to create "*a new image and ideal of the free spirit.*"[19] Each also seeks to set the claims of scientific humanism, Spencerian evolutionism, and positivist nihilism, in critical perspective; and it is here that both Nietzsche and Schreiner articulate the conceptual problem of nihilism as the principle of rationality turned, not only against superstition, but also against reason itself.

This shared concern emerges in affinities of stylistic experimentation: Schreiner's penchant for parable, dream, and allegory finds corresponding echoes in Nietzsche, particularly in that most celebrated, extended experiment in parable, fable, and aphorism, *Thus Spoke Zarathustra* (1883–1885). One such echo is the parable of the hunter that opens the second part of Schreiner's *The Story of an African Farm*, in which Waldo's "stranger," putting into narrative form what he sees in Waldo's fantastical primitive carving, retells the story of Waldo's own crisis of faith and nihilism—an experience figured, for instance, as the hunter's wandering through "the Land of Absolute Negation and Denial" (*The Story*, 162). Recalling the allegorical wanderings of Zarathustra, it also echoes the signature of Nietzschean nihilism—the announcement of the death of God. The parable of the hunter translates into allegorical form the experience of nihilism presented in the enigmatic first-person plural of the interchapter between the first and second parts of Schreiner's novel:

> Now we have no God. We have had two: the old God that our fathers handed down to us, that we hated, and never liked; the new one that we made for ourselves, that we loved; but now he has flitted away from us, and we see what he was made of—the shadow of our highest ideal, crowned and throned. Now we have no God. (*The Story*, 149)

Thus Spoke Zarathustra introduces its death-of-God theme in the second section of the prologue, when Zarathustra, descending from his mountain height into the land of people, is shocked to discover that the holy hermit he meets in the woods has not yet heard the news—"Could it be possible! This old saint has not yet heard in his forest that *God is dead!*"[20]

If both seek to put in perspective a characteristically nineteenth-century crisis of religious faith, there is nothing simple about either formulation. The first-person plural "we" of Schreiner's nihilist experience is a complex effect of the novel's unraveling of the European "Bildungsroman." As Claire Kahane puts it, Schreiner subjects the genre of the novel to an experimental "gender reversal," assigning to a male character "the features of the idealized Victorian heroine" and to a female character "the typical features of the hero of the nineteenth-century bildungsroman."[21] The first-person plural "we" of the novel's central nihilist experience is thus split between the perspective of Waldo's spiritual experience, on the one hand, and that of Lyndall, the novel's female protagonist whose identification with Napoleon constitutes perhaps the most obviously "typical feature" of the male hero of a "Bildungsroman."

Schreiner's split voice of Victorian authorial omniscience provides a revealing point of comparison with the increasingly strident, militant, and masculine voice to emerge from Nietzsche's Zarathustra persona. The voice of Zarathustra is split, too, however. It is the voice of prophecy dissected. Thus, Zarathustra announces the death of God not as a prophetic proclamation, but to himself, in surprise that the "holy man" of the forest has not yet heard the news. In each case, the meaning of nihilism depends on a complex staging of narrative voice and fictional setting. Indeed, as we shall examine later, the setting of Schreiner's African farm helps explain in what sense Nietzsche's impersonation of the ancient Persian Zoroaster is a complicated fiction of contrasting religious, historical, and cultural perspectives. The meaning of Nietzsche's "European nihilism" will depend on how we evaluate that fiction.

First, I want to consider the conflicting evaluations of Nietzsche's Zarathustra fiction as judged from the opposing perspectives of two of Nietzsche's closest "sister" figures: Nietzsche's sister Elisabeth Förster-Nietzsche, for whom Zarathustra represented "the preacher of his gospel to the world";[22] and Lou Salomé, the close friend Nietzsche himself styled his "sibling-brain,"[23] for whom Zarathustra represented a symptom of Nietzsche's decline into madness.

In Förster-Nietzsche's books, introductions, and editorial work generally, Nietzsche's Zarathustra persona occupies a central place in organizing the coherence of her brother's philosophy. In the 1905 introduction to *Thus Spoke Zarathustra*, for example, her account of the origins of "my brother's most personal work" becomes an occasion for reviewing Nietzsche's writings in light of the meaning of the figure of Zarathustra as "the image of his greatest hopes and remotest aims."[24] The figure of Zarathustra unifies her brother's leading ideas—the "doctrine of the Superman... understood in conjunction with... the Order of Rank, the Will to Power, and the Transvaluation of all Values."[25] For Lou Salomé, by contrast, the figure of Zarathustra signals a rupture in the development of Nietzsche's philosophy, a rupture Salomé associates with the increasing turn to poetry and verse, and sees marked by the first appearance of Zarathustra at the end of the fourth book of *The Gay Science*.[26] For both, *Zarathustra* is an intensely personal record of Nietzsche's encounter with the moral and spiritual experience of nihilism. For Förster-Nietzsche, Zarathustra succeeds in "transfiguring" "the history of his most individual experiences, of his friendships, ideals, raptures, bitterest disappointments and sorrows"; *Zarathustra* tells the story of her brother's overcoming of nihilism, a view echoed by Wilhelm Dilthey's judgment of *Zarathustra* as the culmination of the philosophical form of the "Bildungsroman" established by Hölderlin's *Hyperion*.[27] For Salomé, by contrast, Nietzsche's creation of the Zarathustra persona constitutes the symptomatic failure to overcome the problem of nihilism; aesthetically flawed, the work symptomizes Nietzsche's inability to resolve "the conflict between the need for God and the compulsive need to deny God."[28]

These contrasting interpretations of the significance of Zarathustra for Nietzsche's philosophy present alternative ways of conceiving the meaning of nihilism and the significance of Nietzsche's breakdown for the coherence of Nietzsche's late work. The enmity between Förster-Nietzsche and Salomé has attracted inordinate attention largely because, as Biddy Martin and others have discussed, it is written into the very different styles with which each woman represented Nietzsche and his philosophy. Such questions of style and meaning are all the more important in that the very status of Nietzsche's texts is imbricated in biographical disputes about Salomé's relationship with Nietzsche, and Nietzsche's sister's attempts to contain the significance of that relationship.

The most sensational point of reference for what both Nietzsche and his sister styled the "European scandal"[29] of Nietzsche's friendship with Salomé is the notorious May 1882 photograph of Paul Rée and Friedrich Nietzsche posing together at the head of a cart in which Lou Salomé sits holding what appears to be a whip. This group portrait of free spirits has become the focal point for contending views of the philosophical, sexual, and social significance of the collaboration between the three, which fell apart following Salomé's rejection of Nietzsche's marriage proposal in 1882. Whatever role the photograph may have played in creating a "scandal of truly European proportions," its afterimage is inscribed in the contending ways in which Salomé and Förster-Nietzsche each represented Nietzsche's philosophy.[30]

Their sharply differing evaluations of the Zarathustra figure are all the more significant because they are shaped by different perspectives on the state of Nietzsche's personal crisis of 1882, the moment when Zarathustra first appears in Nietzsche's text (at the end of book 4 of *The Gay Science*). Each claims authority for a personal insight into this moment; and each has been accused of manipulating the text and authority of Nietzsche's work. Yet each sister-figure played a decisive role in shaping the afterimage of Nietzsche's life and work: Salomé, in her 1894 study of Nietzsche, and Förster-Nietzsche, in her books about her brother as well as in the editorial work of publishing (or delaying the publication of) the collected works. As Biddy Martin puts it, "This was not simply a clash between ... two different women ... ; it was a conflict between contending constructions of gender, sexuality, family, race, and nation."[31]

This conflict emerges clearly enough, for Förster-Nietzsche, as a matter of "morality," the defining feature of her lengthy discussion of "the whole Lou affair" in her two-volume *Life of Nietzsche*, itself shaped by her repudiation of "that tissue of falsehoods, [Salomé's] *Friedrich Nietzsche in His Works*": "We must, as it were, dissect Frau Lou Andreas in order to give a clear explanation of Nietzsche's attitude towards morality."[32] Förster-Nietzsche's "dissection" of Frau Lou, by no means only concerned with defending Nietzsche from scandal, elaborates a set of assumptions about morality, women, and education by which Nietzsche's philosophy is then measured ("As soon as she saw what a stern and serious self-discipline my brother demanded from his followers, she felt decided qualms"[33]). Just as interesting as Förster-Nietzsche's stereotypically Victorian moral principles, however, is the antithetical stereotype that gives them shape: the stereotype of the emancipated "New Woman." This is itself inseparable from another closely related stereotype, that of the Russian "nihilist" woman who abandons family, marriage, and country in search of independence and education. Such a stereotype begins to emerge in Förster-Nietzsche's list of "characteristics that were essentially distasteful to [Nietzsche]; such as her contempt for the ordinary ties of kinship, and her desire to defy social conventions by going to the University with the two scholars, Rée and Nietzsche, and even, as she proposed, living with them in the same house."[34] It is reinforced in a description of Förster-Nietzsche's own reaction to Salomé's manner of expression: "Perhaps Fräulein Salomé was only a forerunner of a certain section of the modern emancipated women?"[35]

Each one of these elements in Förster-Nietzsche's "dissection" of Salomé amplifies different parts of the contestation over Nietzsche's philosophy. Yet the stereotype of the emancipated, Russian nihilist woman constellates a particular set of questions about women, education, and morality, which form the kernel of contention over the significance of Nietzsche's life and work generally, and the meaning of nihilism in particular. As Friedrich Kittler has pointed out, one consequence of Nietzsche's departure from Basel University in 1879 was that his colleagues and students now included women: "Whenever the hermit of Sils went out among people, he consorted with emancipated women—that is, with women who wrote."[36] The decisive importance of this for Nietzsche, according to Kittler, was that it set the terms for a clear break from the masculine enclaves of the Prussian educational system: "Nietzsche learned with great care the negative lesson of the Pforta school, where pupils could become acquainted with everything but women. His 'philosophy,' therefore set between quotation marks, reversed the university discourse."

This opening-up of academic discourse takes place, as a matter of "style," in the leverage Nietzsche gives to the figure of "woman"—notoriously, in the preface to *Beyond Good and Evil*, "Supposing that Truth is a woman—what then?"[37] Inseparable from those stylistic questions, however, are the social, political, and institutional issues that give them their polemical, critical edge. An important contradiction emerges here, which has crucial consequences for the changing meaning of nihilism in all its senses. As Kittler's remarks already indicate, one of the central social issues concerns women's access to the institutions of higher learning—that profound change taking place (unevenly) throughout the world that produced the phenomenon of the "New Woman." The contradiction for Nietzsche's work lies in the fact that this newly educated, cosmopolitan class of women provided Nietzsche an animating spur, so to speak, with which to attack the very academic institutions to which they had gained entrance.

The other side of that contradiction, however, is that Nietzsche's work solicited the interest of just this class of "New Women." This side of Nietzsche's feminist anti-feminism is the more interesting for the question of nihilism, because it connects the emerging diagnosis of nihilism in Nietzsche's philosophy with the "New Woman"'s challenge to academic discourse. Lou Salomé's reading of Nietzsche is particularly relevant, since she was the figure with whom Nietzsche worked, in the early 1880s, to articulate a positivism of "free-spirits" intended to free up the spirit of the human sciences ("Geisteswissenschaften"). What Salomé found in Nietzsche's work was "a new style in philosophical writing, which up until then was couched in academic tones or in effusive poetry."[38] Salomé's judgment pinpoints a crucial aspect of Nietzsche's "new image and ideal" of philosophy, and its challenge to academic discourse. Here is how Salomé characterized the challenge: "The cultural picture he elicited from Greek life, which he generalized into a profound view of the world and of human life through the eyes of a metaphysician, would have broadened eventually, with further humanistic research, into a total picture of the development of mankind's history."[39] To the extent that this reading seems to mistake the direction of Nietzsche's critique of humanism and scientific positivism, it is all the more interesting an alternative perspective, predicated as it is on her argument (particularly irksome to Förster-Nietzsche) that "one cannot escape the feeling that the greatness reserved for [Nietzsche] passed him by."[40] Salomé's hypothetical image of Nietzsche as humanistic researcher laboring to produce "a total picture of the development of mankind's history" provides the opportunity to see how his style of freeing academic discourse might be understood not so much as the repudiation of the humanist ideal, but rather as the attempt to realize and affirm it as fully as possible.

Salomé's evaluation of Nietzsche's "greatness" here stands in contested contrast to the figure of greatness Elisabeth Förster-Nietzsche forges around the figure of Zarathustra and the doctrine of the Übermensch.[41] The general contours of Salomé's argument illustrate important affinities between Nietzsche's "new image and ideal of the free spirit" and the challenges of "New Women" seeking to realize the nineteenth-century ideals of humanism (the "new philosophy" of a previous generation). It is surely no accident that Salomé's formulations echo Humboldt's idea of "Bildung." The resonances reflect (with some complexity) not only Nietzsche's frequent, usually derisive reformulations of that ideal (which abound in *The Gay Science* and find fictional form in Zarathustra's travels to "the Land of Culture," where he recoils horror-stricken from the seductions of a naked skeleton concealed beneath the motley trappings of "all customs and beliefs"[42]). There is also something strikingly typical in Salomé's invocation, as confirmed by the figure of Sue Bridehead in Hardy's *Jude the Obscure* (1896). Writing to her husband, the schoolmaster Phillotson, at a particularly tortuous moment in the collapse of their marriage, Sue holds up the Humboldtian educational ideal to deflect Phillotson's concerns for Victorian respectability and justify her request to live with Jude: "I know you mean my good. But I don't want to be respectable! To produce 'Human development in its richest diversity' (to quote your Humboldt) is to my mind far above respectability."[43] The figure of Sue Bridehead is not so much, as Hardy claimed, "the first delineation in fiction" of that "woman of the feminist movement—the slight, pale 'bachelor' girl—the intellectualized, emancipated bundle of nerves."[44] Sue Bridehead has important precursors, both in fact and in fiction—including the Russian nihilist women of Turgenev, Chernyshevsky, Dostoevsky, and Tolstoy. There is, also, importantly, Lyndall of Schreiner's *The Story of an African Farm*, according to Elaine Showalter, "the first wholly serious feminist heroine in the English novel."[45] What Salomé's remarks underscore is the way in which it is just these feminist heroines who are Nietzsche's sisters.

However configured, the image of this "new," "nihilist," or "bachelor" woman is, as Hardy's portrait of Sue and Salomé's portrait of Nietzsche suggest, a complex distillation of contradictory effects. The almost stock quotation from Humboldt illustrates that, at the contradictory heart of these "new" challenges, lies the European hypothesis of culture. The figure of Humboldt is all the more revealing in *Jude*, in that Sue is likely quoting not from Humboldt at all, but from John Stuart Mill's *On Liberty* (1859), whose epigraph made Humboldt a familiar name to English readers—and attached that name to one stock sentence: "The grand, leading principle, towards which every argument unfolded in these pages directly converges, is the absolute and essential importance of human development in its richest diversity."[46] The nuances Hardy condenses into the conflict between Sue's Mill and Phillotson's Humboldt (a conflict compressed still more into Sue's own "intellectualized bundle of nerves") dramatize a particularly vexed moment in that novel's plotting of ever-more agonized contradictions between intellectual freedom and social convention.

These knotted involutions of the Victorian marriage plot—and *Jude*, Hardy's farewell to novel writing, marks a sort of formal end to the Victorian novel—have their counterpoint in the Nietzschean question of the "free spirit," the freeing of spirit from academic discourse. In book 2 of *The Gay Science*, which contains some of the richest and most problematic of Nietzsche's remarks on women, Nietzsche seems to indicate, in his own way, an appreciation of Sue's dilemma, when, considering the "monstrous" and "amazing" thing "about the education of upper-class women," he writes that "a psychic knot has been tied that may have no equal."[47] Not perhaps the most insightful of Nietzsche's offensive polemics on the subject, it is an important part of Nietzsche's more sustained improvisation on "the ultimate philosophy and skepsis of woman":

> On female chastity.—There is something quite amazing and monstrous about the education of upper-class women. What could be more paradoxical? All the world is agreed that they are to be brought up as ignorant as possible of erotic matters, and that one has to imbue their souls with a profound sense of shame in such matters until the merest suggestion of such things triggers the most extreme impatience and flight. . . . And then to be hurled, as by a gruesome lightning bolt, into reality and knowledge, by marriage—precisely by the man they love and esteem most! To catch love and shame in a contradiction and to be forced to experience at the same time delight, surrender, duty, pity, terror, and who knows what else, in the face of the unexpected neighborliness of god and beast!
>
> Thus a psychic knot has been tied that may have no equal. Even the compassionate curiosity of the wisest student of humanity is inadequate for guessing how this or that woman manages to accommodate herself to this solution of the riddle, and to the riddle of a solution, and what dreadful, far-reaching suspicions must stir in her poor, unhinged soul—and how the ultimate philosophy and skepsis of woman casts anchor at this point![48]

If Nietzsche's "psychic knot" is the "riddle" from which the "New Woman" is supposedly freed by gaining access to the institutions of higher learning, that wrinkle to this unexpectedly Nietzschean appreciation for the "poor, unhinged" souls of Victorian novels indicates all the more the strange inner affinity between Nietzsche's and Hardy's formulation of the "psychic knot" tied around the "new"-ness of women's challenge to the educational ideals of the century. For what the example of Sue Bridehead illustrates (in her name, for example) is the fact that the "solution to the riddle"—intellectual emancipation, the freeing of the "spirit"—only intensifies the "psychic knot" of women's oppression.

To cast Nietzsche's "philosophy and skepsis of woman" as a problem of Victorian plotting—that staple problem of respectability discussed in Chapter 2—surely misses the fuller peculiarities of Nietzsche's use of the metaphor of "woman," and, indeed, fails to plumb the depths of Nietzsche's misogyny or measure its relation to the moralism of the Victorian obscene.[49] Yet the passage above suggests how the "New Woman"'s challenge to educational ideals shapes a key feature of Nietzsche's nihilist hypothesis: that the "philosophy and skepsis of woman"—putting the "truth" of academic discourse and scientific inquiry in quotation marks—might provide an "anchor" for *realizing* the humanist ideal and the claims of what Heidegger calls "positivism."

This, indeed, is the significance of considering Nietzsche's evolving diagnosis of nihilism from the point of view of Nietzsche's "sisters"—in this case, from the point of view of that educational question, the ambiguous question of "Bildung," around whose nihilist hypothesis Nietzsche's work hinges, as, again, Salomé describes it:

> In his need to generalize and to establish everything scientifically, Nietzsche attempted to place something into the development of history, something whose significance for him lay within a hidden psychic problem. For that reason, it is regrettable that Nietzsche's unique manner of thinking has been obscured by a false emphasis upon his "objectivity." Especially his hypotheses ought not to be taken as abstractions, if one is to draw from them the original kernel. For him the basic question was not the psychic history of mankind but how his own, personal history might be perceived as belonging to all of mankind.[50]

Salomé's argument here reformulates a number of key positions developed by Nietzsche—mostly in *The Gay Science* (in book 4, for example, under the title "*As interpreters of our experiences*": "We . . . who thirst after reason, are determined to scrutinize our experiences as severely as a scientific experiment"[51]). What Salomé captures—here, and throughout her study—is the extent to which Nietzsche's work may be considered as the attempt not so much to *repudiate* the humanist educational ideal of Humboldt, but—through his "personalized style"—to radicalize and reaffirm it as fully as possible.

Nietzsche's nihilist hypothesis is constituted, in its "original kernel," by what we have been calling the hypothesis of culture. This is one aspect of the peculiar fate of the word "Bildung" in translation from Humboldt, via Mill's *On Liberty*, and posited as the keyword to unlock the "psychic knot" of Sue Bridehead's dilemma. The nihilist hypothesis is, as it were, the scientific, positivist formulation of the hypothesis of culture as universal human development. In its blandest, and at the same time, most current latter-nineteenth-century formulation, this is what Herbert Spencer's *First Principles* calls "The Development Hypothesis."[52] In Nietzsche's elaboration from that "kernel," moreover, toward the projected diagnosis of "European nihilism," his work enacts a gathering of different senses of "nihilism" analogous to the blurring of those senses of "culture" we have already discussed in terms of the Arnoldian confusion of "culture."[53]

The contrast between Nietzsche and Arnold draws attention to the wider ambiguity of the mid-nineteenth-century moment—the ambiguous moment of the Victorian blot, in which the variety of different ideas of culture get blurred into a single word, "culture," whose distinctive English formulation looks simultaneously back to the hypothesis of universal human development and forward to its eclipse. The nihilist hypothesis in Nietzsche, like the hypothesis of culture (or "Bildung," more narrowly) in Arnold, is also ambiguous; but what links the two in a revealing, if knotted, double bind is the future temporal orientation of the Arnoldian blurring of "culture" and the retrospective orientation of Nietzsche's projected drawing together into a single diagnosis of all the various brands of "nihilism" which, together, will constitute that "total picture of humankind's historical development"—in the style, not of history, but of genealogy. Culture and nihilism, indeed, might be said to form the complementary concept-metaphors for nineteenth-century attempts to work out Europe's place in the world and in world history, although the particular formulations of each tend to parse them as abstract *opposites*—Nietzsche's genealogy of culture as an iconoclastic dismantling of tradition; Arnold's blurring of culture as an enshrining of tradition.

From the point of view of what we are calling Nietzsche's sisters, the Nietzschean hypothesis of nihilism and the Arnoldian hypothesis of culture describe two sides of the same contradictory relation to academic institutions, discourses, and traditions. The Arnoldian idea of culture is to be realized in the institution of schools and universities—modeled on the very idea of "Bildung" whose spirit the Nietzschean "image and ideal" seeks to radicalize by freeing from those institutions. Although, to be sure, there is some important unevenness of development in the history of schooling systems that accounts for the strangeness of affinities and contrasts, what is important is that the contradictory position of middle-class women vis-à-vis these "universal" educational ideals locates the formal gap, as it were, on which the European humanist ideal is premised; and grasps as the *same* ambiguous problem Arnold's effort to bring culture *into* the educational institutions and Nietzsche's efforts to release it *from* the educational institutions.

The kind of freeing of spirit Nietzsche in fact offered as a model led, according to most diagnoses, to a flight into incoherence—"incoherent rebellion" is aptly the phrase Elaine Showalter uses to describe another of Nietzsche's "sister" writers, the more obscure George Egerton (Mary Chavelita Dunne), who was one of the first writers to import the burgeoning "phenomenon" of Nietzsche into England, in her first two books, *Keynotes* (1893) and *Discords* (1894).[54] Showalter's judgment on Egerton also links her "incoherent rebellion" to the example of Olive Schreiner: "As with Olive Schreiner, her lack of growth seems perversely deliberate."[55] This is a judgment, reflecting as it does on a whole chapter of late-nineteenth-century women's writing (Showalter entitles the chapter "The Feminist Novelists"), that reflects, too, on that imaginary, extended community of Nietzsche's sister writers. The problem of form and style Showalter dubs "incoherent" provides the keynote for examining the problematic status of Nietzsche's text, as it becomes entangled in the very real, very knotted issue of madness.[56] On the one hand, the madness is real—as real for Nietzsche after 1889 as for many "New Women," in fact and in fiction. On the other hand, as Lou Salomé's 1894 study of Nietzsche points out, it is also a matter on which the stylistic and formal coherence of Nietzsche's own philosophical project comes to depend.

These matters are foregrounded in the problematic prophetic voice and attempted cultural-historical perspective of Nietzsche's *Zarathustra* fiction, as variously understood by Lou Salomé and Elisabeth Förster-Nietzsche. Förster-Nietzsche's claim that Zarathustra is Nietzsche's "mouthpiece," "the preacher" of Nietzsche's "gospel to the world" is perhaps the easier to deflate by quoting Nietzsche himself, who writes about *Zarathustra* in the preface to *Ecce Homo*, "Here no 'prophet' is speaking, none of those gruesome hybrids of sickness and will to power whom people call founders of religions."[57] Yet Salomé's critique of *Zarathustra* in many respects agrees with Förster-Nietzsche here, since, for Salomé, the symptomatic failure lay in the vicious circle of Nietzsche's inability to differentiate himself from the "prophet" voice of his creation.[58]

Arguably, though, the point of *Thus Spoke Zarathustra* is not the sermonizing nor even the subversion of the prejudices of the preacher, but rather the rhetorical effect of that voice for those who expect to hear the sermon. As in Zarathustra's claim to sing his song for "lone-dwellers" (Einsiedler) and "twain-dwellers" (Zweisiedlern),[59] the sayings of Zarathustra are an extended play on the language of religious prophecy—an extended dissection of the rhetorical voice of preaching, and of the ear that internalizes its work of ressentiment, reinterpretation, and revaluation.

Bound to the rhetorical impersonation of that "prophet" voice, however, is also the cultural-historical perspective of Nietzsche's choice of the Persian Zoroaster. From the grand opening gesture of Nietzsche's first reference to Zarathustra, in the final section of book 4 from *The Gay Science*, the geographical location of the Zarathustra fiction is more allegorical than historical, creating the fiction of a region of thought beyond the mere realism of region and place: "When Zarathustra was thirty years old, he left his home and Lake Urmi and went into the mountains."[60] Where the *Zarathustra* "poem" succeeds, it is in sustaining this allegorical fiction for the staging of the voice of prophecy, parable, and aphorism. The fictional settings—the mountains, the forest, the marketplace, the land of culture, the wilderness, and so on—are rhetorical devices for positioning, or rather dislocating, that prophet voice. The linguistic play on "dweller" / "-siedler," noted above, extends to place, too, as in the pun on wood and world that produces the coinage "Hinterweltlern," combining the sense of "those who believe in the afterlife" with the sound of "backwoodsmen."[61]

Part of this rhetorical improvisation of perspective, the Persian fiction or phantasmagoria of Nietzsche's *Zarathustra* draws attention to a problem of literary form, whose aesthetic flaw Salomé associates with the dithyrambic verse that breaks out at the end of the fourth book of *The Gay Science*.[62] Conceptually, the cultural-historical significance of *Zarathustra* provides the perspective from which to explain the Nietzschean diagnosis of European nihilism. As Förster-Nietzsche points out, citing Nietzsche's own comments from *Ecce Homo*, the choice of Zarathustra, "the first to see in the struggle between good and evil the essential wheel in the working of things," underscores the conceptual theme of the "overcoming of morality through itself": "Zarathustra *created* the most portentous error, *morality*, consequently he should also be the first to *perceive* that error"; and again: "the overcoming of the moralist through his opposite—*through me*—: that is what the name Zarathustra means in my mouth."[63] By contrast to Förster-Nietzsche's ready acceptance of the fitness of Zarathustra as the proper fictional prophet-persona for Nietzsche's views of himself and his philosophical legacy, Salomé judges the Zarathustra fiction a delusive—and self-delusive—impersonation, precisely because of the "deceptive double character" of the work's literary-aesthetic and mystical-religious registers.[64] There is a disjuncture, Salomé implies, between the symbolic-religious significance of Nietzsche's prophet-figure and the aesthetic consistency of its impersonated Persian fiction.

The aesthetic difficulty Salomé helps illuminate is the problem of how to sustain the credibility of the Zarathustra fiction, "an eternal and free-spirited figure," as Salomé characterizes it, who stands "outside of all time and influence, absolutely independent, all-knowing, and all-encompassing."[65] Zarathustra's time-traveling to "you men of the present, and to the land of culture" (ins Lande der Bildung)[66] still enables sufficient distance to parody contemporary European cultural relativism. But the stylistic premise of the Zarathustra fiction is itself bound to the very problem of cultural relativism this section seeks to critique. The Persian prophet's significance for world history—as a prophet who stands outside all cultural and historical perspectives—needs to be sustained by a fiction of perspectival difference from other world-historical prophet figures (such as the hermit in the opening sections, and the various other figures—the Pope, Luther, Buddha—who come to populate the last book).

In Salomé's aesthetic sense, the cultural-historical consistency of the Zarathustra persona must emerge from a kind of pastiche—from precisely those "motley" characteristics derided in "the Land of Culture" section: "All ages and all peoples gaze motley out of your veils; all customs and all beliefs speak motley out of your gestures."[67] The style of *Thus Spoke Zarathustra* might indeed best be described as a characteristically late-Victorian Orientalism. There are some interesting contemporary English examples that might justify the classification. Robert Browning's "Ferishtah's Fancies" (1884), with its "thin disguise of a few Persian names and allusions" (as Browning himself put it)[68] is a sort of low-key version of Nietzsche's Zarathustra poem. Its fleeting references to Zoroastrianism, moreover, are likely drawn from another piece of late-Victorian Orientalism, Helen Zimmern's *The Epic of Kings: Stories Retold from Firdusi* (1883), whose "theme," according to the author's introduction, "is the old Persian civilization, the cultus of fire, sung by a descendant of those who overthrew this worship. . . . It was deemed that even from beyond the grave the very name of Turan would arouse the warlike ire of the Iranian champion; for the combat of the good and evil principle, that dualism which is the foundation of the Zoroastrian theology, is also the soul of Firdusi's poem."[69] Helen Zimmern, a friend of Browning, was also one of Nietzsche's Sils-Maria companions, very much a sister-spirit, who had translated Schopenhauer and would later translate *Beyond Good and Evil.*

If Zimmern's *Epic of Kings* hardly offers a source for Nietzsche's *Zarathustra*, it does shed light on the late-Orientalist, cultural-historical perspective of Nietzsche's Persian fiction. The problem of impersonation Salomé identifies in *Zarathustra*, and particularly in the later sections of the poem, is a problem of voice and staging. Salomé writes of the "shrill, uncanny dissonances" of the last part of *Zarathustra*, where "the intended jubilation of the dithyrambs [are] drowned out by a cry of pain. They are the last ravagings of Nietzsche by Zarathustra."[70] Where *Zarathustra* succeeds, it is in providing a voice for parables, aphorisms, and riddles. Yet to stage that prophet voice, and its dissolution, requires a fiction of place that strains credibility, and borders on kitsch.[71] The whole of *Thus Spoke Zarathustra*, considered as a mixed (and not exactly successful) literary genre, might be considered characteristically Victorian—something uneasily caught between Thomas Carlyle and Robert Browning. Even the mode of address is the characteristic mode of the Victorian prophet (from Carlyle to Ruskin to Morris), the *moral preacher*. Nietzsche's philosophy, of course, wants to dismantle this sermonizing voice. Where *Zarathustra* fails, however, is in locating the scene of that moralizing, Victorian voice.

This problem of fictional setting is foregrounded in the final part of *Zarathustra*, in the conclusion to the song "Among the Daughters of the Desert," which Kittler describes as Nietzsche's "dithyrambic, flight-of-ideas wish to be out of Europe and in the desert, to lose one's head among its daughters":[72]

> Roar morally!
> Roar like a moral lion
> Before the daughters of the desert!
> For virtuoso howling,
> You dearest maidens,
> Is loved best of all by

> European ardour, European appetite!
> And here I stand now,
> As European,
> I cannot do otherwise, so help me God!
> Amen![73]

Like much of the final section of the book, this "song of the wanderer and shadow" would seem to express the dissolution of Nietzsche's philosophizing into madness. Here, within the Persian phantasmagoria of *Thus Spoke Zarathustra*, the repetition of Luther's famous words at the Diet of Worms ("I cannot do otherwise, so help me God!") evokes a phantasmatic Europe. The insistence on this "European" designation disrupts the extended allegorization of the whole Zarathustra fiction and locates the stylistic problem of *staging*—how to give "perspective" to the problems that are so necessarily "European."

In *Ecce Homo* Nietzsche repeats Luther's famous words in another context, attempting to explain the problem of his own readership generally, and, more specifically, the un-German qualities of his dithyrambic poetry: "I fear that even into the highest forms of the dithyramb one finds in my case some admixture of that salt which never loses its savor and becomes flat—'German'—namely, *esprit*.—I cannot do otherwise. God help me! Amen."[74] The double echo of Luther is a revealing self-reflection on the problem of audience and style. In their combined German, anti-German, European, and "good European" polemic, they reduplicate the contested terms of Förster-Nietzsche's and Salomé's readings of Nietzsche. Immediately before the Luther echo in *Ecce Homo*, Nietzsche seems to evoke both to characterize the problem of his own readership: "It is not for nothing that the Poles are called the Frenchmen among the Slavs. A charming Russian woman would not doubt for a moment where I belong.... To think German, to feel German—I can do anything but not that."[75]

To rehearse this problem of European perspective within *Thus Spoke Zarathustra* threatens to expose the excuse for Orientalist stage sets in the first place. The phantasm of the wanderer-shadow's "Europe" either exposes the stage sets of *Zarathustra* as merely decadent Orientalism; or the Orientalist imposture exposes the fiction of the wanderer-shadow's "Europe." This is the aesthetic dilemma with which Nietzsche's Zarathustra work poses the philosophical problem of "European nihilism." Is this phantasmatic "European" thing a sign of the collapse of Nietzsche's Zarathustra-dream of overcoming? Or is the phantasm of Europe a sign of its accomplishment? The question replicates the ambiguous terms of Nietzsche's incomplete diagnosis of "European nihilism"—is the "Europe" on which the diagnosis is predicated the *foundation* of culture, or a *fiction*? To consider this question, which is all at once Nietzschean and Victorian, we should turn to Olive Schreiner.

Olive Schreiner's "Strangers"

When Olive Schreiner came to Britain in 1881 with the unpublished manuscript of *The Story of an African Farm*, she encountered a turbulent social and political scene whose reverberations through the 1880s, as Anne McClintock so vividly describes, resonate throughout Schreiner's work.[76] The English scene she encountered was also, however, the scene of those "English psychologists" to whom Nietzsche turns, in the opening flourish of *On the Genealogy of Morals*, to set the scene for his genealogy of morals: "These English psychologists, whom one has also to thank for the only attempts hitherto to arrive at a history of the origin of morality—they themselves are no easy riddle; I confess that, as living riddles, they even possess one essential advantage over their books—*they are interesting!*"[77]

No doubt Schreiner's interest in the "English psychologists" was different from Nietzsche's. The coincidence is nonetheless revealing. The English scene Nietzsche evokes to inaugurate his "genealogy of morals" may illuminate and be illuminated in turn by the work of Olive Schreiner. As Ruth First and Ann Scott point out, Schreiner's voluminous reading, in "English political economy and historiography," in particular, led to "the outlines of a project—to trace the evolution of morality."[78] This "project" refers, in part, to the book *Woman and Labour*, which, though published in 1911, represents only a fragmentary reconstruction of an ambitious work that was destroyed by British soldiers in the Boer War of 1899–1902—an incomplete project, then, like Nietzsche's projected diagnosis of European nihilism. The "project" also refers, however, to the fictional work Schreiner brought to England in 1881. *The Story of an African Farm*, published in 1883, provides a fascinating glimpse of the sister-projects of Nietzsche's and Schreiner's genealogies of Victorian morality.

Nietzsche's phrase "English psychologists" caricatures the cluster of intellectual currents that were still shaping the debates Schreiner joined when, for example, she was admitted to the elite Men and Women's Club. What McClintock calls the "privileged language" of that club—"Darwinism"[79]—might loosely be considered the dominant Victorian discourse that both Schreiner and Nietzsche found so "interesting." The shaping influence of the Darwinian theory of evolution on Victorian ideas, as embodied most notably in Herbert Spencer's *First Principles*, is central for each writer's understanding of the meaning of nihilism.

Olive Schreiner does not just help locate the English scene of Nietzsche's philosophy in terms of specific books like Spencer's *First Principles*. As Schreiner's own reading demonstrates, this Victorian scene of reading—the scene of Nietzsche's "genuinely *English* type" of nihilism—is not, of course, "genuinely English." It involves, as well, for Schreiner, a course in Great European books: "Olive spent the winter of 1881 at Rose Cottage, Ventnor, reading Herbert Spencer's *Sociology*, G. H. Lewes's *History of Philosophy*, and George Eliot's *The Mill on the Floss*, and taking desultory German lessons to enable her to read Goethe."[80] In his preface to the *Genealogy* Nietzsche reveals the constructedness of his own "English" scene:

> The first impulse to publish something of my hypotheses concerning the origin of morality was given me by a clear, tidy, and shrewd—also precocious—little book in which I encountered distinctly for the first time an upside-down and perverse species of genealogical hypothesis, the genuinely *English* type, that attracted me—with that power of attraction which everything contrary, everything antipodal possesses.[81]

The book Nietzsche refers to, by Paul Rée, reveals that what Nietzsche calls "English genealogists" is a rhetorical way to foreground the kind of positivism Nietzsche dubbed "Reelism" and around which *The Gay Science* is ambiguously woven.

Just that "perverse species of genealogical hypothesis" is what might be seen to unify the books that appear on the scene of Schreiner's Victorian reading: a particular *Victorian* translation of the hypothesis of "culture," "development," "evolution" for which each of the figures mentioned (Lewes, Eliot, Spencer) might stand as characteristic "*English*" types: Lewes, in his translation of Goethe; Eliot, in her translation of Feuerbach; Spencer in his translation of Darwin. Nietzsche provides a useful way of formulating the significance of Schreiner's own arrival on this Victorian scene. For, although she herself did not characterize her project in terms of an encounter with an "upside-down," "perverse" hypothesis that needed to be set on its feet, her work might indeed be described as enacting a powerful, and influential, reversal of the principles and hypotheses she found in books and people alike. Moreover, to others her approach to the English scene did indeed appear strange—and for her estrangement of Victorian perversities she offers the revealing counterpoint to Nietzsche's English affinities.

What best illustrates the significance of Olive Schreiner's arrival as a stranger on the English scene is the novel appearance of her book, *The Story of an African Farm*. Its success stands in interesting contrast to the peculiar failings of Nietzsche's *Thus Spoke Zarathustra*. One reviewer, Philip Kent, devoted an entire article to the appearance of what he described as "*a new book*," emphasizing the motif of estrangement by quoting lines from Tennyson: "There strode a stranger to the door / And it was windy weather."[82] The strange appearance of the book was emphasized by its packaging, as First and Scott explain: "Published in a small edition in two volumes early in 1883, its spine embossed in a gold ostrich, the front cover incorporating a palm tree and a desert landscape, *The Story of an African Farm* appeared under the pseudonym Ralph Iron, as did the second edition."[83] In some respects a minor detail, these features—designating a landscape, and projecting a male persona "Ralph Iron"—situate a strangeness about the book that not only gestures toward its subject-matter but announces its own particular appeal to the Victorian scene. These composite elements also set in interesting perspective the peculiarities and problems of Nietzsche's Zarathustra stage sets generally—and, most particularly, the "shrill"-ness of the wanderer-shadow's poem, "Among the Daughters of the Desert."

The book's cover design reveals, in the male persona of "Ralph Iron," a further affinity to Nietzsche's *Zarathustra*. As Susan Horton reminds us, the name "Ralph Iron" recalls Schreiner's hero Ralph Waldo Emerson, an echo confirmed in the naming of the characters Waldo and Em. The echo, moreover, has a special resonance for the book's African landscape—its "langscape" as Horton suggestively calls it—since the "Nature" so often invoked in the novel ("And now we turn to Nature . . . " [*The Story*, 151]) is very close to the transcendentalism of Emerson's "Nature."[84] Emerson, indeed, is one of the strange affinities between Schreiner and Nietzsche, whose title page for the 1882 edition of *The Gay Science* also alludes to Emerson, in the form of its epigraph.[85] Still more striking, as Walter Kaufmann discusses, is the possibility that both Nietzsche's "Joyful Wisdom" and his Zarathustra persona are drawn from the Emerson who styles "the peculiar office of scholars in a careful and gloomy generation" as "Professors of the Joyous Science, detectors and delineators of occult symmetries"; and the Emerson whose *Nature* improvises a Zarathustra-like persona to sing "Thus my Orphic poet sang."[86]

The Emersonian landscape in Schreiner and Nietzsche extends the English scene of Victorian positivist science to an American setting that is all at once more rooted in the European spirit of philosophical questioning and almost stereotypically uprooted and free of that very spirit. Schreiner's evocation of Emerson echoes the transcendentalist side to Nietzsche's "nihilism," shaping both the positivist free spiritedness of *The Gay Science* and the unlikely stage sets of *Zarathustra*. For Schreiner the transcendentalist moment of nihilism emerges most clearly when, in the penultimate chapter of *The Story of an African Farm*, Waldo's spiritual struggles are recapitulated in the successive voices of "the true Bible Christian," "the heavenly song . . . of the nineteenth-century Christian," and "the Transcendentalist's high answer" (*The Story*, 287–88).

The power of Schreiner's narrative voice, as many critics have noted, comes from the strong biblical cadences of her prose, and it is this missionary Christian voice that helps locate the moral landscape Schreiner and Nietzsche share. Both were children of German Lutheran pastors, a biographical coincidence that confirms the corresponding crises of religious faith that inform each writer's articulation of nihilism. There is surely a great deal of truth to the biographical explanation that Schreiner learned her biblical prose from the example of her father, a Lutheran missionary on whom Waldo's father, in *The Story of an African Farm*, is apparently modeled. The story of Waldo's spiritual crisis and awakening is, in this sense, very close to elements that keep recurring in Nietzsche's various formulations—the story of the madman proclaiming the death of god, for instance,[87] or the double echo of Luther's "Here I stand" at the end of *Zarathustra* and in *Ecce Homo*. What Schreiner realizes about this experience, however, is the typicality of its colonial missionary meaning. By locating that crisis of religious faith in the colonial scene, *The Story of an African Farm* begins to make sense of the phantasmatic "Europe" of

Zarathustra and, generally, the "European" delineation of Nietzsche's diagnosis of "nihilism."

Thus, the motif of the "stranger" is first established when Waldo's father, on the basis of a text from the Bible, embraces the man who will go on to destroy him, his son, and the tranquillity of the farm:

> Opening a much-worn Bible, he began to read, and as he read pleasant thoughts and visions thronged on him.
> "I was a stranger, and ye took me in," he read.
> He turned again to the bed where the sleeper lay.
> "I was a stranger."
> Very tenderly the old man looked at him. He saw not the bloated body nor the evil face of the man; but, as it were, under deep disguise and fleshly concealment, the form that long years of dreaming had made very real to him. (*The Story*, 56)

What this ensures for the narrative unfolding of the story in part 1 is a devastating, but also sublime revelation of the delusions of missionary Christianity ("the true Bible Christian" [287] of the penultimate chapter). It is devastating in demonstrating the complicity of Waldo's father's Christian piety and the exploitative opportunism of the character of Bonaparte Blenkins, who easily displaces the loose family structure of the farm, dispossessing the three children, Waldo, Lyndall, and Em, of their respective claims to position on the farm (as, respectively, the overseer's son, and the English and Boer nieces to the farm's Dutch Boer owner, "Tant' Sannie"), and usurping the German's position as overseer.

It is also full of sublime pathos in unfolding that delusion as Waldo's spiritual crisis of awakening, leading to the nihilist experience that characterizes the division of the novel's two parts. Bonaparte's ascendancy, assured with the death of Waldo's father, is clinched in an extraordinary evocation of the homesteading experience of colonial farming, when Waldo, unaware of his father's death (described in the previous chapter), returns to the farm under the eager eye of Bonaparte. Waldo's religious musings are overlaid by the reader's awareness of the tragic ambiguity of their simultaneously divine and human reference:

> Then came over him suddenly what he called "The presence of God"; a sense of a good, strong something folding him round. He smiled through his half-shut eyes. "Ah, Father, my own Father, it is so sweet to feel you,

like the warm sunshine. The Bibles and books cannot tell of you and all I feel you. They are mixed with men's words; but you—" (*The Story*, 97)

Interrupted by the revelation that he has reached the "old home farm," Waldo's musings modulate into an evocation of homecoming—a return to the colonial "homestead" figured almost as a classical *nostos*—which is in fact the beginning of his dispossession from the farm.

The power of this narrative unfolding of the motif of estrangement is not precisely to be located in the realism with which it exposes the story of colonialism—colonial possession and dispossession of the land. That is there already in the first appearance of the "stranger" motif, an unacknowledged recognition that the missionary represents the arrival of the "stranger" and political intruder on the colonial landscape. In the narrative reach of the novel, it unfolds in what Georg Lukacs delineates as the characteristic form of the historical novel: the stranger of part 1, whose grotesquely apt name Bonaparte Blenkins captures the world-historical type of the freebooting European conqueror, delineates the anarchy of opportunistic colonialism in its earlier stages; in part 2, the corresponding figure, Gregory Rose, will figure the adoption of colonialism as everyday life in the domestication of Blenkins's tyranny.

In some crucial respects, *The Story of an African Farm* may indeed be viewed as a historical novel of the South African colonial experience—its limitations (as McClintock notes them) and its artistic power (as Horton explores it) as great as any of the European historical novels that are Lukacs's models. But the "story" of the title cannot complete such a historical imperative precisely because the novel insists on a universality of narrative vision and voice.

The prophet voice of Nietzsche's Zarathustra finds its counterpoint in the unfolding narrative voice of *The Story of an African Farm*. Schreiner's narrative voice modulates the omniscient telling of the individual characters' stories in part 1 into the universal, Emersonian "we" that holds together the disparate experiences of the characters in part 2, when they can no longer be contained in the single "story" of the African farm. The result is that the "African farm" of the title simultaneously estranges the traditional setting of the Victorian novel and recalls what connects it materially, spiritually, and in its origins, with the familiar space of English fiction, the colonial estate. Schreiner's narrative perspective creates a novel that may then simultaneously be read as the epitome of the Victorian novel and as its death and transfiguration.

The novel's universality of experience is predicated on incommensurabilities of individual, subjective, or "spiritual" experiences which come, ultimately, to dominate narrative structure and sequence. The reader's expectation that the lives of the novel's three children will be followed to fill out that singular "story" of the novel's title is undermined, not only in that these characters come to be dispossessed of the social sense of family and home provided by the farm, but also as their individual stories are seen to diverge spiritually, socially, and geographically. In the shift from part 1 to part 2 it becomes clearer in what sense "stranger" is not a term generated by contrast to some more primordial sense of relation either to people or to place. Although Waldo's and Lyndall's estrangement from the farm is figured by their respective "strangers," "stranger" as a term comes to designate all the characters' relation to the farm.

This underscores the fact that the novel is built around the virtual absence of any lived experience of antagonism between colonial settlers and indigenous peoples. Where the novel goes furthest in specifying the conditions around which twentieth-century South African apartheid would crystallize, actual forms of social and political domination appear through the distorted dream-work of colonial ideology. One example is Lyndall's racist characterization of a native "Kaffir" farmer as "a splendid fellow" with "a magnificent pair of legs" with which she supposes he will "kick his wife . . . when he gets home. He has a right to; he bought her for two oxen." "There is something of the master about him," she continues, "in spite of his blackness and wool" (*The Story*, 227).

The racism here is deliberately provocative, but rather than dramatizing any point about the relations of European settlers to African natives, its main concern is to develop the difference of sensibilities between Gregory Rose and Waldo. Lyndall is here improvising a response to Gregory Rose who, before his cross-dressing transformation into acting as Lyndall's devoted nurse, has tried to engage Lyndall in the sort of sibling dialogue Lyndall has with Waldo throughout the novel. Many of the novel's most disturbing effects emerge from such attempts to condense and displace the knotted interrelation of racial identification, gendered domestic hierarchy, and sexual domination.[88] The result is, as with Lyndall's racist caricature of domestic violence, to evoke a phantom colonial subject.

The Story of an African Farm is concerned less with the real social relations of colonial rule than it is with this colonial phantasm. Its articulation of racial, domestic, and sexual forms of domination have, for this very reason, something in common with Nietzsche's discourse of "mastery" (Herrschaft), the "drive to dominate" (Herrschafts-Trieb[89]), and the "theory of forms of domination" (Herrschaftsgebilde) projected in *The Will to Power*.[90] "Stranger," in *The Story of an African Farm*, designates the novel's colonial phantasm as a "European" difference—one between colonial settlers of various types and kinds. Thus, although the novel surely is an evocation of what Dan Jacobson calls "a colonial culture"[91]—for that very reason, its exploration of different colonial types does not constitute a genealogy of colonialism. Rather, it provides a genealogy of European types—more precisely, of European types of estrangement. In this, Olive Schreiner's colonial phantasm may provide the counterpart to the phantasmatic "Europe" evoked at the end of Nietzsche's *Thus Spoke Zarathustra*.

In the characters of Bonaparte Blenkins, in part 1, and Gregory Rose, in part 2, the novel's genealogy of European types is most apparent. Blenkins's claim of relation to Napoleon Bonaparte, the Duke of Wellington, and Queen Victoria condenses into a single absurd genealogy a comic delusion of European world-historical power. Gregory Rose, in part 2, provides the domesticated, bourgeois, cultured version of this in the form of his letter-paper: "There was a family crest and motto on the latter, for the Roses since coming to the colony had discovered that they were of distinguished lineage. . . . There were Roses in England who kept a park and dated from the Conquest. So the colonial 'Rose Farm' became 'Rose Manor,' in remembrance of the ancestral domain, and the claim of the Roses to noble blood was established—in their own minds, at least" (*The Story*, 175).

The parodic register of these deluded genealogies (and pathologies) of European world history (Bonaparte) and English claims to world culture (Rose) has its more serious counterpart in the obscure genealogies of Waldo, Lyndall, and Em. Conceived as a collective genealogy of the African farm's extended colonial family, the children of part 1 might appear to present an allegory of successive European intrusions on the South African landscape—something suggested in the novel's opening satirical comment on successive husbands (first Boer, second English) who are displaced in Tant' Sannie's sleep by the dream of "the sheep's trotters she had eaten for supper that night" (*The Story*, 36). This allegorical possibility lingers throughout the novel as part of its incomplete and ambiguous historical and political allusion to the Dutch–Boer/English rivalry. It is necessarily incomplete and ambiguous, one might note, since the novel was written between England's annexation of the Transvaal in 1877 and the Dutch Boer recovery of the Transvaal in the first Boer War of 1880–1881. At the moment when the novel might designate the historical conjuncture for reconstructing such an allegory as prehistory to the present—in chapter 2, whose opening sentence refers to "the great drought" in "the year of 1862" (*The Story*, 44)—Schreiner displaces the historical and political imperative of that allegory by rearranging the question of the children's family background around their response to the name of Bonaparte. Prefiguring Blenkins's absurd genealogy, this introduction to the main characters provides a more revealing scene of instruction in genealogies of European history.

For Em, Bonaparte is a "funny name" from a "Hottentot" "reel"; for Lyndall, by contrast, "He was the greatest man that ever lived" (*The Story*, 47), and she proceeds to retell the story of Napoleon's exile (an exile with which Lyndall clearly identifies). If the difference between Em's and Lyndall's views is clear enough—for Em, Bonaparte's history is "a nice story . . . but the end is sad" (*The Story*, 48)—the dialogue between Waldo and Lyndall introduces a further difference, showing how Schreiner prefigures the collective story of these children by measuring their characters against this touchstone of the grand European narrative of world history. In their disagreement over how to read the version given in their history book ("the brown history"), Schreiner provides, *in nuce*, a formula for the unfolding of narrative:

> As [Lyndall] spoke the boy's dark, heavy eyes rested on her face.
> "You have read it, have you not?"
> He nodded. "Yes, but the brown history tells only what he did, not what he thought."
> "It was in the brown history that I read of him," said the girl; "but I *know* what he thought. Books do not tell everything."
> "No," said the boy, slowly drawing nearer to her and sitting at her feet. "What you want to know they never tell." (*The Story*, 48)

This inaugural scene of reading indicates how the novel follows the form of the "Bildungsroman." In the distance between what each of the three children learn about Napoleon, one measures the constellation of different positions each has already developed, and might yet develop, in relation to the "story" of the African farm. Only as the novel develops does it become clear that theirs is not a collective story. Yet if theirs is not the collective story of the African farm, the narrative nonetheless does trace each character's growth and development (Bildung) in determinate relation to a single unfolding story. The location of the farm is, however, always a split scene; and this important scene of instruction and of reading presents the split scene of a European narrative of universal history—a well-known story read in three very different ways.

Waldo's "Bildung" is in some respects the organizing pattern of the novel—organizing the novel around a spiritual awakening to nihilism and thus reversing the pattern of "Bildung." As the model of "Bildung" and its undoing, this strand of the novel illustrates Homi Bhabha's argument about the split scene of colonial discourse[92]—unexpectedly, in some respects, given the novel's silence on the colonial contest. It is Waldo's narrative, however, that is premised on this silence, providing, as a counterpart to what European history cannot tell, a problem of geography—"This 'kopje', if it could tell us how it came here!" (*The Story*, 48). Such Emersonian transcendentalism, reading hieroglyphs in nature, has its explicit relation to the Bushmen paintings to which Waldo refers and which is balanced, in the chapter's title ("Plans and Bushman-Paintings"), against the European ideal of historical development. What this shows is not that Waldo's "Bildung" is split between an African and a European scene, but rather that it splits the phantom colonial dream of coordinating European history and geography in a universal story. It splits this fundamental element of the European hypothesis of culture (world history, universal geography), but it does not abandon it. Waldo's narrative suggests how what Bhabha examines as the splitting of colonial discourse and the "estrangement of the English book"[93] is the kernel of both culture and nihilism.

For Waldo, in part 1, it is the book of the Bible whose missionary estrangement—dictated by the very authority of the text "I was a Stranger, and ye took me in"—calls into question the authority of "the true Bible Christian." Waldo's questioning of missionary authority does not, to be sure, yield "insurgent interrogations" of colonial practices such as Homi Bhabha finds in the mimicry of subaltern missionary discourse.[94] The missionary location of Schreiner's scene of estrangement nonetheless gives rise to a series of questions about interpretation, or hermeneutics: for example, in Waldo's question about the discrepancy between the gospels of Mark and Luke—"Could a story be told in opposite ways and both ways be true?" (*The Story*, 67). To the extent that such questions are tied to an implied English-reading colonial presence, its "national" authority can only ever be read through the "mixed and split texts of hybridity."[95] Both the Bible and the "brown history," and then also John Stuart Mill's *Political Economy*, which Bonaparte Blenkins confiscates from Waldo later in part 1, provide textbook illustrations for such "mixed and split texts." The appearance of the "brown volume" of Spencer's *First Principles* in part 2 of the novel offers a still more fitting enactment of the scenario Bhabha outlines for the grounding of colonial authority through the "fortuitous discovery of the English book."[96] Displacing the "brown history" of part 1, the "brown volume" of *First Principles* condenses into a single English book the authority of a claim to an understanding of the universal condition of estrangement.

The book Waldo's self-styled nihilist stranger gives him is significantly not named until, obliquely, its title crops up toward the end of the novel.[97] If this dislocation of authority indicates a displacement of Schreiner's own investment in the scenario,[98] the "brown volume" lends a deferred and divided authority to European books, characteristically split between non-fiction and fiction—like the "bright French novel" Waldo's stranger keeps for himself; or the "Black-eyed Creole" whose title is juxtaposed with "First Principles" when that book is finally named toward the end of the novel. It is a deferral and a split sustained throughout as the unresolved European difference of colonial authority and presence on the African scene. *First Principles* thus constitutes a deferred and split point of reference for the Victorian authority of the universal "we" of Schreiner's narrative voice.

As with Waldo's story generally, this authority for the universality of his existential nihilist experience is made dependent on Lyndall's story. Lyndall's story embodies the emancipatory narrative imperative echoed in Sue Bridehead's "human development in its richest diversity"; indeed, Lyndall gives voice to the universal feminist challenge of the nineteenth-century culture hypothesis when she explains at length to Waldo why "woman's work needs a many-sided, multiform culture.... *We* bear the world, and *we* make it" (*The Story*, 193). Not the universal "we" of Schreiner's novel, this voice is nonetheless essential in reproducing the dominant voice of Victorian narrative authority, that of the pseudonymously male woman novelist. If the moral authority of the Victorian novel typically depends on measuring this universal imperative (the rights of women) against the claims of social reality, Lyndall's story itself cannot be measured against the social coordinates of the novel's "African farm" setting.

Enacting a phantasmatic colonial contradiction between freedom and confinement, her great trek out of the novel's frame of reference (into the Transvaal Free State) figures a quest for freedom as the very terms of her confinement through pregnancy, the loss of her child, and death. Much of the power and pathos of the novel comes from the fact that, with news of Lyndall's death, the novel defers forever the possibility of reading Waldo's experience from Lyndall's perspective. Schreiner's novel thus defers the authority of a narrative perspective that might measure Lyndall's universal feminist imperative against the claims of Waldo's universal existential nihilism.

This appropriation of the moral authority of Victorian novel form produces, around a phantom colonial subject, the narrative voice of the novel's disembodied, phantasmatic "we." It also produces what Elaine Showalter, writing about the unfinished novel *From Man to Man*, suggestively describes as "a fictional world obsessed with a femaleness grown monstrous in confinement—a world full of Bertha Masons."[99] This description, together with Schreiner's earlier title for the novel—*Mirage: A Series of Abortions*—recalls the terms of Gayatri Spivak's landmark essay aligning *Frankenstein*, *Jane Eyre*, and *Wide Sargasso Sea* as novels that figure the cost of assuming the female authority of the English novel-writing tradition in terms of the devastating conjuncture of "soul-bearing" and "child-bearing."[100] This conjuncture is what Nietzsche sought to diagnose as the "psychic knot" of women's experiences; and the terms of this "knot" tying together the priorities of "soul-bearing" and "child-bearing" are lucidly explained by Lyndall's claim "*We* bear the world, and *we* make it":

> The souls of little children are marvellously delicate and tender things, and keep for ever the shadow that first falls on them, and that is the mother's or at best a woman's. There was never a great man who had not

a great mother—it is hardly an exaggeration. The first six years of our life make us; all that is added later is veneer; and yet some say, if a woman can cook a dinner or dress herself well she has culture enough. (*The Story*, 193)

These split imperatives of "soul-bearing" and "child-bearing" are written into the terms of what Claire Kahane, describing the relation between Waldo's and Lyndall's story, calls the "split subject" of the novel. Kahane examines how these conflicting imperatives, premised on a narrative inversion of the usual gender roles of Victorian hero and heroine, constitute the split authorial voice of the novel. Yet what she takes to be the novel's flaw—its failure to articulate Schreiner's "political and creative voice"—might alternatively be read as the novel's formal success in locating the colonial phantasm of the novel's split subject:

> In spite of the [novel's] experimentation with splitting and reversal, with multiple genres and different voices, the novel about the New Woman ultimately takes refuge in an old story: Lyndall's quest for self-liberation ends in pregnancy and death; Waldo's quest for a figure of truth is so totally thwarted that at the end he longs only for an escape from consciousness and dies in a welcome submersion into sleep. The salutary hysterical tension of part 1 yields to a masochistic resolution in part 2 that privileges stasis, silence, and death.[101]

The terms of this argument might also suggestively be transposed to describe the constitutive features of narrative voice in Nietzsche's *Zarathustra*, particularly for those "shrill, uncanny dissonances" Salomé hears in the dithyrambic "last ravagings of Nietzsche by Zarathustra."[102]

Schreiner provides a fictional setting—the African farm—for this narrative voice split between hysteria and masochism; and it is the colonial setting that might explain in turn the hystericized split subject of both Schreiner's novel and Nietzsche's *Zarathustra*. With the impending marriage of Em and Gregory Rose, the novel's conclusion returns, even more so than Kahane suggests, to conventional Victorian plot form. The formula of marriage frames the dialogic split between Lyndall and Waldo through the voice of another—Em, the one whose story most closely sticks to the "story of an African farm"—and through whose perspective the reader is compelled to imagine the final split scene between the voice of Lyndall's "hysterical aphasia" and Waldo's "masochistic silence."

The dialogue between Lyndall and Waldo by which the narrative measures the distance between what Spivak calls "soul-bearing" and "child-bearing" is, according to the logic of the abandoned title, aborted in perhaps the most moving moment of the novel—significantly in a scene of writing, when Waldo, in the midst of an unfinished, long letter to Lyndall, learns from Em that Lyndall is dead. Both the pathos and the narrative implications of this formal undoing of novel form are managed in the virtuosic manner with which Schreiner reconstitutes the collapse of the Victorian novel around its most characteristic closure, marriage. Em's announcement of the anticipated marriage to Gregory Rose is neither ironic nor of course does it provide any compensation, emotional or ideological, for the devastating loss the narrative has traced in its "strange coming and going of feet."[103] What is offered instead is an image that almost incidentally figures what we might call, recalling Nietzsche, the "psychic knot" of the Victorian novel:

> "I remember once, very long ago, when I was a very little girl, my mother had a work-box full of coloured reels. I always wanted to play with them, but she would never let me. At last one day she said I might take the box. I was so glad I hardly knew what to do. I ran round the house, and sat down with it on the back steps. But when I opened the box all the cottons were taken out." (*The Story*, 296)

This "empty box" that Waldo "perhaps" is thinking of when he kisses Em's forehead "gravely" in the moments before his own death, provides a fitting image for the success with which Olive Schreiner, crafting a perfect Victorian novel, perfectly demonstrates the emptiness that is its "psychic knot." Around this empty box Schreiner coordinates the nihilism and estrangement of European identity that constitutes the kernel of Victorian novel form.

Aesthetic Form, European Nihilism, and Pathologies of Power

The colonial setting and narrative voice of *The Story of an African Farm* provide an aesthetic counterpart to the phantasmatic Europe evoked in *Thus Spoke Zarathustra*. Both constitute a fiction of power and imperial politics premised on an estrangement of European cultural identity and identification. What erupts in the "shrillness" of dithyrambic song and what constitutes the Victorian stage sets of Zarathustra's prophet-persona is an estrangement of European cultural identity that Olive Schreiner formulates as the pathos of our attachment as readers to the "strange coming and going" of the three characters, Lyndall, Waldo, and Em. This pathos—what Nietzsche formulates as a pathology of power—remains for the twentieth century a core feature of the fiction of geopolitics.

Novel form is the one genre with which Nietzsche seems least familiar, something particularly striking given its importance for so many of his women friends. Opera, rather than the novel, is the aesthetic form that Nietzsche finds most revealing for what he sought to diagnose as "European nihilism." The coordination of different arts—theater, music, stage sets, lighting—is both part of the appeal and part of the problem with the medium of opera. Like the phantasmagoria of the Zarathustra books, opera may be grasped, in terms of aesthetic form, as ambiguously situated between all those decadent forms of pastiche that sprouted up in the late-Victorian period and the twentieth-century struggle over the new, non-literary media.

Nietzsche not only diagnoses the aesthetic problem of opera, however. He experiences it himself as a "crisis of taste."[104] Wagnerian opera, which in *The Birth of Tragedy* (1872) had promised a rebirth of culture out of the spirit of music, comes to symptomize for Nietzsche, in *The Case of Wagner* and *Nietzsche contra Wagner*, both written in 1888, the year before his collapse, "the whole of European decadence."[105] Nietzsche's evaluation of Wagnerian opera prefigures in aesthetic form what is projected for the diagnosis of "European nihilism"—having "lived through the whole of nihilism, to the end, leaving it behind."[106]

The aesthetic form of the opera stages a problem of European cultural perspective common to a range of nineteenth-century art forms, including the late-Victorian Orientalism of his own Zarathustra books: "Winckelmann's and Goethe's Greeks, Victor Hugo's orientals, Wagner's Edda characters, Walter Scott's Englishmen of the thirteenth century—some day the whole comedy will be exposed!"[107] Edward Said's *Orientalism* has exposed the "comedy" of such cultural-historical anachronisms, generally, as the staging of European world power and colonial domination. His more recent discussion of Verdi's opera *Aida*, in *Culture and Imperialism*, is still more relevant. Exploring the incongruities of producing and staging Verdi's Orientalist vision of Egypt in Egypt, Said shows how the monumental exhibition of European cultural capital abroad became "an imperial spectacle designed to alienate and impress an almost exclusively European audience."[108]

Like Verdi, Wagner, too, stages an "imperial spectacle"—and this, for Nietzsche, is a central feature of its decadence. At the end of *The Case of Wagner*, Nietzsche explains the connection between Wagnerian opera and the spectacle of the new German Empire ("Reich") and the nationalism and militarism following the Prussian defeat of France in 1870:

> It is full of profound significance that the arrival of Wagner coincides in time with the arrival of the "*Reich*": both events prove the very same thing: obedience and long legs.—Never has obedience been better, never has commanding. Wagnerian conductors in particular are worthy of an age that posterity will call one day, with awed respect, *the classical age of war*.[109]

The case of Wagner here delineates the imperialism of operatic spectacle. At the same time, it is itself a showcase for that rhetoric of domination and war that increasingly punctuates Nietzsche's late work. Like Nietzsche's various "declarations of war" just before his collapse, *The Case of Wagner* itself "declare[s] war upon Wagner—and incidentally upon a German 'taste.'"[110] The pathology of power Nietzsche ascribes to Wagnerian opera, then, is the pathology of his own discourse of power, "great politics," and global warfare.

Verdi's Egyptian staging of opera abroad to "alienate and impress an exclusively European audience" is instructive here. Nietzsche is one of those "almost exclusively European" listeners the operatic spectacle is designed to alienate and impress. Unlike Verdi's *Aida*, Wagnerian opera is an imperial spectacle staged within Europe. Its effects, as Nietzsche so painstakingly describes, are no less alienating and impressive. The discourse of war, power, and "great politics" in Nietzsche's philosophy is surely both a diagnosis and also a symptom of a pathology of imperial power. The pathology is less that of the preacher, or would-be prophet; it is that of the listener, or would-be opera-lover. Nietzsche's diagnosis of "European nihilism" is, then, a self-diagnosis of the dissolution of his own "good European" cultured "tastes" as effects of the alienation and impressive power of opera. He examines—and experiences—the spectacle of European high culture as the pathology of European power.

Nietzsche's perceptions of the dissolution of European culture look back to the nineteenth-century idea of "Bildung"—as part of the "crisis of taste" with which he diagnoses the breakup of his own educated, acquired, and affected cultural tastes. Midway between Nietzsche's enthusiasm for Wagner, in *The Birth of Tragedy* (1872), and the late polemic against Wagner, in *The Case of Wagner* (1888), "theater and music" constitute the point of leverage in the critique of "Bildung," in book 2 of *The Gay Science*: "Theater and music as the hashish-smoking and betel-chewing of the European! Who will ever relate the whole history of narcotica?—It is almost the history of 'culture' ['Bildung'], of our so-called higher culture!"[111] Here already, however, Nietzsche looks toward the sort of "new evaluation" announced in *The Case of Wagner* under the title "Toward a Physiology of Art"[112] and outlined in *The Will to Power*—"In place of 'epistemology,' a perspective theory of affects."[113] This "theory" or "doctrine" (the German "Lehre" is ambiguous) is premised on a "theory" or "doctrine" of power: "In place of 'sociology,' a theory of the forms of domination [eine *Lehre von den Herrschaftsgebilden*]."[114] Nietzsche's "forms of domination"—his "power-complex," we might call it, to capture the ambiguity of his diagnosis of pathologies of power—is also accompanied by a revealing reformulation of culture: "In place of 'society,' the culture complex, as my chief interest (as a whole or in its parts)."[115] Nietzsche's late-nineteenth-century "power-complex" is perhaps still a measure of our twentieth-century "culture-complex." As Friedrich Kittler argues, in breaking from the older discourse of "Bildung," Nietzsche "stood at the threshold of a new discourse network"[116]—in which the question of style is no longer a matter of literary genres.

Kittler traces Nietzsche's preoccupation with the new media networks back as early as *The Birth of Tragedy*, noting Nietzsche's description of the hero of Greek tragedy by comparison to the familiar effect of the entoptical afterimage (colored spots produced "as a cure, as it were" by the attempt to gaze directly at the sun). Disregarding the Apollonian surface, the Greek hero is "after all, . . . in the last analysis nothing but a bright image projected on a dark wall."[117] As Kittler comments:

> Moving "images of light" by which the eye forms an image of its own retina have little to do with productions of Sophocles at Athenian festivals. Nietzsche's Apollonian art describes something quite different—the technological medium of film, which the Lumière brothers would make public on December 28, 1895. Nietzsche and the Lumières based Apol-

Ionian art and the movies on applied physiology: the entoptical afterimage, or the illusion, created by afterimage and strobe effect, in which discrete images proceeding with sufficiently high frequency appear to form a continuum.[118]

The heroic blot of Nietzsche's Hellenic ideal suggests a physiological principle for measuring the pathology of European greatness as an optical illusion of world history. In this sense, the twentieth-century fiction of geopolitics might still be measured against the pathologies of Nietzsche's own attempts at a diagnosis of "European nihilism."

The work of Olive Schreiner helps set these pathologies within the context of the novel form and what we have examined, in the previous chapter, as the Victorian blot. Nietzsche's pathologies, after all, are not only the pathologies of what Salomé called "the last ravagings of Nietzsche by Zarathustra."[119] They belong, too, to the pathos of identification shared by a great many late-Victorian novel-readers, Olive Schreiner's "strangers" and Friedrich Nietzsche's "sisters" alike. In the preface to *On the Genealogy of Morals*, this pathos is what Nietzsche diagnoses as "the morality of pity":

> I understood the ever spreading morality of pity [Mitleid: pathos] that had seized even on philosophers and made them ill, as the most sinister [unheimlich: uncanny] symptom of a European culture that had itself become sinister [unheimlich], perhaps as its by-pass to a new Buddhism? to a Buddhism for Europeans [Europäer-Buddhismus]? to—*nihilism*?[120]

The fantasmatic "Europe" of Nietzsche's *Zarathustra*, like the colonial phantasm of *The Story of an African Farm*, is that pathological point of sentimental and philosophical pity that produces the novel-reading subject. It is that subject torn between the unfinished letter of Waldo and the departed spirit of Lyndall. Another version of the endless improvisation of the shame of individual identity and identification that we have already explored in the work of Wilkie Collins, it is also the pathology Nietzsche sought to diagnose as "European nihilism."

PART III

UTOPIA AND SABOTAGE

Contesting Geopolitics

4 Broadcasting News from Nowhere
Utopian Narrative and the Sketch-Artistry of R. B. Cunninghame Graham

"The time to act is now, whilst the present generation is young; in order that the lives of the workers may not be consumed in fruitless agitation. What a wild, unknown Western world . . . is there open to the man who will discover the means whereby the working-classes may possess this America, nay even will take them with him and plant them on it—without a journey. The America is here, richer far than the wildest imagination of the bold adventurers of the 16th century painted Eldorado. The treasure is here, too, richer far than Potosi. But a legion of demons guard it—demons of prejudice and bigotry, of class hatred and all uncharitableness."
—R. B. Cunninghame Graham,
Introduction to *A Labour Programme* by J. L. Mahon, 1888

"When Dante walked about the streets . . . the people used to point him out as the man who had seen Hell. You may, perchance yet live, and living, may see . . . me pointed out as the man who [has] seen Socialism."   —R. B. Cunninghame Graham,
"Life in Tangiers," *The Labour Elector*, 11 January 1890

"Why is it that perhaps the most practical book that was ever written on the social question till modern times, has become the synonym for everything that is absurd and Utopian?—you see I too fall into using the adjective even about the book I admire."
—R. B. Cunninghame Graham,
"Utopia," *The People's Press*, 11 October 1890

The meaning of utopia for Marxism finds its classic statements, first, in *The Communist Manifesto*, which critiques utopian socialism for its rejection of revolutionary action[1]; and then also in Friedrich Engels's *Socialism: Utopian and Scientific* (1880), which contrasts the "Utopians' mode of thought" that "has for a long time governed the socialist ideas of the nineteenth century" to the "scientific basis" of dialectical materialism.[2] Marxism's anti-utopian imperative is itself, however, an imperative bound constantly to elaborate on the meaning of utopia. In 1848, commenting on a utopian communist project by one Citizen Cabet, Karl Marx had explained at some length why emigration to America could not succeed in realizing communism, concluding, "I cry out to the communists in every country: Brothers, stay at the battlefront of Europe. Work and struggle here, because only Europe has all the elements to set up communal wealth. This type of community will be established here, or nowhere."[3] This oddly utopian, anti-utopian imperative is deeply embedded in the matrix of revolutionary challenges from which Marxism was to emerge as one of the master discourses of the twentieth century.

In the accentuated Eurocentrism of his appeal to "communists in every country" to "stay at the battlefront of *Europe*," Marx seems to exaggerate a contradictory logic of place inscribed already in the word utopia, and happily highlighted in English by the interplay between the "no-where" of the imagined ideal community and the urge to realize that community "now-here." The particular urgency with which Marx opposes the "battlefront" of Europe to the American scene of Cabet's proposed emigration scheme has a good deal to do with the emergencies of 1848, when revolutionaries faced repression and exile. In drawing on and inverting that commonplace utopian trope of European emigration to America, Marx forges a simultaneously utopian and anti-utopian revolutionary imperative.[4]

This anti-utopian utopian imperative remains as a complicated, riddling afterimage in a whole cluster of utopian narratives that flourished over the turn of the century. The narrators of these utopian tales come across as impatient storytellers: eager to get "nowhere" fast, they are as eager to get back to tell the news of their discoveries. In Bellamy's *Looking Backward, 2000-1887* (1888), William Morris's *News from Nowhere* (1891), and H. G. Wells's *The Time Machine* (1895), the narrators are placed in the position of having to explain their relation to two very different kinds of society, the actual existing social condition of the late nineteenth century and that society "nowhere" which is their cherished or (with Wells) feared imagined community. This embarrassment constitutes something of a departure from the classical utopian model, More's *Utopia*, in that it concerns the problem of getting the narrator back and forth from the future to the present. One thing that is striking about these utopian narratives is how *little* their narrators are embarrassed by discovering themselves in the same geographical location: Bellamy's Boston, and the Southeast England of Morris and Wells. A necessary condition for the message each brings from the future, this privileging of history over geography leaves entirely out of their picture of the 1890s that immense transformation taking place at the time and bringing together, often with unimaginable violence, different peoples and linking different regions of the world.

The imperative to imagine Utopia as the future shape of the now and *here* belongs to a rather special sort of impatience with storytelling in the 1890s, and it is in this sense that Marx's anti-utopian utopian imperative is at work in these narratives, socialist or anti-socialist. Utopian anxiety about the "nowhere" of the future expresses a profound inability to link the challenge of international socialism with a new geography of politics. The revolutionary legacy of nineteenth-century humanism, as socialism appeared in the 1890s to revolutionaries and reactionaries alike, was charged with the considerable theoretical and practical challenge of realizing a new globalism of social and political relations. To examine how the "battlefront" of revolutionary struggle was drawn in the 1890s I should like to consider, in counterpoint to the Marxist imperative "here, or nowhere," the representative example of R. B. Cunninghame Graham.

Afterimages of R. B. Cunninghame Graham

Scottish aristocrat, socialist agitator, close friend of Joseph Conrad, and voluminous correspondent with many famous people (and many more forgotten) of the turn of the century—the figure of Cunninghame Graham crops up in the margins of many different histories.[5] The eccentric images of the wild barricade socialist and wild colonial adventurer which constitute the legend of "Don Roberto," as he was and still is popularly known, have in fact worked to obscure the links his writing makes between two particular histories—that of the labor movement in its historic struggle for parliamentary representation, and "impressionist" experimentation in the historical formation of high literary modernism. G. K. Chesterton wrote of Cunninghame Graham: "No Cabinet Minister would ever admire his Parliamentary style; though he had a much better style than any Cabinet Minister. Nothing could prevent Balfour being Prime Minister or MacDonald being Prime Minister; but Cunninghame Graham achieved the adventure of being Cunninghame Graham."[6] That "style" which Chesterton praises precisely because it disqualifies him from a prime place in political history applies also to evaluation of his place in literary history—he lived, so the legend reads, the adventure that others sought to realize in artistic form or practical politics.

The persistence of this legend may be illustrated by a set of images of R. B. Cunninghame Graham from the 1890s, which I offer in place of a biographical sketch. The first is the portrait of Graham by Sir John Lavery (see Figure 12). Painted in 1893 "in the manner of Velasquez, full-length and life size, a harmony in brown," Lavery renders Graham with a Whistler-like aristocratic aestheticism.[7] Along with the characteristic traits of Don Roberto's pose as *gaucho* horseman of the South American pampas, the portrait registers the influence of Graham's adventurous aura on a range of turn-of-the-century artists and writers.[8] (During the 1980s this Lavery portrait was used to illustrate the front cover of the Penguin edition of Joseph Conrad's *Nostromo*, all at once framing the South American setting and indicating Conrad's debt to his close friend Cunninghame Graham.) The second image is that of "Cunninghame Graham, M.P." side by side with Keir Hardie, two prominent founders of the Scottish Labour Party and thus figureheads on the first party ticket, which has since been reproduced as a tea towel by the People's Palace in Glasgow to commemorate the party's founding in 1888 (see Figure 13). It is an image which places Graham in suggestive, if eccentric relation to that icon of Labour history, Keir Hardie, the first member of Parliament to be elected as representative of a labor party.

These afterimages of the Don Roberto legend, each characteristically eccentric, situate Cunninghame Graham at key turning points in the histories of early modernism and democratic socialism. Indeed, what makes that legend representative is the intersection of those histories, a conjuncture of literary and political representation best grasped in the form of the literary sketch, which Graham developed in the 1890s. To emphasize the role of Graham's own sketch-artistry in the fashioning of these images, there is a third image of Graham, an earlier portrait by John Lavery of Graham and a horse, about which Lavery wrote: "Graham had purchased from the tramway company a wild Argentine pony that refused to go into harness. He named him Pampa, and insisted on my painting a picture of himself in complete cowboy outfit on the pacing steed" (see Figure 14).[9] It was this portrait which Graham himself chose to illustrate *The Ipané*, the

FIGURE 12. Sir John Lavery's portrait of R. B. Cunninghame Graham (1893). Courtesy of Glasgow Museums: Art Gallery & Museum, Kelvingrove, Scotland.

FIGURE 13. Scottish Labour Party ticket with Keir Hardie and R. B. Cunninghame Graham. Courtesy of Glasgow Museums: The People's Palace, Scotland.

early volume of sketches which marks Graham's transformation from political journalist to literary stylist and perhaps most fully articulates the geography of politics in Graham's sketch-artistry.

John Lavery echoed G. K. Chesterton's assessment of the "adventure of being Cunninghame Graham" when he wrote, "I think I did something to help Graham in the creation of his own masterpiece—himself."[10] Graham's own assessment of what went into the creation of this "masterpiece" is also, however, worth recording. In characteristically casual style, Graham offers such an assessment in his preface to Walter Shaw-Sparrow's *John Lavery and His Work*, alluding in passing to his departure from parliamentary politics: "Once, I suppose in his perennial search for 'raw material,' the hegemonist of the Glasgow School set out for Fez to paint the Orient. I as it happened being unemployed, went with him and with us went the correspondent of the Times."[11] Condensed in this one passage are the set of questions about geography, politics, and artistic representation over the turn of the century which get constellated in the various afterimages of Cunninghame Graham and which I propose to examine in the following pages, with particular attention to the publication of *The Ipané* in 1899. In all these images, in the combined anomalies of an aristocratic Scottish M.P. representing labor and dressed up in *gaucho* drag, emerge that problem Graham's writing explores in seeking to imagine a geography of politics after the anti-utopian utopian imperative of Marx's "here, or nowhere."

His first three full-length books would seem to suggest that Cunninghame Graham's socialist utopia is most likely to be found, if anywhere, in the past. Vanishing, precapitalist forms of life seem increasingly his preoccupation in *Notes on the District of Menteith, for Tourists and Others* (1895), his parodic genealogy of his own ancestors and their lands; in

FIGURE 14. Sir John Lavery's portrait of R. B. Cunninghame Graham with his horse "Pampa" (probably 1893 or earlier). Courtesy of Museo Nacional de Bellas Artes, Buenos Aires, Argentina.

Mogreb-el-Acksa: A Journey in Morocco (1898), an account of his notorious failure to reach the forbidden holy city of Tarudant; and in *A Vanished Arcadia: Being Some Account of the Jesuits in Paraguay, 1607 to 1767* (1901), the first of his many histories of the Spanish in America. These vanished arcadias—antiquated Scottish customs, the Moroccan empire of Islam's "far west," and the maligned history of Jesuit missions in South America—seem very far removed from the socialist futures imagined by utopian narratives of the 1890s. To understand what links the progressive socialist figure of Cunninghame Graham, M.P., and the image of "Don Roberto" acting out the romance of a vanished arcadia, we should turn to the style of storytelling Graham forged into a unique form of sketch-artistry, from the political journalism of the late 1880s and early 1890s to the "impressionism" of the late 1890s.

It is really the sketch that defines the genre of all Graham's works, and his sketch-artistry is the medium through which "the adventure of being Cunninghame Graham" links the battlefronts of socialist struggle and colonial politics. A characteristic of the Graham sketch is its combination of realistic reportage and stylistic impressionism—the political column is broken up by the storyteller's yarn, and the crafted tale can become at any moment the stage for direct political commentary. Graham's hybrid style of narrative representation, self-representation, and news telling articulates the missing dimension of Bellamy's, Morris's, and Wells's utopian tales. The news those narrators bring from the "nowhere" of the future stands in contrast to the "nowhere" of news telling in Graham's sketches, which turns the narrator's problematic position in relation to a future communist society into the problematic geography of the narrator's present political standpoint.

If the "sketch" as a literary genre is still more eccentric in literary history than the utopian tale, Graham's sketch-artistry helps illuminate a structural inversion that might in turn place the generic importance of those eccentric utopian tales. The connection between Graham's narrative point of view and his art of political news writing calls attention to what Bellamy, Morris, and Wells all owe to the "low" literary form of political journalism in the age of the "new journalism." Graham's friendship and collaboration with Joseph Conrad illuminates the link between the "low" and the "high" literary craft of early modernists.[12]

In the "impressionist" art form of the sketches perfected in the period of collaboration with Garnett and Conrad, there is an emphasis on personal reminiscence, and particularly reminiscences of his adventures in South America in the 1870s amongst the *gaucho* riders of the Pampas. (This is the scene of adventure that provides the "raw material" for Lavery's paintings of Don Roberto.) Yet Graham's South American sketches of unsettled and violent frontier encounters between Indians, *gauchos*, and Europeans depend for their effect on the editorial intrusion of the political journalist, a style of writing Graham developed in his participation in the ferment of demonstrations, strikes, and union organization during the late 1880s and early 1890s.

The News of "Bloody Sunday": Lessons in Working-Class Consciousness

In William Morris's *News from Nowhere*, "Bloody Sunday," the violent police breakup of the Trafalgar Square demonstrations of 13 November 1887, provides the starting point for the Great Change, or revolutionary struggle, that ultimately transforms England into a communist utopia. "Bloody Sunday" was not the watershed moment of history Morris makes it, but as British labor historian Chushuchi Tsuzuki explains, it did provide the occasion for a realignment of political affiliations in the atmosphere of antagonism and "petty squabbling" that characterized the socialist organizations of the 1880s following the split in the Social-Democratic Federation.[13] The planned march on Trafalgar Square had been called, not by Morris's Social-Democratic Federation, but by the Metropolitan Radical Federation, to protest the arrest of William O'Brien, a militant organizer of the Irish Home Rule movement. To the political issues of free speech and Irish Home Rule were added the voices of the unemployed, whose grievances had sparked the West End riots of 1886 and who had been gathering in increasing numbers in Trafalgar Square throughout October 1887.

For his part in the fray, arrested, beaten, and convicted for assault, Cunninghame Graham earned a reputation as wild socialist in Parliament, where he was then a Liberal M.P. In a sense, the prominence of the event in the Don Roberto legend has diminished rather than increased appraisal of his activism in fighting for the eight-hour day and working with John Burns on labor and trade-union alliances with Keir Hardie in the foundation of the Scottish Labour Party. These shifting political alliances around the event of "Bloody Sunday," rather than the adventure of demonstration and imprisonment, explain his place next to Keir Hardie as figurehead for the Scottish Labour Party.

What made "Bloody Sunday" the occasion for these shifting political alignments were the lessons drawn from the event by emerging leaders of the labor movement. For William Morris, as E. P. Thompson has emphasized, the "'Battle' of Trafalgar Square" was a lesson in how working-class consciousness could lead to the "overturn" of capitalist society.[14] By contrast, Watts and Davies, in their reconstruction and analysis of the events of "Bloody Sunday," argue that the violence of the day "strengthened the hand of those who spoke for reformist rather than violent methods: for radicalisation of the unions, and, ultimately, labour representation in Parliament."[15] Rather than a test over the alternatives of reform or revolution, the event became a test for political leadership within the labor movement, a test of how to achieve working-class unity.

Tsuzuki emphasizes the lesson in political leadership drawn from "Bloody Sunday" by labor activist John Burns, one of Graham's close allies in working-class politics and with whom Cunninghame Graham was arrested on "Bloody Sunday." Burns, in his speech at their trial, emphasized the role of the unemployed: "These men, the unemployed . . . taught the politicians the very element of government: how to organize society during the transitional period from the present competitive system where the policeman is absolutely necessary, to the co-operative system where the teacher will take his place."[16] This was a lesson which became central for the activist work of both John Burns and Tom Mann, impressed by Burns's speech, in their role in helping organize the London Dockers' Strike of 1889. The importance of this successful, in Burns's words "spontaneous" strike, which drew together unskilled, semi-skilled, and unionized dock laborers to achieve a symbolic victory in paralyzing the docks and achieving the demand for the docker's "tanner" wage of sixpence an hour, clearly outweighed the drama of "Bloody Sunday." It was a test of the principles of leadership articulated by Burns after "Bloody Sunday," in which a set of heterogeneous interests and working-class positions could provide the basis for the first articulation of the British Labour Party. What makes Graham's role of interest is precisely his compromised position, as aristocrat but most importantly as Liberal M.P., within the new group of leaders (notably John Burns, Tom Mann, and Keir Hardie).

All pulling in slightly but significantly different directions, they nonetheless achieved a success which Tsuzuki characterizes, with specific reference to the London dock strikes, in terms of a "new awakening of the working class as a class."[17]

"Bloody Sunday," Graham's essay on the event written a year later (1888) for William Morris's *The Commonweal*, is a revealing example of Graham's early political journalism. Like Burns, Graham contrasts the measured conduct of the demonstrators to the brutal reaction of the police, not, however, to work their conduct into a lesson for the organization of society during "the transitional period" to "the co-operative system," as Burns did—and, indeed, as Morris echoed him in *News from Nowhere*. Graham rather mocks the docility of the crowd—"I never till that time completely realised how utterly servile and cowardly an English crowd is"[18]—and resorts to classic rhetoric of class struggle: "As I stood there . . . I thought yet, still—I have heard that these poor working-men, these Irishmen and Radicals have votes, and perhaps even souls, and it seemed impossible but that some day these poor deceived, beaten, downtrodden slaves would turn upon their oppressors and demand why they made their England so hideous, why they ate and drank to repletion, and left nothing but work, starvation, kicks, and curses for their Christian brethren?"[19] Set next to Burns's argument for organization and even Morris's visionary projection, Graham's rhetoric seems to confirm the reputation he gained as wild socialist but poor strategist.

Yet Graham's "Bloody Sunday" is more complicated than this. The rhetoric of class conflict is suspended as a question in Graham's mind "as I stood there"; and it is picked up and turned around: "Somewhat in this style I thought; this I saw as I stood wiping the blood out of my eyes in Trafalgar Square. What I did not see was entirely owing to the quietness of the crowd. I did not see houses burning; I did not hear pistols cracking. I did not see this—not because of any precautions the authorities had taken, for they had taken none, but because it was the first time such a scene had been witnessed in London during this generation."[20] There is something characteristic of Graham's style in the interjection of the personal standpoint, all at once claiming the experience of "Bloody Sunday" as his own—"as I stood wiping the blood out of my eyes"—and suspending that perspective from its historical significance.

Reading "Bloody Sunday" as a narrative of personal revelation might seem to compound the image of Don Roberto as wild socialist with that of a literary poseur in the act of memorializing his own adventure. Yet that very trait is after all inseparable from the strategic political point with which the article is framed. It opens with a curious dismissal of his capacity to tell the news of "Bloody Sunday"—"Except the facts already known to the public, I fear I can tell little of the occurrences in Trafalgar Square last November."[21] What he does begin to tell, however, is the tale of how "a newly elected Liberal member" became "undeceived" about his own party—"for at that time I did not know that Liberals, Tories, and Unionists were three bands of thimbleriggers."[22] And that is how Graham's "Bloody Sunday" ends, concluding that the event "had no result, so far as I can see, but to make the Liberal party as odious and despised as the Tory party in the metropolis," with the important addition which completes the narrative of personal conversion to socialism: "All honour to the Socialists for being the first body of Englishmen in the metropolis to have determined that the death of three Englishmen . . . shall not go unregarded."[23]

This was, in fact, a political position he had outlined in the *Pall Mall Gazette* the day before "Bloody Sunday":

> In times like these, when Irish members of Parliament are in prison for daring to speak free, and when men in Chicago, against whom no crime has been proved, are to be executed to allay the blind panic of the capitalist classes, I think that it is high time for everyone calling himself a Liberal to protest, and for that reason I intend to address the meeting on Sunday.[24]

The demonstration, then, is already before the event presented as a test for "everyone calling himself a Liberal," so that when "Bloody Sunday"—Graham's 1888 article, that is—picks up this narrative thread, it is to point out that the Liberals failed that test, with the result that Graham will no longer call himself a Liberal.

Watts and Davies argue that Graham's "whole political position was a compromise with an institution, Parliament, which in its present form he found infuriating."[25] This compromise, everywhere visible in his anomalous position as Liberal M.P. amongst labor leaders, is representative of the political compromise toward which the labor movement was tending, as symbolically captured in the twin images of Graham and Hardie as figureheads on the S.L.P. ticket. Graham's almost daily correspondence with John Burns between 1888 and 1892 reports the news of how labor legislation was proceeding in Parliament, and, as Watts and Davies show, that news was increasingly punctuated by assessment of Graham's compromised position in representing the labor movement. In 1891, for example, Graham writes of the impasse over legislation for an eight-hour day: "Look how the matter stands at present. Last year I introduced the Trades Congress Bill. *Not a soul* in Parliament believed I had any authority to do so, & does not now believe it. The only thing that induced them to listen to me at all, was because I am personally not disliked there."[26]

Graham's "authority" to represent working-class interests had led, as early as September 1887, before "Bloody Sunday," to confrontation within Parliament over the Lords amendment to the Coal Mines Regulation Bill. For his protest that "an Assembly which is not elected by a popular vote should dare to dictate to us, who are elected"[27]—he was suspended from Parliament in a dramatic confrontation that became a key element in the formation of the "Don Roberto" legend, thanks to G. B. Shaw's dramatization of his statement "I *never* withdraw" in Saranoff's "I *never* apologise" in *Arms and the Man*. Watts and Davies, in an effort to balance out Graham's moments of level-headed political strategies, suggestively characterize this outburst as one of those moments when "he had too much blood in his eyes, as he pressed forward with his red banner, to see exactly where he was going."[28] Yet it might also be argued that the incident was significant precisely in defining the limits of where Graham could go with Parliament. Graham's news to Burns from Parliament made those limits painfully clear, and his complaints about Parliament's disbelief in his authority to represent the interests of labor tell a story, too, of the increasing distance between Burns and Mann and Graham: "I decline to press the 8 Hours question at all (in Parliament) till either I or someone else ... is given some authority by the advanced party."[29] Nonetheless, as an increasingly isolated Member of Parliament—representing no party at all—Graham's news from the parliamentary battlefront of the labor movement served a crucial purpose, and precisely in clarifying the compromises of representative social democracy in Britain in the 1890s.

The shifting political alignments around "Bloody Sunday" presented lessons of leadership that reflect a more general shift of alignments within international socialism. Ernesto Laclau and Chantal Mouffe have argued that the crisis of Marxism over the turn of the century may be traced to the presumed unity of working-class interests—the proletariat—laid down by the laws of the economic base, or "historical necessity," that "cornerstone" of Second International Marxism.[30] In some ways, the events of "Bloody Sunday"—and Cunninghame Graham's participation in them—reproduce in miniature the theoretical lessons Laclau and Mouffe draw from the crisis in Second International Marxism. They show the heterogeneous elements at work in the set of political demonstrations and strikes from the 1880s into the early 1890s which gave impetus to the formation of new social-democratic political parties—the Scottish Labour Party and the Independent Labour Party—as well as to the so-called "new unionism" of the 1890s. Cunninghame Graham was no Marxist theoretician, but his practice of political activism during a peculiarly important moment in the history of the British labor movement situates the eccentric myth of "Don Roberto" in suggestive relation to the underlying theoretical question of the class unity of the labor movement.

Turning from Graham's essay "Bloody Sunday" to a later sketch, "Sursum Corda," his reflection on his imprisonment written a decade later, it is easy to note the difference between the political rhetoric of the one and the almost resigned irony of the other ("What triumphs in the world can be compared to those speech gives?"[31]). Equally as significant is the difference of venues—"Bloody Sunday" appeared in the pages of Morris's organ for the Socialist League, *The Commonweal*; "Sursum Corda" appeared in the highbrow pages of *The Saturday Review*, by then Graham's "favourite exhibition-ground."[32]

The representative compromises with Parliament that led to Graham's simultaneous exit from Parliament and from a leading position in the labor movement, clearly took him on a very different path from that of John Burns. Yet, while Graham rejected compromise with parliamentary politics, John Burns ascended to the compromised position of most reactionary member of a Liberal cabinet. For that betrayal of the causes both had worked on together in the name of the labor movement, Graham was to associate Burns with Conrad's Nostromo (in the phrase "John Burns Nostromo Esq"[33]), that man of the people whose heroic adventurism ends up betraying his own name. In a sense, the strange reversal of roles that characterized the future careers of the two heroes of "Bloody Sunday" made them both the Nostromo of the British labor movement.

To characterize this crossing of paths as a betrayal of the working class, however, is to miss the lessons of leadership they each drew (even if they did not learn from them) from "Bloody Sunday." Those lessons belonged all at once to the historical moment of the Second International Workingmen's Association (news of whose meetings Graham and Burns reported for *The Labour Elector*) and to the new logic of political struggle Laclau and Mouffe trace in the emergence of the concept of "hegemony" from the theoretical crisis over the presumed class unity of working-class positions. E. J. Hobsbawm articulates the problem of class unity from a somewhat different perspective, when he writes: "What from one point of view, looked like a concentration of men and women in a single 'working class,' could be seen from another as a gigantic scattering of the fragments of societies, a diaspora of the old and new communities."[34] When Cunninghame Graham wrote to John Burns in 1892, "I am just off to Morocco as special correspondent for the daily Graphic. I have *given* up all thoughts of reentering public life," the new battlefront of Graham's journalist ventures (joined by the painter Lavery, "the hegemonist of the Glasgow School") may appear less like a betrayal and more like a working out of the geography of politics in the 1890s.

News from Overseas: *The Ipané* and Edward Garnett's Overseas Library

The Ipané (1899), his first volume of sketches,[35] illustrates the idiosyncrasy of Graham's sketch-artistry in its political and geographical range. Consisting of previously published sketches, the organization of sketches emphasizes the sometimes bewildering juxtaposition of divergent concerns that is a hallmark of Graham's writing. The first of many such volumes to come, it is also revealing in emerging from the period of Graham's most intense correspondence, friendship, and collaboration with Joseph Conrad and Edward Garnett. If the volume marks Graham's transformation from political journalist to literary stylist, it also shows how Graham's style of political news writing informed the artistic ambitions shared with the more famous figures of early modernist experimentation, Garnett and Conrad.

Selection and organization of the tales in *The Ipané* is revealing not only because it took place against the backdrop of Graham's friendship and correspondence with Edward Garnett and Joseph Conrad. Edward

Garnett had chosen *The Ipané* for the first volume of a new series,[36] which he had been pressing his employer Unwin to launch since 1897.[37] Garnett's aims are revealed in the prospectus and call for submissions which appeared on the flyleaf of *The Ipané* and begins:

> Where are the "Ends of Empire"? and which are the Over-Seas? At "the Ends" of one may arise the beginnings of other Empires to come. It is notorious that wherever an English-speaking community settles and opens up new lands, it speedily speaks for itself as a Centre; and so rapid is the growth of the great Colonies, that Ministers to-day writing despatches to Dependencies over-seas, receive their answers from nations to-morrow.[38]

In looking toward the "Ends" of Empire, Garnett's idea, otherwise entirely in keeping with the mass industry of publishing colonial and imperial tales, takes on a critical edge closer to Garnett's personal views on the cant of imperialism. Graham's *The Ipané* was perfect for piloting such an idea. It was perfect not only in approaching Garnett's high artistic ambitions, but also for the popularity to which the sketches and their author might appeal.

The nature of Don Roberto's possible popular appeal emerges in Garnett's humorous but revealing comments on Graham's deliberations on a picture for the frontispiece. Initially, Graham had suggested using a photograph, but Garnett writes:

> Madame Stepniak to whom I showed it, exclaimed in horror "But where are the *curls*? I have heard the factory girls at a meeting call him "*the curly darling.*" I explained that the curls were probably abandoned in the prison where you sojourned—but she was dissatisfied. If you have another photograph by you one that gives more the character of the face and less of the riding breeches I think the women here would probably examine more seriously the arguments on polyandry and polygamy that crop up in your sketches—and who knows but that your portrait may spread an "overseas" movement which the colonial Tories may never check."[39]

The complex and humorous fantasy of Graham's popular photogenic appeal to women locates a hypothetical readership somewhere between a famous Russian nihilist fantasy of factory girls' fantasies and the uncertain class and national implications of Garnett's "women here." Still more complex is the male supervision of this sex appeal, which adds a knowledge (of prison, of ethnographic data gathered in travels) whose specifically male experience is invested (however ambiguously) in the popular and political appeal of Cunninghame Graham's image.[40] Perhaps the ambiguity of these complicated sexual, popular, and political fantasies is captured in John Lavery's portraits. What Graham finally chose to illustrate *The Ipané* was Lavery's "Don Roberto" on his horse Pampa; and Garnett was delighted: "The Lavery delights me. I gaze at it with affection.... It is a thing of art and as the democracy will not understand it, that makes all the difference. I think the aloof air goes with the atmosphere of the Sketches. Now the photograph was too personal—it was a thing on which to found paragraphs about 'that brilliant personality CG etc etc.'"[41]

Garnett's conscious attempt to articulate an anti-imperialist artistic movement, through *The Over-Seas Library* and elsewhere, emerges in the imaginary geographical and cultural coordinates by which Garnett locates the importance of Graham's work and that of Joseph Conrad. In a letter to Graham from July 1898, he wrote: "Ah the South! But you are North & South both in your writings. You double the parts & leave us to be onesided. By the way Conrad to my mind is born on the dividing line between East and West."[42] Garnett's abstractions North South East West reduce, of course, the specific cultural and political experiences of Cunninghame Graham's sketches and Joseph Conrad's tales. Yet around 1898 it is possible to discern in all three writers an adoption of just this kind of reductive generalization.[43] This simplification is a studied response to the rhetoric of the "new imperialism," whose high-tide mark was 1897, the year of Queen Victoria's Golden Jubilee celebrations. What these writers were up to in consciously appealing to the charm of the "new imperialism" is indicated by their discussions of Kipling. Complex though Kipling's own political vision was—it was, moreover, undergoing a crucial change in reaction against the popular enthusiasm of the 1897 Jubilee celebrations—nonetheless Kipling was still the Bard of Empire. Indeed, Garnett's geographical abstractions might justly be described as Kiplingesque. As Orwell would note in the 1930s, Kipling was "the only English writer of our time who has added phrases to the language,"[44] and it is notable (although Orwell does not note it) that almost all the examples he gives are catchphrases whose simplifications articulate a new sense of global political proportion—"East is East and West is West," "What do they know of England who only England know," "Somewheres East of Suez," "the white man's burden."

It is revealing that in their first exchange of letters Graham and Conrad are attempting to evaluate Kipling's art. Garnett, writing to Graham in January of 1899 after two years of intense literary collaboration between the three men, comments:

> As for Kipling, as I think I've reiterated to you Kipling is *the* enemy. But he did create India to the Saxon world that world of dulness that said it *owned* it! He is a creator; & he is *the genius of all we detest.* (Some day I hope to analyze his genius, & I shall write with keen joy, for how joyous it is to hate perfectly.) I hate his essence.[45]

Garnett never produced his critical analysis, but the prospectus for the *Over-Seas Library* shows how he had been waging his war by other means:

> It is the artist alone, great or small, who, by revealing and interpreting the life around him, makes it living to the rest of the world. And the artist is generally absent! In the case of the English in India, ten years ago, while the literature of information was plentiful, the artist was absent; Mr. Kipling arrived and discovered modern India to the English imagination. And today, in the midst of a general movement for Empire expansion, with talk of Federation, Jingoism, and with the doing of real work, the artists in literature are generally absent, the artists who should reveal the tendencies, the capacities of the new communities.[46]

Garnett's work in helping Graham select, arrange, and edit his sketches forms a significant part of the story of Graham's transition from political journalist to literary artist, as suggested by Garnett's comment in a letter from 23 June 1898: "I sue for the artist in you, the artist you concealed so long under the man of action, the artist that is most important."[47] At the same time, the politics of Graham's style challenged Garnett's sense of the artist's role. Garnett's first response to Graham's sketches was to exclude the "social & political papers" (as he put it to Graham in May of 1898), to conform to his evolving Overseas idea: "The character of the volume of sketches I had projected was necessarily *exclusive of Social, Political & Historical Sketches.* I thought of a volume to be made of *sketches of a local character & atmosphere*—outside England."[48] But Garnett soon came to recognize that Graham's method of sketch-artistry depended on juxtaposing reminiscence and political essay, and this collaboration over the shape of *The Ipané* illuminates how Graham's imaginative geography of politics informed Garnett's Overseas idea.

Deliberation over Graham's most polemical attack on British imperialism, "Bloody Niggers," reveals Garnett's evolving insight into the artistry of Graham's style. The biting satirical sketch, originally published in *The Social-Democrat* in April 1897, creates, as Watts and Davies summarize it, "a tapestry-like picture of the world, its inhabitants, and its history, while announcing, ironically of course, that all these riches were designed by their Creator for British use."[49] In June, Garnett praised the piece—"The *quintessence* is there of your attitude, your insight"—but resisted its political rhetoric as inappropriate for the volume: "But the core of it, the blasphemy against the stupidities might damage all the other sketches with those who do not understand—i.e. with Everybody.... It is too good to leave out, but it would be a sheer luxury to tempt every ordinary creature to make himself more ordinary over it."[50]

The lever of Graham's polemic is his use of the racist term "nigger" to concentrate the "stupidities" of British attitudes toward "foreign and native races" (to use Garnett's formulation from the Overseas prospectus). In the coda to the sketch, he returns to the title: "What is a 'nigger'? Now this needs some words in order to explain his just position. Hindus, as Brahmins, Bengalis, dwellers in Bombay, the Cingalese, Sikhs and Pathans, Rajpoots, Parsis, Afghans, Kashmiris, Beluchis, Burmese, with all the dwellers from the Caspian Sea to Timur Laut, are thus described. Arabs are 'niggers.'" Pausing for a new paragraph, the sketch launches into another list of peoples obliterated by the term, and in a further paragraph dwells on how "'niggers' of Africa occupy first place."[51] The polemic necessarily provokes extreme unease about the ingrained racism permeating all shades of imperialist and colonial ideology. It is worth noting that a prominent supporter of the Zulus, Harriette Emily Colenso, writing to Graham about Olive Schreiner's political attitudes toward race and racism, expressed concern about Graham's title: "I am rather inclined to think that 'we' ought to exclude the word 'nigger' from general conversation, & literature. It is not required, & only expresses contempt."[52]

The sketch illustrates something of the limits to Garnett's Overseas idea not so much because of Garnett's concerns for his ignorant readers, but rather because it strikes at the very "range" of the series. No editor can manage all the news coming out of the colonies, and Garnett's project, however anti-imperialist in its inspiration, assumes a sort of hegemonic control over the artistic talent he hopes might re-imagine the relation between center and periphery. Scanning the list of proposed books for the series, and those ultimately published by Unwin, it is perhaps too easy to recognize how Garnett's Overseas idea would only follow in the "general movement for Empire expansion" rather than redirect it politically. The limitations of the series' ability to imagine the "new communities" forming at "the Ends of the Empire" are visible already in Garnett's proposal to address "the actual life of the English outside England, whether of Colonial life or the life of English emigrants, travellers, traders, officers, overseas, among foreign and native races, black or white." One of the series' books, Sir Hugh Clifford's *In Court and Kampong*, in some respects a worthy example of Garnett's artistic aims, illustrates how the Overseas Library could provide the platform for a new stage of colonial hegemony over the "new communities," since its sketches of Malay life, though written by a colonial administrator increasingly uneasy with the system of colonial governance in the Malay Federated States, still provided the ethnographic detail and ideological rationale that would make the "benevolent" governor-system of British Malaysia a model for sustaining British colonialism both in British Malaysia and in Africa.

These limitations in imagining an anti-imperialist geography of politics go to the heart of Garnett's perceptive insights into Graham's style of sketch-artistry. Garnett recognized, from the start, the strength of Graham's juxtaposition of widely different cultural settings.[53] The substance of most of Garnett's advice to Graham for editing, amending, and arranging *The Ipané* concerns the relation between that diversity and the personal point of view that Graham brings to that diversity:

> A volume of such sketches give [sic] *through its diversity*, (& through the writer's strong central point of view) a really connected harmonious picture of life—*the sketches fall into harmony*, & form an artistic whole. The wider the range the more powerful artistically does the volume become—with each fresh atmosphere the reader yields more and more to the eyes that saw, to the spirit that interpreted.[54]

In light of this characteristic emphasis on Graham's personal experience (recalling Chesterton's "adventure of being Cunninghame Graham"), it is striking now to turn to the argument Garnett makes for including "Bloody Niggers" after all:

> I sat down & read *Niggers* when it came & was so ravished that the folly of criticism passed leagues away ... now you sting us & glide away like a beautiful snake. Formerly you *remained* on the spot after an outburst, defying the Anglo-Saxon world, with your best card played. But *now* you have struck & vanished! The booted perspiring Britain gazes round, with the heavens grinning at him.[55]

It is, like most of Garnett's remarks, an astute appreciation which shows his growing recognition of Graham's art of political rhetoric, even as it also testifies to the value of Garnett's advice, since Graham had revised the essay slightly to produce an argument that, according to Watts and Davies, "is clearer, because more controlled."[56] What is remarkable, however, is Garnett's stress on Graham's strategy of striking and vanishing, since this is the one element of Graham's method of shifting narrative perspective which, in other sketches, Garnett sought to control by stressing "the eyes that saw, the spirit that interpreted."

Garnett's clearest exposition of his sense of Graham's method is in a letter from 1901, when, having praised the sketch "The Gualichu Tree," he writes: "But analysing your work, & demanding the finest forms for your fineness, I think that where your work succeeds is where *everything* converges to a centre [Garnett sketches a circle of arrows aimed at a central spot] & where your work sometimes is unsatisfactory in form is where you have turned & shot arrows at many targets."[57] Yet this fault defines the very success of Graham's sketch-artistry, and above all its geography of politics. If the unpredictable juxtaposition of widely different cultural contexts seems to deflect from the coherence of "the eyes that saw, the spirit that interpreted," that is part of the success with which Graham's sketch-artistry probes a perceived new geography of experience in the 1890s.

"Sursum Corda," although it was one of the sketches Garnett had Graham exclude from *The Ipané* (it was collected in *Success* in 1901) is a revealing example. Ten years after the demonstrations called to affirm the principle of free speech, the sketch takes up the topic of speech in an extended editorial comment which almost only incidentally achieves something of the effect of a carefully crafted modern short story. As "Sursum Corda" tightens the wide latitude of its editorial meditations on speech and silence, political editorial turns into the form of a tale crafted around an almost epiphanic moment: the title's allusion to the opening call in the preface to the Mass, "lift up your hearts," unfolds in Graham's reminiscence of hymn-singing amongst fellow-prisoners; and it is through this that the sketch figures the bond of humanity—through speech—denied to the prisoner but reconstituted through the uplifting message of the hymn. In characteristically turning that message against the Christian moralizing of the enforced Sunday exercise, the epiphany of "Sursum Corda" affirms a consciousness of human bonds different from either the bondage within prison or the hypocrisies of Church singers outside prison, creating an aesthetic effect around the question of class consciousness:

> So in a side street when the frequent loafer sidles up, and says mysteriously "Gawd bless yer, chuck us arf a pint; I was in with you in that crooil plaice," I do so, not that I think he speaks the truth nor yet imagine that the prison, large though it was, contained two million prisoners, but to relieve his thirst and for the sake of those condemned to silence, there "inside," and for the recollection of the "bloomin' 'ymn."[58]

The story's "sursum corda," turning a religious into a political incitement to courage and fervor, makes the sketch an unregenerate account of what Graham learned from "Bloody Sunday." In crafting the lesson of his prison experience into a lesson in class consciousness, he thus confirms and sustains one of the central questions of the Trafalgar Square demonstrations.

To the extent that "Sursum Corda" reflects the lessons of "Bloody Sunday" ten years later, however, it is in a sketch-artistry whose stray lines follow a different, if related problem of class unity and consciousness. One such stray line occurs in the penultimate paragraph, appearing to deflect the coherence of the epiphany: "Does you good, No. 8, the bloomin' 'ymn," an old lag says, but for the moment dazed by the ceasing of the noise, as Bernal Diaz says he was when the long tumult ended and Mexico was won, I do not answer...."[59] The reference to the conquest of Mexico would be a defect in a pure short story—for precisely the reason Graham, I think, insists on it: one would want to find a more self-consistent image to secure the point that the Anglican hymn grafts an exalted sense of worship onto a fundamentally different sense of human community. Yet the image is not simply drawn uneconomically from Cunninghame Graham's store of adventurous interests. It echoes an earlier discordant image deliberately placed to mark the stray lines of the sketch: "Think on a silent world, a world in which men walked about in all respects equipped with every organ, every sense, but without speech. They might converse by signs as Indians do upon the trail, but I maintain no city of tremendous night could be more awful than the horror of a speechless world."[60] These discordant images belong to the geography of politics characteristic of Graham's style. The sketches, straying now to the rhetoric of class struggle and now to the contemplation of vanishing forms of social life, are shot through with a double vision of what Hobsbawm characterizes as the different perspectives of working-class unity on the one hand and, on the other, "a gigantic scattering of the fragments of societies."[61]

The connection between Graham's narrative point of view and his art of political newswriting calls attention to what the utopian narratives of Bellamy, Morris, and Wells all owe to the "low" literary form of political journalism—the effort to overcome the narrator's difficulty in interpreting the existing, volatile events of the present moment. Though with varying degrees of complexity and success, each of these utopian tales probes a perceived gap between events and the reporting of events.

The title of Morris's *News from Nowhere*, which draws much of its resonance from the role of the newspapers in responding to the events following "Bloody Sunday," best captures the key element of the utopian narrative's logic—the narrator's embarrassment at not having realized the significance of the social upheavals of contemporary society. Morris's attention to the mediating role of the newspapers[62] is surely in part a response to Bellamy's inability to translate the news of the labor upheavals of 1887—in response to the narrator's question "What solution, if any, have you found for the labor question?" Doctor Leete responds, "It may be said to have solved itself."[63] *The Time Machine* displaces the embarrassment of relating the news of the future to the news of the present by focusing on the newsworthiness of time travel itself, but this very fascination for the machinery of technology dictates the manner in which Bellamy's "labor question," "the Sphinx's riddle of the nineteenth century," gets transformed into the traveler's own bloody intervention in the transfigured class warfare between Morlocks and Eloi. Wells's technological resolution of the utopian problem of broadcasting "news from nowhere" is still more vividly portrayed in *When the Sleeper Wakes* (1899), in which the narrator—"a fanatical Radical—a Socialist—or typical Liberal" named Graham (perhaps after Don Roberto)—awakens as "Master of the Earth" faced with a vast instantaneous news broadcasting propaganda system.[64]

Graham's sketches are still more eccentric in terms of literary history than the utopian tales of the 1890s, but his sketch-artistry foregrounds a change in the nature of narrative form that might in turn situate the historical place of those eccentric utopian tales. For the Graham sketch springs from the widening split between "low" and "high" literary production at a time—the moment of early modernism—when narrative form is tilted from the axis of time and history to an axis of space and geography.

News of Death: "Heather Jock" and Cunninghame Graham's Utopian Sense of Community

Part of the success with which Graham's sketch-artistry probes a perceived new geography of experience lies in the unpredictable juxtaposition of widely different cultural contexts, even as this deflects from the coherence of, in Garnett's words, "the eyes that saw, the spirit that interpreted." This, it seems to me, is the greatness of another sketch from *The Ipané*, "Heather Jock," one of the finest examples of Graham's craft of unsettling the tale through the insertion of personal reminiscence. It unfolds with all the unpredictability of Graham's characteristic obsessions, weaving the character sketch of an eccentric mad pedlar from the West of Scotland into a personal reminiscence from the Argentinean Pampas, where the narrator learned of the news of the man's death, itself the occasion to relate another death, the violent killing, by Indians, of one of the men who brought Graham the news. The juxtaposition of place—the Argentinean Pampas, the frontier of violence between Indian and Gaucho, and the West Highlands of Scotland—coordinates a strange and disturbing miscellany of memories, culminating in the funeral song for the dead *gaucho* rider, in which the narrator "seemed to hear the jangling of the dead fool's bells, and listen to the minstrelsy, such as it was, of the hegemonist of Bridge of Weir."[65]

Much of the curious power of the sketch turns on the ironic use to which Graham turns the word "hegemonist." A word used to signify the power of one political state over another,[66] Graham applies it, incongruously, to the newsworthy fame attained locally by an eccentric madman. This incongruous juxtaposition of the local and the global lies at the heart of Graham's utopian anti-geopolitics. Perhaps, too, Graham's idiosyncratic use of the word "hegemonist" (here and in the description of the painter Lavery as "the hegemonist of the Glasgow School"), sheds light on the way the word "hegemony" forms part of a wider turn-of-the-century contest over the conception of cultural and political leadership.

It is likely that Conrad drew something from Graham's method of relating the news of Heather Jock's death in developing the art of having Marlow relate his news from the nowhere of Patusan, in *Lord Jim*, or the Inner Station of *Heart of Darkness*.[67] Yet in their collaborative efforts to devise ways of bringing the horrors of imperialist exploitation home to their readers, Graham's sketch-artistry remains distinctive in its insistence on the "nowhere" of news telling itself. In what seems like a stale political side-thrust at the established press in the beginning of "Heather Jock," Graham offers an editorial comment that will introduce the figure of the mad Scottish weaver-turned-traveling-merchant of the story's title: "The wandering semi-madman was a feature in Scotch life. In ancient times he filled, to some degree, the function of a newspaper, retailing news distorted to the taste of those he catered for, after the fashion of the modern editor."[68] Given the story's emphasis on the imponderable cost of bearing the news, this apparent throwaway provides a guiding parable for the story's contemplation of the geography and politics of storytelling.[69]

The effect of piling up stories in "Heather Jock" goes beyond the self-reflexive strategy for commenting on the function of news reporting set within the parameters of a storyteller retailing experiences of past memories, as Graham reflects on his Argentinean adventures of the 1870s and early 1880s. It is crucially determined by the "immediate" place of the narrator as reporter, inviting the reader's search for the present location of the special correspondent. But that search is constantly deflected by the style of Graham's rendering of personal experience, as we see in the description of the character of Heather Jock—"What he had seen during his wandering life he treasured up, relating it, on invitation, to his hearers in the same way an Arab or a Spaniard quotes a proverb as if it were a personal experience of his own."[70]

This deflection of personal experience through multiplying geographical contexts defines the political practice, as well as the limits, of his anti-imperialist sketch-artistry. The style of impressionism is designed for readers eager to see the world of Empire reflected in an actuality of experience. This is illustrated perhaps best through the appreciation of a rare audience. Writing to Graham in 1898, Conrad described his enthusiasm upon reading Graham's *Mogreb-el-Acksa* with "a man":

> A man staying here has been reading over my shoulder; for we share our best with the stranger within the tent. No thirsty men drank water as we have been drinking in, swallowing, tasting, blessing, enjoying gurgling, choking over, absorbing, your thought, your phrases, your irony, the spirit of your vision of Your expression. . . . You are magnificently generous. You seem to be plunging your hand into an inexhaustible bag of treasure and fling precious things at every paragraph. We have been shouting slapping our legs, leaping up, stamping about. There was such an enthusiasm in this solitude as will meet no other book. I do not know really how to express the kind of intellectual exultation your book has awakened in me; and I will not stay to try; I am in too great a hurry to get back to the book. My applause, slaps on the back, salaams benedictions, cheers. Take what you like best of these, what you think most expressive. Or take them all. I *can't* be too demonstrative. Ever Yours with yells Conrad.[71]

Here is evidence of the manner in which Graham became "a writer's writer," the treasure of his experiences generously scattered for the great masters of style to set into works of art. Conrad's enthusiasm suggests not only that Graham's adventures themselves could provide a model for Conrad's rather different art of narrative. In Conrad's metaphors one may also read the shared interest in displaying the loot and plunder of experiences culled from distant places.

The "intellectual exultation" provoked in Conrad by Graham's style—both here and throughout the letters collected by Cedric Watts—provide an invaluable record of the archive of literary modernism in its formative stages. In the almost sensual excitement of what might be done with the treasure trove of Graham's news from nowhere, we might recognize the changing shape of what Jameson styles "narrative as a socially symbolic act."[72] The image of Graham's readers "shouting slapping our legs, leaping up, stamping about" recalls the situation of Marlow retailing his story to his auditors whose grunts and interjections are the echo of that howling and dancing Marlow heard from the natives as he maneuvered his steamboat upriver to "the back of nowhere."

The controlled narrative structure of Conrad's *Heart of Darkness* most fully illustrates the reorientation of the utopian narrative structure of a Bellamy, a Morris, and most particularly Wells's *The Time Machine*, from whose narrative frame Conrad may well have drawn for his own tale. Conrad's achievement, moreover, though it owes some debt to the "intellectual exultation" over Graham's sketch-artistry, is I think clearly more powerful in conveying the horrors of imperialist exploitation. In "Heather Jock," one of Graham's characteristic stray sentences catches at an economic point about that "gigantic scattering of the fragments of societies" Hobsbawm sets in perspectival relation to "the increasing concentration of men and women into a single 'working-class.'" Describing the *gaucho* rider who brings the news of Heather Jock's death, along with the news of his own brother's death, Graham pauses on the detail of the messenger's handkerchief, "a handkerchief which had been white when it left Manchester some years ago."[73] This detail might be compared to one of the most powerful moments in *Heart of Darkness*, when Marlow encounters, cast aside with the crowd of slave-laborers because they are too weak to be useful, a dying worker with a piece of white thread tied around his neck— "He had tied a bit of white worsted round his neck—Why? Where did he get it? Was it a badge—an ornament—a charm—a propitiatory act? Was there any idea at all connected with it? It looked startling round his black neck, this bit of white thread from beyond the seas."[74]

In moments like these it seems that Conrad's skepticism was able to transform Cunninghame Graham's rough sketch-artistry into a powerful rendition of the political logic of violence separating First and Third Worlds. And there is some truth to the idea that, while Graham sought to realize an impossible geography of political connection between the proletarian battlefield of Europe and the frontiers of colonialism, only Conrad, of the two, could break the spell of Second International Marxism: "The Internationale will be the human race." Both writers sought a form of storytelling that might push the reality of lived experience a little beyond experience, to paraphrase Conrad reflecting on *Heart of Darkness*, in order to "bring home to the readers" the horror of imperialist exploitation.[75] In Conrad's controlled narrative structures the axis of the utopian tale is most fully reoriented from its attempt to bear news of the communist future to the problem of bearing the news from overseas. Indeed, Conrad goes further, enacting a direct reversal of at least Wells's *The Time Machine* when Marlow's journey up the Congo River is projected as a journey back in time. Here we might note how Conrad's controlled narrative structure departs from the principles of Cunninghame Graham's sketch-artistry, insofar as the symbolic logic of Marlow's journey into the time of "pre-historic man" defines the geography of imperialist horror as, precisely "nowhere": "this nowhere," "some ghastly Nowhere, where he [Kurtz] intended to accomplish great things."[76]

The "nowhere" of Graham's sketches is defined differently, in its hybrid of political commentary, personal reminiscence, and the stray lines juxtaposing quite different geographical locations. In "Heather Jock," the news is neither from "nowhere" nor addressed to "nowhere." Rather, the weight—and narrative effect—of the news is constituted by the diverse spaces across which it is borne. Contemplating the "unpleasant news" of the Gaucho's brother's death at the hand of an "infidel," Graham as narrator describes with uncanny leisure his receipt of "home news" before the discovery of the announcement of Heather Jock's death in "a scrap of newspaper":

> Whilst he [the Gaucho] caught a horse—a lengthy operation when the horses have to be driven first to a corral and then caught with the lazo—I took the bag, with the feeling, firstly, that it had cost a man his life, and then with the instinctive dread which, when in distant lands, always attends home news, that some one would be dead or married, or that at least the trusted family solicitor had made off with the money entrusted to him for investment.[77]

In certain respects, the effect is one of simple macabre humor, but through Graham's narrative art it lends the story a pace and suspense that calls attention to the stray details of discrepant geographical and cultural contexts.

In between the telling of the two deaths, Graham takes the time to interject an editorial comment on the meaning of the word "Christian" in the *gaucho* rider's expression that his brother "died like a Christian": "Christian, I may explain, upon those frontiers is rather a racial than a religious status. All white men are *ex officio* Christian, with the possible exception of the English, who, as they listen to their mass mumbled in English, not in Latin, are less authentic."[78] This almost perversely ironic ethnographic comment illustrates a sort of negative dialectic of ethnography, whereby all the markers of collective status and identity (religious, racial, national, and linguistic) are successively emptied of descriptive power through an ironic incongruity of comparative cultural contrasts, a metaleptic collapse that reveals the target of Graham's irony to be the English-reading public for whom the ethnographic explanation serves as proof that they can themselves logically be neither "white," nor "Christian." In the context of the story's preoccupation with the most incongruous forms of remembering the dead, however, such extreme satire has the odd effect of creating a space of community where one would least expect it: along the "frontiers" of extreme violence, those "frontiers of America" Graham had earlier evoked, with anti-utopian zest (in *The District of Menteith For Tourists and Others*), as "a sort of kaleidoscope of human atoms looked at through the hind sights of a Winchester rifle."[79]

If the ultimate "frontier" of the story is death, rather than territorial state power, the sketch does not present death's "frontier" as transcending the divisions of race, religion, or language. Rather, the sense of community evoked by each instance of "racial" or "religious" status can only make communal sense as the riddling cultural memory of another's death. This is the problem of posterity we are left with in the story's concluding ironic caricature of Heather Jock as the "hegemonist of Bridge of Weir"—and it gives shape to the peculiar force of that word "hegemonist," too. Highly ironic, it is nonetheless clearly a salute to the memory of the individual. He survives. His memory has been important enough for that report of his death to have been sent overseas. It is a memorial, however, incongruously mixed up with the death of a man bearing the news of his death; and it is only in memory of that other man's death that Heather Jock's status as "hegemonist of Bridge of Weir" makes sense. If there is a utopian sense of community here, it remains in the indeterminate religious, racial, and then also class identification with which Graham suspends his own role as intermediary in receipt of the news of death, refusing anything but a contingent hegemony of the local. In its most powerful effects, this deflection from personal experience points to the present "nowhere" of shifting geographical and political identifications.

News of War: Cunninghame Graham's "Victory" and the Spanish-American War of 1898

The shifting lines of geographical and cultural alignments in Graham's sketches help explain the irony of his success as a writer remembered not as a writer but as "a man of action," or, when invoked as a writer, consistently described as underrated. The success of the "Don Roberto" legend—and here both Lavery portraits are telling—owes much to the global political realignments marked by the Spanish-American War of 1898. The United States's defeat of the vestiges of Spain's Empire in Cuba, the Philippines, and elsewhere marked a decisive new stage in the policies and practices of imperialist nations, articulating virtually overnight the terms of the United States's emergence as a world power. It stood as a striking example of Garnett's point, from the Overseas prospectus, that at the ends of one Empire may be found the beginnings of another. Graham's response to the war found fullest literary expression in "Victory," a sketch whose bitterly ironic title is given affirmatively to a Spanish nobleman. "Success," a slimmer reflection on the war, is another ironic title, more resignedly bitter, which became the title of his third collection of stories, published in 1902. In a sense, the combination of bitterness and irony in this title reflects how Graham's own literary success was bitterly won.

More significantly, Graham's response to the war was decisive in the Graham-Garnett-Conrad collaboration, determining the political geography of Graham's contribution to this formative moment of modernism. "Victory," a sketch that Watts and Davies select as exemplary for Graham's impressionism, became the occasion for a disagreement over method between Garnett and Graham which led to a certain victory, so to speak, in Graham's articulation of his artistic style. Set in Paris, the story unravels the effect of the news of an American victory over the Spanish in the war. Garnett insisted that the Spanish nobleman, whose response to that news produces what Watts and Davies interpret as the "moral victory," ought to be introduced *first* in order to make sense of the narrator's digressive reminiscences of reminiscences. Graham stood his ground, insisting "I am not a story teller, but an impressionist," terms he had already used in defending "Heather Jock."[80] In response, Garnett wrote: "I admire, I admire fully & deeply. Your method is so much your own nobody will ever come after you—& You will remain *alone*."[81] Watts and Davies illuminate the significance of this exchange when, having quoted from "Victory" the complex digression of a memory of being in Cadiz remembering the scent of the mimosa of the pampas, they pose the question: "Beyond establishing . . . that Graham knows the Hispanic world, what on earth has this to do with either Paris or the War of 1898?"[82] Their answer explains the way the sketch works, and they provide a fine demonstration of Graham's impressionistic technique. Yet they strangely reduplicate Garnett's concession: the center of the story, they claim, is not the Spanish noble, but "Graham himself," a conclusion which locks up the experience of the story into Chesterton's "adventure of being Cunninghame Graham."

There is, I believe, another answer to the question Watts and Davies pose. For Graham's digression (the story uses the Scots word "dwawm") momentarily offers a glimpse of that space of news telling in "Heather Jock" where the intertwined stories linking Indians, *gauchos*, and Scottish semi-madmen constitute an open-ended geography of political affiliations governing the reporting of news. The center of the story, then, is neither the Spanish nobleman nor "Graham himself," but the way in which, in the words of Watts and Davies, "we have to re-align our perception of the way the sketch works"[83] in shifting from the one to the other. In a sense, Garnett knew too well where Graham's political sympathies lay, and at first wanted those sympathies clarified by making the Spanish nobleman the story's center. In his later response, he recognized, and admired, the central place of Graham's personal impressions: the story's problem is not so much the conflict between Latin and Anglo-Saxon worlds, but rather a reflection on the vanishing place of Graham's memories within the convergence of responses to the news of the war. Garnett's recognition of Graham's success is, in effect, double-edged, and when he claims "You remain *alone*," there is the suggestion that Graham's world has been eclipsed by the events of the Spanish-American War. The passion of Graham's identification with the old Spanish Empire against the industrialized power of North America had an immense symbolic appeal for Conrad, as suggested by Conrad's letters to Graham on the subject, and confirmed most notably in the striking achievement of *Nostromo*. Conrad's novel reconstitutes the imaginative appeal of Graham's Spanish and Spanish-American sympathies as an identification with the old, eclipsed New World *against* the new world order of "Pax Americana." The result is a powerful and complex articulation of the new North-South axis of imperialist struggle across the emerging global formations of an industrialized "first" world and an economically dependent "third" world.

Yet Conrad's ability to transform the politics of Graham's response to the war into the "nowhere" of *Nostromo*'s fictional Latin America crucially obscures the geography of politics in Graham's sketch-artistry. Graham's South America includes a sense of space outside the imagined political logic of *Nostromo*. Indeed, the *gaucho* costume of Lavery's portrait of Don Roberto draws attention to that sense of space—the pampas of the *gaucho* rider, whose local color does not, after all, well illustrate Conrad's novel. If the scene of *gaucho* riding is quintessential Cunninghame Graham "adventure," it is neither as local color, nor as setting—nor as ethnographic detail—that the pampas provide a key sense of the "nowhere" of Graham's sketches. In "A Vanishing Race," we read, "Pampa, in the quichua tongue, signifies 'Space.'"[84] The detail calls attention to the many vanishing moments of Graham's sketches, particularly those that allude to the decimation of Native Americans, either explicitly in "A Hegira," or in drawing toward the vanishing trail of Indians—for instance, in "Heather Jock": "Just at the crossing of the Guaviyú, close to a clump of "Espinillo de Olor" [mimosa], we found the body, cut and hacked about so as to be almost unrecognizable, but holding in the hand a tuft of long black hair, coarse as a horse's tail, showing the dead man had behaved himself up to the last like a true Christian."[85] The "space" of the pampa captures Graham's sense of "nowhere" by being triply removed through Indian (Quichua), Spanish (Gaucho), and English (Scottish) tongues.

The geography of politics in Graham's sketch-artistry is not explained, however, by a *quichua* concept of space, by the *gaucho* lifestyle, or through Graham's nostalgia for the pampa of his youth (signaled by the naming of his horse and stylized through the Lavery portrait). If Graham shared a nostalgic, utopian view of the South American pampa with his friend W. H. Hudson, the "nowhere" of Graham's Spanish and Spanish-American world cannot be characterized, as Fredric Jameson characterizes Hudson's work, as a "return to some earlier precapitalist form" with "an appeal to a generalized and global nostalgia."⁸⁶ Even to the extent that the Spanish and Spanish-American world of Graham's sketches is projected as a "vanished arcadia" not unlike the world of Hudson's pampa in *Far Away and Long Ago: A History of My Early Life*, it is important to specify the negative dialectic by which the aura of the "Don Roberto" myth registers a resistance to the global political realignments following the Spanish-American War—a resistance to a whole range of Anglo-Saxon imaginings, most notably Rudyard Kipling's address to Americans to "take up the white man's burden." Yet the Hispanic aura of "Don Roberto's" Spanish America is rarely an exotic utopia, as indicated by the title "The Ipané." Far from an exotic evocation of the name of a place or of a people, it is the name of the old steamer whose explosion yields the macabre climax to the title story of the volume, with its gruesome depiction of the scattered bodies of its passengers, some of that "nondescript society" of life in Paraguay, which includes "all the waifs and strays of cosmopolitan humanity who, 'outside our flag,' pursue their useless lives, under the sixfold international code of law so neatly codified by Colonel Colt."⁸⁷ As a name, of course, it is not unimportant, lending a local color entirely in keeping with Graham's geography of politics: primarily a place-name from the Guaraní, it translates into the Spanish *laguna hedionda*—as one might say, "fateful waters"; or, alternatively, "stinking hole."⁸⁸

The realignment of geography and politics in Graham's sketches provides a counterweight to the paradigms of geopolitics emerging in the 1890s. Still more importantly, their stray lines present open-ended possibilities of political affiliation across disparate cultural experiences. The myth of Don Roberto does not simply register a global nostalgia of a lost Spanish-American world. Nor can the glamour of "R. B. Cunninghame Graham, M.P." as socialist activist appeal in terms simply of a lost art of political struggle. These eccentric afterimages of Cunninghame Graham register, rather, an imagined geography of politics articulated against the emergent dominance of twentieth-century discourses of geopolitics. To the extent that such a "utopian" perspective may be ascribed to Cunninghame Graham, it is because his sketches link the battlefront of socialist struggle with the frontier of colonial violence to transform that utopian imperative of the 1890s—Marx's "here, or nowhere"—into the problematic lesson of the "here" as "nowhere."

5 The Geopolitics of Screenplay
Sabotage from Joseph Conrad to Alfred Hitchcock

> "When he is conducting his locomotive through space, doubling or slacking speed at his pleasure, does the engine-driver believe himself the inferior of the sovereign shut up behind him in a gilded railway carriage, and trembling from the knowledge that his life depends on a jet of steam, the shifting of a lever, or a bomb of dynamite?"
> —Elisée Reclus, *Evolution and Revolution* (1885)

> "Query: Which is really more criminal?—the Bomb of Madrid or the Meat of Chicago."   —Joseph Conrad, letter to Galsworthy (1906)

> "I would like to come back to Britain and weave a film around a pit disaster or an incident of sabotage in the Glasgow dockyards."
> —Alfred Hitchcock, "The Censor Wouldn't Pass It" (1938)

In the following pages I examine the historical emergence of the term "sabotage" from roughly 1907 (the publication date of Conrad's *The Secret Agent*) to 1942 (the year Hitchcock's *Saboteur* was released). My concern is to show how the word works to articulate the general management of social agency in modern industrial society. Alternatively represented as the action of a foreign agent or a domestic traitor, sabotage comes to signify, by the 1940s, a sensational threat against national security. As a word in some senses productive of the very idea of national security, "sabotage" is a peculiarly unstable and contradictory signifier for the industrialized nation-state, for the relation between nation-states, and for the abstract conception of social agency on which these depend.

Alfred Hitchcock's movies *Sabotage* (1936) and *Saboteur* (1942) provide classic examples of how "sabotage" came to articulate a complex set of anxieties and fantasies about national security and world politics. Hitchcock's use of the motif of sabotage, which becomes a governing motif for the movies of his transatlantic period, also invites investigation into the significance of film for the subject of geopolitics. In *The Geopolitical Aesthetic* Fredric Jameson turns to cinema to seek an explanation for what he calls "the geopolitical unconscious."[1] This reformulation of Jameson's earlier diagnosis of the "political unconscious" turns on an examination, in particular, of conspiracy film—"the 'conspiratorial text,'" as he dubs it, "which, whatever other messages it emits or implies, may also be taken to constitute an unconscious collective effort at trying to figure out where we are and what landscapes and forces confront us in a late twentieth century whose abominations are heightened by their concealment and their bureaucratic impersonality."[2]

There is good ground for considering Jameson's "conspiratorial text" of postwar American movies in terms of a "geopolitical unconscious." As O Tuathail shows in his study of the rise of a U.S. discourse of "geopolitics," 1942 constituted something of a watershed year in the "raging fashion" for geopolitics promoted by the American sensational press and by Hollywood movies.[3] O Tuathail's study reveals the projection—and screening (in Frank Capra's army propaganda film, *Plan for Destruction* [1943])—of an imaginary Geopolitical Institute at Munich, which quickly acquired the status of a received, mythic truth. Discussing the various ways in which American geopoliticians sought to realize an American counterpart to this imaginary Geopolitical Institute, such as the short-lived Geopolitical Section within the Military Intelligence Service, O Tuathail concludes that "what remained . . . was the dream of a global panopticon of intelligence, a desire the Office of Strategic Services had already begun to institutionalize and a desire that would later propel the establishment of the Central Intelligence Agency and the National Security Agency."[4]

The history of "sabotage," a keyword in the "conspiratorial text" of American Cold War representations, offers a case study in the formation of a "geopolitical unconscious" (to borrow Jameson's formulation), and a test case, too, in "critical geopolitics" (following O Tuathail). One thing this history helps show is how, for discourses of geopolitics, cinema becomes the classic medium. In the various espionage films of Hitchcock's period of transatlantic crossover into American moviemaking (from 1935 to 1942), the familiar subject of the spy film develops around a set of concerns about territorial loyalty, ethnic affiliations, and the coordination and management of the various media of propaganda. These concerns trace back to an earlier moment of ideological containment: reaction, in particular, to the anarcho-syndicalism of the early years of the twentieth century; and to the origins of cinematography. What Jameson calls the "conspiratorial text" is, as he himself points out, an outgrowth of a variety of genres of spy plots and mystery thrillers. This prehistory of movies and mysteries, as a matter both of generic form and political history, is what gets formulated, along with the American rage for "geopolitics," as the sensational problem of "sabotage."

Simply put, this prehistory involves the ideological containment of the use of the term "sabotage" amongst anarchist and syndicalist circles to signal a revolutionary tactic in working-class revolt. By the late 1930s, the revolutionary figure of the striker as hero of international working-class solidarity can be ideologically contained by the sinister figure of the treacherous saboteur. The geopolitical resonance and prominence of the terms "sabotage" and "saboteur" in the 1940s arise from a complex of contested meanings, already embedded in the prior terms of turn-of-the-century geography and politics. In the retrospect of the long turn of the century, the twentieth-century threat of sabotage in time of world war seeks to lay to rest the nineteenth-century specter of international class warfare announced in the opening to *The Communist Manifesto*. The fiction of geopolitics turns that "spectre ... haunting Europe"[5] into the worldwide menace of wartime sabotage.

The Meaning of Sabotage

By 1942, when Hitchcock's *Saboteur* was released, the term "sabotage" had become something of a keyword in the lexicon of wartime mass propaganda. George Orwell, in a radio address on "The Meaning of Sabotage" produced for the Indian section of the B.B.C.'s Eastern Service on 29 January 1942, claimed, "Everyone has heard the word sabotage."[6] Connecting the word to other contested slogans of geopolitics—"scorched earth policy" and "Lebensraum"—Orwell defined the meaning of sabotage, succinctly, as "the tactic of a conquered people."[7] The definition stands in contrast to the way the term works in Hitchcock's *Saboteur*. There, sabotage embodies the threat of Fascism. The movie's opening act of sabotage against an American munitions factory provides the *mise en scène* for a characteristically Hitchcockian case of mistaken identity—the wrong man is accused and hunted across America as a saboteur. He becomes in turn the hunter of the actual saboteur, who is finally chased to the top of the Statue of Liberty from which he plunges to his death (though not without successfully having carried out a final act of sabotage at the launching of a newly built ship). Hitchcock successfully transforms the fears of Nazi sabotage against American industry into the material for a classic thriller film plot.

For Orwell and Hitchcock sabotage appears to mean something very different. What for Orwell is the "tactic of a conquered people," for Hitchcock is the tactic of an invading people. And while Orwell openly advocates the tactic of "sabotaging the war machine" of the Nazis, Hitchcock's film appeals to the near-hysteria about Nazi infiltrators and the vigilance needed to prevent the sabotaging of the American war machine. The different inflection each one gives the meaning of sabotage provides a study in contrasts. Yet rather than presenting opposed ideological positions, Hitchcock and Orwell elaborate in fact on a shared wartime sense of the term as it helps conceptualize what Orwell calls the "war machine."[8]

The historical contestation over the meaning of "sabotage" is brought more sharply into focus by contrasting Orwell's "The Meaning of Sabotage" with Hitchcock's earlier movie, *Sabotage* (1936), adapted from Joseph Conrad's 1907 novel *The Secret Agent*. This movie's title sequence presents a dictionary definition of "sabotage," which reads: "willful destruction of buildings or machinery with the object of alarming a group of persons or inspiring public uneasiness." The definition emphasizes the meaning of sabotage as the criminal act with which the movie proper opens—the blackout of London's electricity, narrated through the montage sequence of a light bulb, a nighttime view of the city lights, the light bulb going out, and the city lights extinguished. The act of sabotage is revealed in a further succession of visual and auditory montages: following the discovery at the electrical plant, conveyed in truncated dialogue ("sand"—"destruction"—"sabotage"—"who did it?"), Oskar Homolka, as Mr. Verloc, is filmed emerging from the London Underground, clearly interpellated by the music, sinister facial expression, and montage sequence, as the one "who did it."

The movie's framing definition of the meaning of sabotage in fact echoes, more closely than any dictionary definition, the wording of the "criminal syndicalism" statutes passed in many states during the First World War. So, for instance, Montana's statute reads:

> Sabotage is hereby defined to be malicious, felonious, intentional or unlawful damage, injury or destruction of real or personal property, of any

form whatsoever, of any employer, or owner, by his or her employee or employees, or any employer or employers or by any person or persons, at their own instance, or at the instance, request or instigation of such employees, employers, or any other person.[9]

By contrast, Orwell seeks to remind his radio listeners of the word's heroic origins ("One understands better how it works if one knows something about its origins"):

> Everyone has heard the word sabotage. It is one of those words that find their way into all languages, but not all of the people who use it know where it comes from. It is really a French word. In parts of Northern France and Flanders the people, at any rate the peasants and the working people, wear heavy wooden shoes which are called sabots. Once, many years ago, some working men who had a grievance against their employer threw their sabots into a piece of machinery while it was running, and thus damaged it. This action was nicknamed sabotage, and from then onwards the word came to be used for any action deliberately intended to interfere with industry or destroy valuable property.[10]

Orwell's etymological account draws attention to the working-class origins of the term elided in Hitchcock's framed dictionary definition. Yet Orwell's etymology, too, reiterates a myth—the "hoary old myth," according to Geoff Brown's study of the tactic of sabotage in industrial conflict, "that the word 'sabotage' itself derives from the fact that clogs were thrown by French speaking workers into their machines in order to damage them."[11] If both Hitchcock and Orwell offer carefully framed myths of the meaning of sabotage—Orwell's tailored to the propaganda needs of the Indian Section of the B.B.C.'s Eastern Service; Hitchcock's to the needs of American wartime cinema entertainment—what each together illustrates is the fact that the meaning of sabotage is inseparable, in its contested definition, from myth.

In their dictionary and etymological claims, Orwell and Hitchcock reframe a pattern of earlier polemic over the meaning of sabotage. Prominent examples include Bertrand Russell's comments on sabotage in a 1918 essay on "The Syndicalist Revolt," and Thorstein Veblen's "On the Nature and Uses of Sabotage" (1919). Following closely on the heels of the "criminal syndicalism" statutes in the United States, both Veblen and Russell trace the term to the syndicalist movement, Veblen with special attention to its importance for the I.W.W. (Industrial Workers of the World, or "wobblies"). Russell, who focuses on European examples, devotes two pages to discussion of sabotage as one of the tactics of the "syndicalist revolt," in which he usefully catalogues the "many forms" it takes—"some clearly innocent, some open to grave objections."[12] He reserves his "grave objections" to

> such acts as all ordinary morality would consider criminal; for example, causing railway accidents. Advocates of sabotage justify it as part of war, but in its more violent forms (in which it is often defended) it is cruel and probably inexpedient, and even in its milder forms it must tend to encourage slovenly habits of work, which might easily persist under the new régime that the Syndicalists wish to introduce. At the same time, when capitalists express a moral horror of this method, it is worth while to observe that they themselves are the first to practice it when the occasion seems to them appropriate.[13]

The moral ambiguities Russell foregrounds—between "innocent" and "criminal" forms of sabotage—present an important part of the polemical force of the word as it carries over into the late 1930s and early 1940s. Russell's assertion that some forms of sabotage are "criminal" captures a crucial feature of Hitchcock's definition, and one that prepares for the movie's extended meditation on "innocent" and "criminal" actions. Unlike in *Saboteur*, where each of the three acts of sabotage fit a straightforward definition of an attack on the American war machine, in *Sabotage* three acts of sabotage (the London blackout, the attempt to bomb Trafalgar Square, and the Professor's suicidal blowing up of the Bijou theater) pose increasingly problematic moral questions on the nature of "innocent" and "criminal" action. The last act of sabotage poses a particularly problematic set of questions about moral and political agency, since it conceals all evidence of Mrs. Verloc's murder of her husband (arguably the movie's main act of sabotage), leaving the audience to ponder the nature of her crime.

Veblen's essay demonstrates the extent to which Russell's moral questions are embedded in the particular history of the word's polemical formulation. Veblen first offers his own neutral definition of the word, recalling Orwell and Hitchcock: "'Sabotage' is a derivative of 'sabot,' which is French for a wooden shoe. It means going slow, with a dragging, clumsy movement, such as that manner of footgear may be expected to bring on. So it has come to describe any manoeuvre of slowing-down, inefficiency, bungling, obstruction." He then goes on to argue:

The sinister meaning which is often attached to the word in American usage, as denoting violence and disorder, appears to be due to the fact that the American usage has been shaped chiefly by persons and newspapers who have aimed to discredit the use of sabotage by organized workmen, and who have therefore laid stress on its less amiable manifestations.[14]

Veblen's essay offers an important glimpse of the polemicized charge of the word "sabotage" immediately following the First World War, because he directly addresses the way in which the word "sabotage," as Geoff Brown explains, "became the scare word in a period of a general scare about the I.W.W."[15] He shows, moreover, how any attempt to frame a neutral definition of the meaning of sabotage—such as Orwell's or Hitchcock's—is itself a part of the polemicized history of the word.

Veblen's essay is all the more interesting in its rhetorical effort to counter the "sinister meaning" of sabotage by applying the word to an analysis of the "vested interests" of big business:

Sabotage, accordingly, is not to be condemned out of hand, simply as such. There are many measures of policy and management both in private business and in public administration which are unmistakably of the nature of sabotage and which are not only considered to be excusable, but are deliberately sanctioned by statute and common law and by the public conscience.... It should not be difficult to show that the common welfare in any community which is organized on the price system cannot be maintained without a salutary use of sabotage.[16]

With irony and sarcasm, Veblen attempts to control the polemical opposition between workers' sabotage and capitalist sabotage, but the essay's increasingly parodic tone turns the word "sabotage" into a portmanteau word for the whole industrial "price system" itself: "The needed sabotage can best be administered on a comprehensive plan and by a central authority, since the country's industry is of the nature of a comprehensive interlocking system."[17] If Theodor Adorno's critique of the element of "buffoonery" in Veblen's cultural criticism seems applicable here, it is just that kind of wit which enables Veblen to demonstrate how "sabotage" works to articulate the modern industrial system.[18]

Once read in the context of this wider field of polemicized (and transatlantic) cross-reference, the title of Hitchcock's *Sabotage* assumes a more complex resonance. Indeed, the movie's opening sequence sets into play this polemical field of reference—not only in the sinister register of Verloc's (Oskar Homolka's) first appearance as saboteur, but also, as that almost parodic montage effect is in turn undercut, by shifting to the comic register of the dialogue between Ted, the undercover detective (John Loder), and Mrs. Verloc (Sylvia Sidney) over how to treat the customers whose movie viewing has been disrupted by the act of sabotage. Ted's mock legalistic disquisition on the nature of the "act" ("act of God . . . act of Providence . . . acted action"—perhaps a remote parody of the "criminal syndicalism" statutes) sets in comic relief the movie's opening displacement of attention from the menaced machinery of industry to the popular-culture industry of entertainment.

Anarcho-Syndicalist Origins

The title and *mise en scène* of Hitchcock's *Sabotage*, then, draw from the terms of a longer polemical debate reaching back through the 1930s and 1920s—back, indeed, to the polemical debates of the first decade of the century, the period in which Conrad was writing *The Secret Agent*. Although the anarchism Conrad satirizes is quite different from the obscure politics motivating the group of men who briefly appear in Hitchcock's *Sabotage*, the polemical history of the word "sabotage" itself identifies a hidden affinity between the movie and the book used as the text for its screenplay. As revealed in Conrad's letters from 1905 on, *The Secret Agent* emerges from an extended meditation on "anarcho" themes. In June of 1906, writing to Galsworthy about the stalled progress of his "long Anarch: Story" (i.e., *The Secret Agent*), Conrad poses a revealing riddle: "Query: Which is really more criminal?—the Bomb of Madrid or the Meat of Chicago."[19] Referring, on the one hand, to the recent assassination attempt on the King and Queen of Spain, and, on the other, to the adulteration of food in American packing companies (as exposed that year by Upton Sinclair's *The Jungle*), Conrad's "query" anticipates the polemical juxtaposition of "workers' sabotage" and "capitalist sabotage" that surfaces in both Bertrand Russell and Thorstein Veblen. It draws attention, furthermore, to other features of that polemic: connecting the older language of anarchist "direct action" (assassination attempts) with an anarcho-syndicalist focus on the workplace (the meatpacking factories), Conrad's economical "query" also underscores a logic of international political struggle (Madrid and Chicago) revealed in the nexus of political events (regicide) and everyday consumption (eating tainted sausages).

In its origins, the term "sabotage" also evoked that nexus of international commerce, politics, and consumer relations that Conrad makes the prime location of his novel—the Brett Street stationery shop. Possibly the earliest written reference to the term "sabotage" comes from 1907, the year *The Secret Agent* was published. Outlining the "various means" of "direct action" available to workers, a pamphlet entitled "Le Syndicat" lists "*grève*" (strike), "*sabottage*" [sic], "*boycottage*," and "*label*."[20] If this provides only a fleeting reference, the word (now spelled correctly) receives its "syndicalist baptism" in a later pamphlet, *Le Sabotage*, published in 1910 by the same author, Emile Pouget, a veteran anarchist propagandist of the 1880s and 1890s and former editor of *Le Père Peinard*. Here, at the source for most later contestations over the meaning of "sabotage," the conceptual, rhetorical, linguistic, and historical poles of the word's polemical force field of reference become fully visible. Translated into English in 1912 by I.W.W. member Arturo Giovannitti, the pamphlet became, in the words of Louis Adamic, writing in 1934, "a sort of wobbly gospel."[21] It is this pamphlet, too, which sets the terms for later etymological framings of the meaning of "sabotage."

Pouget opens with a brief account of the term's etymology:

> The word "sabotage" wasn't, until fifteen years ago, anything but a slang word meaning not the act of making "sabots"/clogs but, figuratively and expressively, the act of executing work "as if with blows of clogs."[22]

This etymology provides a useful point of reference for the variety of connotations that tend to get delimited in later attempts to contain the meaning of the word: the slang meaning opens up to a range of further senses in the French word *saboter* (for example, "to make a noise with sabots, to perform or execute badly, e.g., to 'murder' [a piece of music]" [see the O.E.D.]—connotations that tend to be screened from view in Orwell's myth of workers throwing their shoes into a piece of machinery, or Hitchcock's indirect citation of criminal statutes).

Pouget's pamphlet recounts how sabotage was adopted by the Confederal Congress at Toulouse in 1897 (its "syndicalist baptism," as he calls it); and this account provides the basis for numerous later recountings, one of the most influential of which was Elizabeth Gurley Flynn's 1916 I.W.W. pamphlet, "Sabotage: The Conscious Withdrawal of Workers' Industrial Efficiency." It is important to note the polemic that marks the origins of syndicalist usage. Directly following the opening summary of the word's "syndicalist baptism" (a phrase full of Pouget's propagandist satire), he writes:

> The new arrival was not, from the start, received by everyone, in working-class circles, with heated enthusiasm. Certain people looked on it with an evil eye, reproached it for its vulgar and anarchic origins . . . and even immorality.[23]

Foregrounding the polemic of its "syndicalist baptism," Pouget makes the word a word of political struggle by framing it in terms of a struggle over meaning and dictionary definition:

> Despite this suspicion, which resembles almost that of hostility, sabotage has made its way in all worlds.
> It has since captured working-class sympathies. It has conquered the right to be cited in Larousse, and no doubt the Academy—as long as it doesn't *sabotage* itself before reaching S in its dictionary—has undertaken to draw from the word "sabotage" its most ceremonial reverence and open up its pages in official recognition.[24]

As a characteristic feature of this rhetorical fabrication of the myth of sabotage, Pouget undercuts his own account of the word's "syndicalist baptism":

> One would, however, be wrong to believe that the working class waited, before practicing sabotage, until this word of struggle had been consecrated by the corporate Congresses. As is the case with all forms of revolt, it is as old as human exploitation.[25]

This claim combines two significant strands of later polemic over the meaning of sabotage: the attempt politically to contain its historical significance (as a recent phenomenon, or one of long-standing practice); and the attempt to frame its geographical import (as something that can or cannot be translated across national borders). Both strands are present in an I.W.W. cartoon from May 1917 which presents Sabotage personified as an Egyptian Sphinx confronting the puzzled capitalist.[26] The cartoon illustrates how claims for the word's ancient lineage of meaning play with and on xenophobia. Suspicion of ethnic origins forms an important element of responses to I.W.W. tactics generally, since the I.W.W.—by contrast to the American Federation of Labor—appealed to an immigrant membership. The association of sabotage with an immigrant-alien politics became increasingly pronounced during the 1930s.[27] This is a side of the polemicized meaning of sabotage echoed in the opening sequence of Hitchcock's *Sabotage*, when the word is metonymically linked to the viewer's first identification of Oskar Homolka's face as both criminal and foreign. In Britain, too, the French-sounding word provided the occasion for nationalist polemic. As an example of the Independent Labour Party's and Social-Democratic Federation's repudiation of sabotage, Geoff Brown cites A. S. Headingley's March 1912 essay in *Justice*, "Syndicalism indigenous to France; inappropriate to England."[28] And in an essay from October 1912 entitled "Is Sabotage Un-English?" in *The Syndicalist*, E. J. B. Allen contended "if the word 'sabotage' is French . . . the practice is undoubtedly English. It is as old as the Labour movement."[29]

If sabotage comes to signal a sinister foreign import, this, too, is there (although with a significantly different accentuation) in Pouget's deliberate rhetorical fabrication:

> [Sabotage] is not, moreover, circumscribed by our borders. In fact, in its contemporary theoretical formulation, it is an English import.
>
> Sabotage has been known and practiced across the Channel for a long time now, under the name of *Ca' Canny* or *Go Canny*, a Scots word whose translation more or less precisely might be put as: "Don't strain yourself."[30]

This English—or rather Scots—precedent for sabotage suggests how polemicized foreignness constitutes a core feature of the rhetorical force of the term.[31] "Sabotage," from its first "baptism" is figured through its international, interlinguistic meaning as, to recall Orwell's formulation, "one of those words that find their way into all languages."[32]

This English-Scots precedent draws attention to the historical significance of this multiple and multiplying polemics of foreign definition. Pouget's point of reference is the 1889 Dockers' Strike, suggesting that the contested meaning of sabotage emerges from the contradictory imperatives and heterogeneity of struggles in the 1890s that we have traced around the figure of R. B. Cunninghame Graham. Indeed, in the immediate aftermath of the Dockers' Strike, Cunninghame Graham himself turned to "Ca' Canny" as a way to contextualize the heterogeneity of labor tactics: "No, 'ca canny' is not a Chinook word, neither Chinese, nor even German. Nothing more awful than North British, otherwise called Scotch."[33] The article he wrote on "Ca' Canny" for *The People's Press* (in November 1890) argued for the importance of a tactic that was neither an all-out strike nor a regulated system of collective bargaining through political representation.[34]

Using the example of "Ca' Canny" as elaborated practically through anecdote and theoretically in the popularized explanation from an 1895 pamphlet (itself perhaps partly modeled after Cunninghame Graham's), Emile Pouget draws on the lessons of the heterogeneity of British tactics to illustrate the logic of sabotage: "'Go Canny' consists, therefore, in putting systematically into practice the formula 'poor work, poor pay!' But it is not circumscribed by that alone. From this formula follows, by logical extension, a diversity of manifestations of the will of the worker in conflict with the rapacity of the boss."[35] Pouget's account thus deliberately interweaves a variety of forms of working-class tactics of resistance and struggle around the polemicized "word of struggle," sabotage.

This deliberate fabrication of a contested and contestatory myth stands in interesting and important relation to that other, in some respects more celebrated syndicalist tactic, the General Strike. For Sorel, writing in *Reflections on Violence* at the same time that Conrad was writing *The Secret Agent*, the general strike constitutes

> the *myth* in which Socialism is wholly comprised, *i.e.* a body of images capable of evoking instinctively all the sentiments which correspond to the different manifestations of the war undertaken by Socialism against modern society. Strikes have engendered in the proletariat the noblest, deepest, and most moving sentiments that they possess; the general strike groups them all in a co-ordinated picture, and, by bringing them together, gives to each one of them its maximum of intensity; appealing to their painful memories of particular conflicts, it colours with an intense life all the details of the composition presented to consciousness. We thus obtain that intuition of Socialism which language cannot give us with perfect clearness—and we obtain it as a whole, perceived instantaneously.[36]

Sorel adds, in a footnote, "This is the 'global knowledge' of Bergson's philosophy." Along with what Chantal Mouffe and Ernesto Laclau characterize as Sorel's break with economism, the syndicalist adoption of the tactic of sabotage poses fundamental problems concerning working-class solidarity and class consciousness—insinuating, for instance, an ethnic and racial challenge to national and international working-class solidarity. The "decisive point" to emerge from Sorel's theory, according to Laclau and Mouffe, is also, if in crucially different ways, the fundamental challenge presented by the tactic of sabotage: "that the very identity of social agents becomes indeterminate."[37]

Sabotage and the General Strike, as the most prominent tactics associated with the anarcho-syndicalism of the beginning of the twentieth century, form the Janus face of a whole series of strikes, labor disputes, and social unrest from the 1890s to 1914 throughout Europe and America. Perhaps the most memorable of all was the great wave of strikes in Russia that precipitated the 1905 Revolution. From the nature of these mass movements, Rosa Luxemburg, in "The Mass Strike, the Political Party, and the Trade Unions" (written in 1906), drew lessons in social agency and political leadership polemically opposed both to anarcho-syndicalism and to German socialism; and it would be from these movements that a heroic mythology of strikes would emerge following the Russian Revolution of 1917—memorialized with Eisenstein's 1925 film *Strike*. Yet the heroic figure of the "striker" to emerge from these mass political movements in Russia[38] stands in important contrast to the figure of the "saboteur" to emerge from the mass political movements of France, Italy, Britain, and the United States.

In this sense, sabotage might be understood as the historical supplement to the Sorelian myth of the General Strike—what, refiguring and displacing the General Strike, constitutes the "co-ordinated picture" that organizes the "painful memories of particular conflicts" into "a whole, perceived instantaneously"—"the 'global knowledge' of Bergson's philosophy." This supplementary meaning of sabotage as working-class betrayal underscores what happens to the idealized General Strike with the outbreak of World War I. Around the myth of sabotage the revolutionary rhetoric of class warfare gets reconfigured into the geopolitical imperative of world war. The wartime appropriation of sabotage transposes the utopian socialist problem of awakening international working-class consciousness onto the problem of loyalty in time of war. The meaning of "sabotage" thus displaces the problem of organizing mass political movements onto questions of territorial loyalty or betrayal.

This territorial logic informs the geopolitical meaning of sabotage for the Second World War. For Orwell, the meaning of "sabotage" is a heroic afterimage of prewar workers' struggle only insofar as it targets the enemy war machine. The solidarity of political loyalties is presumed, but in a way that only reinforces a riddle of territoriality, since his broadcast is addressed to an Indian audience quite likely conflicted in its loyalty to the British Empire. This dynamic of betrayal and loyalty is written into the opening sequences of Hitchcock's *Saboteur*, in a different way, as the figure of the heroic factory worker gets mistaken for the saboteur. From then on, the worker's loyalty is bound to revealing the betrayal of the saboteur, in a hunt that inscribes the territorial riddle of sabotage across the heartland of America.

The Anarchist Premises of *The Secret Agent*: From Agency to Secret Agency

Conrad's *The Secret Agent* provides a unique perspective on the changing meaning of sabotage in its reframing of the Greenwich bomb outrage of 1894, the unnarrated event around which Conrad constructs the fragmented pieces of his narrative. Conrad's plot is premised on an appropriation of anarchism for the purposes of containing revolution: Mr. Vladimir (presumed Russian ambassador) plans the attack to precipitate a government crackdown on anarchists. This counter-revolutionary appropriation and containment of anarchism is not only the premise of the story; its logic also informs the novel's celebrated modernism of narrative form—the "ironic treatment," as Conrad called it simply in the author's note.[39]

As a number of critics have noted, following Conrad's own comments in the 1920 author's note, *The Secret Agent* looks back on the anarchist scares throughout Europe and America in the 1880s and 1890s and the political suppression of anarchists that accompanied those scares. Yet rather than an anachronistic evocation of anarchism, *The Secret Agent* marks an interesting and important conjuncture in the transition from the suppression of anarchism in the 1890s to the resurgent anarcho-syndicalism of the first decades of the twentieth century. This historical conjuncture is refracted through the novel's mimicry of revolutionary propaganda generally. More specifically, the novel effects a kind of dialogization of the "propaganda by the deed" of the 1890s, which resonates throughout *The Secret Agent*, not unlike the way Hitchcock uses the term "sabotage."[40]

Anticipating the moral questions Hitchcock unravels around the "innocent" or "criminal" nature of the movie's three "acts" of sabotage, the novel's first consideration of the "criminal" meaning of the explosion occurs in the dialogue between Ossipon and the Professor, which constitutes a suggestive disagreement over methods of propaganda—between the methods of Ossipon, "editor of the F.P. leaflets," and those of the Professor, who scorns Ossipon's methods: "The condemned social order has not been built up on paper and ink, and I don't fancy that a combination of paper and ink will ever put an end to it" (*TSA*, 71). A caricatured difference between "propaganda by the deed" and, as it were, propaganda by the word, the exchange intimates an underlying congruity between that form of literary propaganda the Professor scorns as "a combination of paper and ink" and the "combination of time and shock" which is the principle of the Professor's "system" for the ideal detonator. Both are bound to the problematic condition of mediating between the present "social order" and an imagined future utopian state.

The Secret Agent everywhere subverts utopian projections of any future social, let alone socialist, order. Thus, the response to Vladimir's query about the title of the secret revolutionary organization to which Verloc belongs:

> "What are all these leaflets headed F.P., with a hammer, pen, and torch crossed? What does it mean, this F.P.?" Mr. Verloc approached the imposing writing-table.
> "The Future of the Proletariat. It's a society." (*TSA*, 26)

There is more to this joke than its ironic comment on the complacencies of a revolutionary organization whose name erases the ideal social future in order to designate its status as secret society. The difference between society and "a society," on which this particular irony depends, indicates the principle of narrative ellipsis with which the novel presents its social vision of late-Victorian London through ironic deployment of utopian discourses of emancipation and revolution.

What Conrad does with the "Future of the Proletariat" is humorously echoed by a fictional case of "sabotage" that surfaces in a utopian narrative Emile Pouget co-authored with Emile Pataud, *Comment nous ferons la révolution*, published in France in 1909 and translated into English in 1913 under the title *How We Shall Bring About the Revolution*. An anarcho-syndicalist utopian narrative, explicitly modeled on the examples of Bellamy's *Looking Backward* and Morris's *News from Nowhere*, the book comments, in its preface, on the future tense of its title:

> At baptism, our book changed its name. This was the fault of the publisher, who, in presenting its title page to the printer's ink—the baptismal font for books—shamelessly committed an act of sabotage.
> Not being of a morose disposition, we bear him no ill-will on this account, and we plead his cause with you; like us, you will grant our publisher free pardon.
> And yet the sabotage is obvious!
> In place of the anachronistic title which appears on the title page, there should have blazed forth, in three lines,
>
> "HOW
> WE BROUGHT ABOUT
> THE REVOLUTION."
>
> Such was the title, this book of ours should have borne.[41]

The printer's "act of sabotage" conveniently resolves that characteristic problem of nineteenth-century utopian narratives (and the utopian imperative of nineteenth-century narrative): the narrator's impatience of getting back and forth from the present to the utopian, future "nowhere" of society after the revolution. Here, as a matter of grammatical and political incorrectness, Pataud and Pouget humorously reveal how "sabotage" reconfigures the problem of utopia, subverting the problem of the message by means of the medium.

The Secret Agent gives sustained attention to this dilemma by folding the propaganda mode of address inside out, as it were. As with "The Future of the Proletariat," there is neither a "proletariat" to address nor a "future" to imagine for it. The parody of Marx in Michaelis's pronouncements at the opening to chapter 3 offers a classic example of Conrad's "ironic method" in this regard. Mimicking Marxist analysis—"History is dominated and determined by the tool and the production—by the force of economic conditions"—Conrad turns the rhetoric of economic determinism (the hallmark of Second International Marxism) against the call for revolutionary action: "No one can tell what form the social organization may take in the future. Then why indulge in prophetic phantasies?" (*TSA*, 41). Although we are likely to recall the speech as addressed to fellow members of the Red Committee, Michaelis twice addresses his comments to "my boy": "Leave that [pastime] to the moralists, my boy." In retrospect these words might best be understood as addressed to Stevie, as if lifted from a later scenario (perhaps during Stevie's visit to Michaelis's little cottage in the country). As throughout the novel, Stevie is the exemplary target of revolutionary propaganda. Karl Yundt's "eloquent imagery," Ossipon's F.P. leaflets, and Michaelis's call for "Patience" (*TSA*, 49), all have their distinct and marked effect on the overly sensitive Stevie. His receptivity and sensitivity leads, of course, not to an awakening but to an obliteration of consciousness—the most violent ellipsis of social agency, around which the novel's narrative parts are arranged in disjointed segments (whether at the level of words, phrases, or whole chapters).

This ellipsis of social agency constitutes the anarchist premise of *The Secret Agent*, generally, in the "house, household, and business" of the Brett Street shop, but also, more specifically, in the early description of "The old affair of fireworks on the stairs" (as it is recalled later, in chapter 10 [*TSA*, 220]). It is memorable as possibly the only act resembling revolt in the whole novel:

> When he had reached the age of fourteen a friend of his late father, an agent for a foreign preserved milk firm, having given him an opening as office-boy, he was discovered one foggy afternoon, in his chief's absence, busy letting off fireworks on the staircase. He touched off in quick succession a set of fierce rockets, angry catherine wheels, loudly exploding squibs—and the matter might have turned out very serious. An awful panic spread through the whole building. Wild-eyed, choking clerks stampeded through the passages full of smoke, silk hats and elderly business men could be seen rolling independently down the stairs. (*TSA*, 9)

The first appearance of the word "agent," this presents an abbreviated formulation for industrial relations ("an agent for a foreign preserved milk firm"), which recalls the nexus of international commerce, politics, and consumer relations in Conrad's "query" from 1906. In a significant proleptic allusion to the Greenwich bomb explosion, Stevie's pyrotechnics is presumed to be a response to grievances against working conditions:

> His motives for this stroke of originality were difficult to discover. It was only later on that Winnie obtained from him a misty and confused confession. It seems that two other office-boys in the building had worked upon his feelings by tales of injustice and oppression till they had wrought his compassion to the pitch of that frenzy. But his father's friend, of course, dismissed him summarily as likely to ruin his business. (*TSA*, 9–10)

The episode is striking not only for the uncharacteristic sympathy it seems likely to solicit for Stevie's action. As the first in a series of evocations of the unnarrated explosion that dismembers Stevie, the episode produces an unresolved question about Stevie's motives in the Greenwich bomb affair. Thus the novel's most secret problem of agency is connected to a form of direct action, or sabotage, in the anarcho-syndicalist sense of the term.

If narrative form in *The Secret Agent* is premised on a fundamental elision of social agency, what is elided, together with the propagandist's idea of an awakening proletarian consciousness, is also the narrative principle of a developing consciousness. The basis for, among other things, the "Bildungsroman" and Hegel's *Phenomenology of Spirit*, this narrative principle might be regarded as the phenomenological condition for what we have elsewhere described as the European hypothesis of culture. This principle is violently eclipsed in the obliteration of Stevie, whose perspective becomes the missing narrative term of the novel. The destruction of Stevie's consciousness is a particularly gruesome version of the crisis of modernity—a grisly resolution to that problem of identity and identification presented in the "green wothe" of Joyce's Stephen from *A Portrait of the Artist as a Young Man*; a particularly vivid display of the philosophical crisis of phenomenology associated with Husserl, the *Lebensphilosophen*, and—as we shall discuss in a moment—Henri Bergson's influential attempts to explain the mechanism of consciousness from *Matière et mémoire* (1896) to *L'Evolution créatrice* (1907).

The formal congruity between the medium of political propaganda and literary art is never far from the concerns of Conrad's narratives, and in reframing the anarchist debates of the 1890s, Conrad is also looking back to the origins of his own work as novelist. Some three months before completing his first novel, *Almayer's Folly*, Conrad improvised, in a letter to his aunt Marguerite Poradowska, his own escape as bomb-carrying anarchist from French police agents.[42] This surreal fantasy, in which a work of art gets transformed into an anarchist's bomb, offers a richly suggestive anticipation of *The Secret Agent*. If on the one hand it suggests the containment of anarchist politics through art, it also indicates the political origins of modernist form in an unresolved fantasy of identification with anarchists and anarchism.[43]

This unresolvable fantasy may partly be explained in terms of the ideological function of modernist irony, as analyzed by James English through his sustained attention to the "witty construction" of the fat anarchist in *The Secret Agent*. Drawing on parallels to Bergson's philosophy of laughter (*Le Rire* [1900]), English argues that the "fat anarchist" is a complex index of the "working community" that enables Conrad to resolve the politics of anarchism in what he suggestively calls the "joke-work of counter-revolution."[44] Although English emphasizes the reactionary politics of Conrad's "joke-work," what makes this argument valuable is that it identifies a crucial ambiguity of political perspective in the "ironic method" of *The Secret Agent*. Following English in this direction, we might consider how literary form, in *The Secret Agent*, enacts the full ambiguity of anarchist politics at the beginning of the twentieth century. If Conrad's "joke-work" is itself anarchist in practice (whether revolutionary or counterrevolutionary), perhaps the irony of *The Secret Agent*—and Conrad's literary practice more generally—may be seen to be intricately connected to the political tactic of sabotage as it defines anarcho-syndicalism in the first decades of the century.

An exemplary point of departure for considering the anarchist practice of Conrad's narrative technique is provided by a particularly Bergsonian moment of laughter in *The Secret Agent* that emerges in the following exchange between the Assistant Commissioner and Sir Ethelred:

> "[Verloc's] state of dismay suggested to me an impulsive man who, after committing suicide with the notion that it would end all his troubles, had discovered that it did nothing of the kind." . . .
> A slight jerky movement of the big body half lost in the gloom of the green silk shades, of the big head leaning on the big hand, accompanied

an intermittent stifled but powerful sound. The great man had laughed.
(*TSA*, 220)

The description of Sir Ethelred's laughter is a condensed illustration of what English shows it means to "laugh at the fat anarchist in 1907"—condensed, because, behind the "big" Sir Ethelred and the burly police spy Verloc, it is the incongruity of a disembodied consciousness that is the object of laughter. The incongruity of that impossible consciousness is, moreover, political in a way that leads back to the novel's political premises. In its attempt to capture Verloc's oddly absent-minded anarchist thinking, what the Assistant Commissioner's riddle of consciousness so aptly and humorously describes is not Verloc's state of mind at all, but rather the state of mind the Assistant Commissioner cannot at all figure out—Stevie's state of mind. As the narrative has just emphasized, the Assistant Commissioner's speculations are premised on

> his ignorance of poor Stevie's devotion to Mr. Verloc (who was *good*), and of his truly peculiar dumbness, which in the old affair of fireworks on the stairs had for many years resisted entreaties, coaxing, anger, and other means of investigation used by his beloved sister. For Stevie was loyal.
> (*TSA*, 220)

Metonymically linked to "the old affair of the fireworks," Stevie's act of self-immolation in the Greenwich bombing serves as an unresolved question of political consciousness at the heart of the Assistant Commissioner's extravagant joke and the mechanical Bergsonian laughter it solicits from Sir Ethelred.

Bergsonian philosophy provides a useful point of reference. If, like Bergson's hypothetical motor-mechanism, "consciousness" is considered the result of a combination of "perception-image" and "memory-image," Conrad's irony is generated through a constant ellipsis of the relation between perception and memory.[45] In the above example, there is an extreme disjuncture between the perceptions of the Assistant Commissioner, Sir Ethelred, or the reader's response to these, on the one hand, and the memory of Stevie's dismemberment on the other. As an instance of what Ian Watt has called "delayed decoding," it is interesting for its elision of the "consciousness" Watt posits for the reader's act of "decoding"[46]: the ironic "joke-work" of the description is effective not so much for what is decoded, but rather for what is left out (the incongruous object of laughter, an impossibility of consciousness). Through a process of extended delay—what Cedric Watts, after Watt, calls the "elision or delay of logical connections"[47] and what Jakob Lothe glosses as "analepsis"[48]—such effects accumulate a series of disconnected "memory-images," afterimages of the explosion that cannot be attached to the memory of any of the characters in the novel.

Henri Bergson is only one of a range of thinkers invoked by Conrad's novel. If such figures as Cesare Lombroso and Alfred Russel Wallace provide the coordinates (psychiatry and ethnography, respectively) for reading the novel as an archaeology of nineteenth-century discourses of the human sciences,[49] this dialogization of such discourses constitutes in fact another side of the novel's dialogization of anarchism. One revealing way in which the Bergsonian elements of *The Secret Agent* belong to this genealogy of the anarchist element of the human sciences is in the manner in which Bergson's experiments in consciousness are submitted to ironic transposition as experiments in political consciousness. Laughter, which for Bergson signals "superficial revolts . . . on the surface of life,"[50] for Conrad constitutes an aftereffect of the deepest, most problematic and unresolvable problem of political agency and revolt. The Bergsonian elements in Conrad's novel approximate, rather, Walter Benjamin's critique of Bergson. Bergson's rejection of "any historical determination of memory," according to Benjamin, led him to block out the very experience from which his philosophy arose—the experience, namely, of "the inhospitable, blinding age of big-scale industrialism." Transposing Bergson's own metaphor of the optical "afterimage" from *Matter and Memory*, Benjamin writes:

> In shutting out this experience the eye perceives an experience of a complementary nature in the form of its spontaneous afterimage, as it were. Bergson's philosophy represents an attempt to give the details of this afterimage and to fix it as a permanent record.[51]

The Bergsonian "afterimage," for Benjamin, constitutes the most enduring, most revealing of turn-of-the-century efforts to construct a philosophy of lived experience; he contrasts Bergson's *Matter and Memory*, significantly, with Wilhelm Dilthey's *Das Erlebnis und die Dichtung*, the touchstone for theories of the nineteenth-century Bildungsroman. In this respect, it constitutes a useful point of reference for a range of turn-of-the-century retrospectives on the "age of big-scale industrialism," the nineteenth century. Conrad's "simple tale of the xixth century"—as the dedication to H. G. Wells puts it—offers just such a retrospect, albeit on a rather different scale from the example of Proust's *A la recherche du temps perdu* which Benjamin pursues. The revealing contrast here is rather to Sorel's *Réflexions sur la Violence*, with its application of Bergson's philosophy to the myth of the general strike. Where Sorel turns Bergson's "afterimage" into the instantaneously perceived totality of socialist struggle, however, Conrad's novel presents the Bergsonian "afterimage" as a product of the breakdown between perception and memory. Sorel's and Conrad's Bergsonism might thus be seen to constitute the Janus face—the General Strike and Sabotage—of anarcho-syndicalism around 1907.

No less collective, no less political than Sorel's myth of the General Strike, the Conradian "afterimage" constitutes a stoppage in the relation of a whole body of images (a "solution of continuity, sudden holes in space and time" [*TSA*, 85]) formulating a set of questions about the nexus of industrial production and consumption, commerce, and international politics—questions, as we have sought to show, of sabotage: "the Bomb of Madrid or the Meat of Chicago"; Stevie's fireworks. Arguably the most powerful moments of Conrad's narratives turn on just such effects, in which narrative sequence is disrupted by an eclipse of social agency giving rise to a series of insoluble questions concerning the nexus of industrial relations—as in *Heart of Darkness*, when Marlow encounters, cast aside with the crowd of slave-laborers because they are too weak to be useful, a dying worker with a piece of white thread tied around his neck—"He had tied a bit of white worsted round his neck—Why? Where did he get it? Was it a badge—an ornament—a charm—a propitiatory act? Was there any idea at all connected with it? It looked startling round his black neck, this bit of white thread from beyond the seas."[52]

If Marlow's hysterical breakdown, in *Heart of Darkness*, ultimately displaces the historical specificity of anti-colonial resistance, it provides an important point of reference for the novella's celebrated genealogy of colonial discourses; in a related way, the "joke-work of counterrevolution" in *The Secret Agent* unearths, in its condensation and displacement of anarchism, a genealogy of revolutionary discourses. As the image of the "white worsted" suggests, in its condensed elision of political agency under the labor conditions of international industrial relations, colonial discourses and revolutionary discourses are intricately intertwined. In *The Secret Agent* the knotted geography and politics of this intertwined history of revolution and imperialism comes most clearly into perspective in chapter 10, added after the novel's American serialization, in which the Assistant Commissioner resolves the Greenwich bomb outrage as a problem of geopolitics.

As the detective solution to the Greenwich bomb mystery, the Assistant Commissioner's assertions provide a particularly revealing formulation for that eclipse of social agency that underlies all the forms of propaganda address mimicked and parodied throughout the novel, whether revolutionary or reactionary. It is here—when the Assistant Commissioner confronts Vladimir with his knowledge of the "sham" anarchist bomb plot—that the novel comes closest to formulating the Greenwich bomb plot as "sabotage" in the Hitchcock sense. Not coincidentally, this supplementary chapter reformulates the anarchist plot as a plot of international politics:

> "Look at this outrage; a case specially difficult to trace inasmuch as it was a sham. In less than twelve hours we have established the identity of a man literally blown to shreds, have found the organizer of the attempt, and have had a glimpse of the inciter behind him. And we could have gone further; only we stopped at the limits of our territory."
>
> "So this instructive crime was planned abroad," Mr Vladimir said, quickly. "You admit it was planned abroad?"
>
> "Theoretically. Theoretically only, on foreign territory; abroad only by a fiction," said the Assistant Commissioner, alluding to the character of Embassies which are supposed to be part and parcel of the country to which they belong. (*TSA*, 227–28)

The territorial riddle—"Theoretically . . . on foreign territory; abroad only by a fiction"—reformulates the political meaning of the bomb outrage as a problem of international political intrigue. If the answer to the riddle is provided by the narrative in terms of the peculiar status of embassies, this fails to answer the riddling set of questions of moral, social, and political agency raised by the novel's central, unrepresented action. What the Assistant Commissioner does, instead, is to resolve the political mystery of the Greenwich outrage as a geopolitical riddle.

Both *The Secret Agent* and "sabotage" emerge from the historical knot of issues around which forms of nineteenth-century revolutionary propaganda get reconfigured into the twentieth-century media of propaganda. Already embedded in the polemical "scare" tactics of prewar usage of the term "sabotage" are a set of contested definitions of new industrial relations, the new machinery of the state and the new media of mass communications. Bergsonian philosophy sheds light, also, on the political implications of the novel's inherent preoccupation with cinematography, historically and in terms of narrative technique. In place of a narrative account of the Greenwich bombing, we have a method that might best be termed montage—that process of narrative disruption, of lifting, of editing out, or simple rearrangement of text. Montage is not only to be associated with the photomontage of early-twentieth-century propaganda (to which Walter Benjamin turned in theorizing "the dialectical image"[53]), but also, perhaps more obviously, to the new techniques of film (as practiced and theorized, for example, by Eisenstein[54]).

Perhaps the most extensive analysis of the relation between *The Secret Agent* and *Sabotage* to date, Mark Wollaeger's recent study of Conrad's and Hitchcock's manipulation and mastery argues that the "shock effects" in both novel and film "struggle to compensate for the audience's potential elusiveness by asserting greater control over the artistic materials."[55] This elusiveness of audience, however, like the elusiveness of social agency in modern industrial society, may be more closely bound to the new medium of cinema than Wollaeger's emphasis on artistic mastery here allows. As Gilles Deleuze has pointed out, Bergson's account of the "cinematographic mechanism of thought" (in *L'Evolution créatrice*, published the same year as *The Secret Agent*) is only the most explicit of the many ways in which Bergson's philosophy theorizes the perceptual and conceptual implications of cinema.[56] What *The Secret Agent* shares with Bergsonian philosophy is a similar concern for the perceptual and conceptual disruptions revealed by new technologies of mechanical reproduction and telecommunication. Bergson's example of the "afterimage" is explained in terms of visual and audio recording systems ("We are dealing here with images photographed upon the object itself, and with memories following immediately upon the perception of which they are but the echo"[57]). The Professor's "perfect detonator" is operated by "the principle of the pneumatic instantaneous shutter for a camera lens" (*TSA*, 66). Indeed, Conrad's novel provides a sort of inventory of the range of technologies of mechanical reproduction related to early cinematography, all the more significant in that these are registered in the moment before they get coordinated into the movie industry. Conrad's novel is itself an attempt to grasp the revolutionary potential of film from the vantage point of the first decade of the century, at a moment when cinema had not yet become organized as an international system of mass entertainment, world industry, and the propaganda machinery of nation-states.

Mass Media, Cinematic Narrative, and the Subject of Geopolitics

Relocating Conrad's Brett Street stationery shop as the Bijou cinema house, Hitchcock's *Sabotage* in many ways brilliantly realizes the novel's inherent preoccupation with cinematographic media. Among the complex ironies of Conrad's use of the Dickensian topos of the London shop, as presented already in the novel's opening descriptions of the shop's wares, is the network of connections made between the selling of light entertainment, writing equipment, pornography, and politics. The movie theater conveniently updates the nineteenth-century image of the stationery shop, refiguring the Verlocs' "house, household, and business" around cinema as the nexus of commercial, consumer transactions (see, for example, Figure 15). The transposition is doubly revealing: on the one hand, Hitchcock's Bijou cinema reveals how Conrad's "simple tale of the xixth century" is preoccupied with the politics and technology of mass media. By the same token, however, what Conrad's novel does with the location of its London shop reveals in what sense Hitchcock attempts to reframe the place of cinema in the nostalgic afterimage of an imaginary Victorian social space.[58]

Although both Conrad's London shop and Hitchcock's Bijou cinema house provide interesting locations for a sociological study of different historical moments, in neither case does the narrative pursue such an anthropology of urban space. These social settings are, rather, the fictional pretexts for another sort of story about society—the geopolitics of secret agents and spies, of international intrigue and sabotage. In *The Secret Agent*, the opening sequence of three chapters systematically unfolds the Verloc "house, household, and business" as the overdetermined cover for Verloc's "business" as secret agent both for a foreign embassy and for the British police. In *Sabotage* the corresponding topography is what gets projected in the opening set of montage sequences that implicate Mr. Verloc

FIGURE 15. Still from Alfred Hitchcock, *Sabotage* (1936). Mrs. Verloc (Sylvia Sidney) behind the ticket booth of the Bijou cinema, and Ted (John Loder), the police detective, disguised as a greengrocer.

in the sensational meaning of the title's "sabotage." These effects cast a sinister light over both the cinema house and the neighboring grocery shop, where "Ted" the undercover policeman works. Suspicions about these everyday places of urban life are increasingly confirmed as the film exploits the story of their involvement in something other than the ostensible business of grocery and entertainment, respectively. The movie makes the cinematic labor process itself (an actor acting a grocer; a cinema that makes cinema its setting) the fascinating, sinister, and mistaken other scene of the daily work of everyday life—that everyday life constructed in the opening montage of contrast and collusion between entertainment and industry, signaled by the term "sabotage" itself.

By contrast to Conrad's plot, these narrative displacements from daily work deliberately obscure the terms of Verloc's political "business": the politics of Verloc's circle of co-conspirators is never divulged, nor is their relation to the spy figure who instructs him to blow up Trafalgar Square. This elision of politics constitutes something crucially different from

Conrad's formalism of montage and ellipsis, as is suggested in the moment when Ted, in discussion with his superior is told explicitly that the shady spy plot is none of their business:

> TED: What's the idea, sir? What's the point of all this wrecking?
> SUPERIOR: Making trouble at home to take our minds off what's going on abroad. Same as in a crowd. One man treads on your toe and while you're arguing with him his pal picks your pocket.
> TED: Who's behind it?
> SUPERIOR: Ah, they're the ones you and I'll never catch. It's the men they employ that we're after.

Here we have perhaps the most explicit explanation within a Hitchcock movie of how the famous "MacGuffin" works. As Hitchcock put it to Truffaut, "The 'MacGuffin' is the term we use to cover all that sort of thing: to steal plans or documents, or discover a secret, it doesn't matter what it is.... The only thing that really matters is that in the picture the plans, documents, or secrets must seem to be of vital importance to the characters."[59] The MacGuffin thus signals the cinematic narrative principle whereby the "picture" is organized around a matter of great geopolitical interest (plans, documents, or secrets) that turns out to be, as Hitchcock goes on to explain to Truffaut, "nothing at all."

If the MacGuffin in *Sabotage* is the sinister foreign plot to cause widespread wreckage and alarm in London, it is instructive to note that this plot is generated by a geopolitical problem—sabotage—which must then in turn be rendered insignificant. Thus, the movie's three acts of sabotage can be read as a series of narrative displacements replicating the ideological containment embedded in the history of the term "sabotage." With each explosion, the ostensible political meaning of the act becomes less and less important for the viewer's narrative and dramatic investment, until, with the Professor's suicidal destruction of the Bijou cinema house itself, the explosion successfully obliterates all meaningful political considerations by leaving us with the psychological trauma of Mrs. Verloc, whose act of murder has now effectively been covered up. The sensational geopolitical catchword "sabotage" is resolved as a metaphor for the psychological drama of Mrs. Verloc's crime, all the more powerful for internalizing an unrepresented, unrepresentable global politics of international relations.

This psychological screening of geopolitics rewrites the effect of Stevie's obliterated perspective from Conrad's novel, with its disturbing accumulation of so many afterimages of Stevie's self-annihilation. Hitchcock reconstitutes these in an oddly Victorianized family plot—transposing, most notably, the detail of the fruitseller's stall from *The Secret Agent* into a greengrocer's stall, the cover for Ted the policeman. Where, in Conrad's novel, the "violent blaze of light and colour" of the Brett Street fruitseller's store, with its "glowing heaps of oranges and lemons" (*TSA*, 150) twice evokes the violence of Stevie's dismemberment, Hitchcock makes the fruitstand a sign of working community, connecting the movie theater to a nexus of everyday buying and selling (see Figure 15). *Sabotage* insists on a kind of stereotyped evocation of Victorian elements—for instance, in the protracted moments of delay during which Stevie is waylaid by all the forms of commercial distraction and entertainment that characterize an imagined plenitude of busy London social life, clocked as these nonetheless are against the inevitable detonation of the time bomb. Stevie, for Hitchcock's *Sabotage*, represents a kind of disproportionate innocence, not so much in psychological terms as in terms of the movie's overall manipulation of the cinematic labor process. He is the slapstick fall guy—comically enacting the everyday slips of domestic labor in his opening debut as substitute cook; later, slipping on the banana peel on his way between the house and the grocer's stall. If Hitchcock was later to regret the extent to which Stevie's fate is deliberately manipulated through the viewer's unwilling suspense of the inevitable, that regret distracts from the more revealing ways in which Stevie's acts call attention to the sinister register attached to all those everyday stagings of family life.

It is by means of this sort of manipulation of the cinematic labor process that Hitchcock reframes the ironies of Conrad's Victorian "anarchism" around the polemical postwar meaning of "sabotage." In the film's inaugurating shift from the machinery of industry to the workings of the entertainment industry, the contrast not only plays on a secret affinity between the technology of film-entertainment and that of modern industrial society. It also formulates the manner in which Hitchcock's movies characteristically turn inside out the expected relation of modes of production to modes of consumption. Turning from the places of industrial production (the factory; the electrical generator; and the transportation network) to the place of everyday entertainment and consumption, *Sabo-*

tage coordinates the relation of work to leisure precisely by disrupting the contrast.[60] There is thus an unconscious logic connecting the final explosion of the Bijou cinema with the opening act of sabotage: even as it buries the plot of political motivations for the wrecking, it enacts the full extent of destructive wreckage of industry by targeting the cinema itself. The syndicalist meaning of "sabotage," repressed in the title sequence, returns to recast the entire movie, in retrospect, as a disruption of the cinematographic labor process.

Thus the psychological drama internalized in Mrs. Verloc is clinched by thematizing the rudimentary cinematographic effect of the afterimage produced in the succession of moving images. Immediately before the explosion, Mrs. Verloc has proclaimed, of Verloc, "He's dead." The confession, however, is misunderstood by the Chief of Police, Ted's superior, who, in the aftershock of the explosion, forgets whether Mrs. Verloc's words occurred before or after the detonation. This effect, essential for sustaining the psychologized trauma of Mrs. Verloc's tortured conscience as the narrative closure of the film, recalls Bergson's example of the optical "afterimage" (or "image consécutive") as an illustration of the motor-mechanism unifying "perception-image" and "memory-image" into "global knowledge." The "motor-mechanism" at work here, of course, is cinematography, as organized by the historical emergence of narrative cinema between 1907 and 1936; the historical development of montage (as traced by Gilles Deleuze, for example); and the historical coordination of the Bergsonian "afterimage" as alternatively explained by Walter Benjamin with respect to the shock effects of the new mass media. The closure of *Sabotage* provides an interesting counterpoint to Benjamin's critique of Bergson. The shock effect that makes the police chief unable to know whether Mrs. Verloc spoke before or after the explosion provides narrative closure around a peculiar auditory afterimage which successfully psychologizes the "blinding age of big-scale industrialism" as Mrs. Verloc's traumatic experience of loss and murder (triangulated through nostalgic and guilty attachment to a familial illusion).

The conclusion of the movie only confirms what is given at the beginning: Mrs. Verloc's compromised position—in the beginning, as ticket-seller in the enclosed glass booth at the front of the cinema—defines the problematic relation of mass consumption to mass production. The fact that Sylvia Sidney, the well-known American film star, is put in the compromised position of directly confronting dissatisfied customers is a witty combination of discrepant elements of cinematography—the Hollywood star system and the business of film distribution in Britain following the Cinematograph Films Act of 1927.[61] Entirely in keeping with the film's preoccupation with the cinematographic labor process, the joke prefigures the ways in which the syndicalist meaning of sabotage gets reconfigured as the unconscious geopolitical meaning of cinema.

Most revealing, in this regard, is the scene of Mrs. Verloc's distracted capture before the movie screen, in the moments before she kills her husband with the carving knife. The figure of woman as worker and as consumer poses, at the nexus of production and consumption, an exemplary problem of the cinematic subject—positioned, indeed, as Mrs. Verloc herself is at the outset, at the impossible virtual coordinating point of a variety of movements of mass and media. The Disney cartoon sequence "Who Killed Cock Robin?" that captivates her momentarily, in the end only confirms, as one might expect, her own narrative dilemma: although the cartoon of one bird serenading another initially distracts her attention, the arrow shot that kills Cock Robin (together with the abrupt change of musical rhythm and chorusing of the title's question) returns her to the fact of Stevie's death.

This complex identification with the cartoon offers something like a counterpoint to the perceptual blur that remains as the afterimage of Stevie's obliterated consciousness in Conrad's novel. The fantasy of identification is not only sexually overdetermined through the auditory, visual, and narrative encoding of a male gaze (the female bird responds to Cock Robin's crooning through animated coy bodily gestures, batting eyelids, and the words "Hmmmm, you flatter me"). The sequence also presents a most suggestive, if highly ambiguous ethnographic fantasm of a cartoon bird masquerading as Southern white belle.

The Disney cartoon that captivates, while confirming the dominance of Hollywood both on the Bijou's cinema screen and in the running allusions to Sylvia Sidney's status as American star, nonetheless stands out from the other citations (as it does in the closing credit sequence, too). The cartoon images stand out by way of framing, in reverse as it were, the surrounding narrative fiction of the daily business of living and entertainment, of customers, dinner, and family. The Disney image, as the foregrounded sign of an international distribution and consumption of cinematography, sets, against the obscure politics of European foreign affairs, an hallucinatory transnational imagined community. This transatlantic fantasy—what might be called, echoing Paul Gilroy's formulation of the "black atlantic,"[62] the fantasy of a white atlantic—frames an ethnographic Victorian phantasm of Englishness—the Verloc family—which is the impossible social ideal in whose afterimage Mrs. Verloc's guilt or innocence, following the murder, will be affixed.

This indicates a key direction in which the movies of Hitchcock's transatlantic period consolidate the containment of the syndicalist meaning of sabotage. Worker and consumer both get positioned within a characteristically controlled family plot. The impossible position of Mrs. Verloc ("The Woman Alone," as *Sabotage* was renamed for American consumption), more generally the impossible position in which Hitchcock's women are characteristically put, is the split scene of production and consumption. By relocating Conrad's Brett Street shop to the Bijou theater, Hitchcock is able to locate the split scene of international labor and domestic consumption as a movie screen and in the home, anticipating the now familiar place and organizing function of the television screen.

Sabotage and the Geopolitics of Screenplay

This split scene of international labor and domestic consumption reveals the logic of sabotage unifying the whole series of movies Hitchcock made in the period of his transatlantic crossover to Hollywood, from *The Secret Agent* (1936) to *Saboteur* (1942). This is the logic of territorial loyalty, sexual betrayal, and impossible ethnic affiliation writ large across the American landscape of *Saboteur*. Pursued as saboteur and himself in pursuit of the saboteur, the hero's flight is mirrored by the heroine who attends him both as partner-in-flight and as a fixture of the American landscape, an image looking on from advertising billboards. The utopian American landscape of Hitchcock's *Saboteur*, prefigured in the earlier English and Scottish settings of *The Thirty-Nine Steps* and remapped in *North by Northwest*,[63] is nothing other than the place of the Hollywood film industry itself. In response to Truffaut's suggestion that he "didn't want to come here as a tourist, but as a film director," Hitchcock responded: "But I wasn't in the least interested in Hollywood as a place. The only thing I cared about was to get into a studio to work."[64] It is the effort to coordinate that "work"—the whole cinematographic labor process—that unifies the series of movies of Hitchcock's transatlantic crossover.

"Sabotage" names the ambiguity of Hitchcock's turn to Hollywood, simultaneously the utopia and the business reality of filmmaking.[65] This ambiguity surfaces in the interplay between literary texts and motion pictures from *The Secret Agent* to *Saboteur*. Discussing the trouble with *Saboteur*, Hitchcock singled out its undisciplined script and went on to argue, "This raises a big problem in American film-making, the difficulty of finding a responsible writer who is competent at building and sustaining the fantasy of the story."[66] Screenplay, an essential part of the cinematographic labor process, must reorganize text into cinematic narrative to shape that transatlantic fantasy of identity and identification framed around the geopolitical Disney image of *Sabotage*.

This emerges even in those movies of the transatlantic sequence that seem the least concerned with sabotage: *Young and Innocent* (1937), *Jamaica Inn* (1939), and *Rebecca* (1940). Hitchcock's appropriation of literary texts written by women (Josephine Tey and Daphne Du Maurier) organizes a gendered rivalry between visual image and literary text—what Hitchcock himself, discussing *Rebecca* with Truffaut, characterized as a rivalry between the "Hitchcock picture" and "a whole school of feminine literature."[67] Of decisive significance for Hitchcock's manipulation of the male gaze that, according to Laura Mulvey's classic argument, structures the narrative form of Hollywood cinema,[68] this complex rivalry between male visual and female literary modes also reveals an imperative to appropriate a feminine narrative geography (the more or less Victorian English landscapes of Josephine Tey and Daphne Du Maurier) to organize cinematography. Although *Young and Innocent* is the film most relevant for discussion here, the increasingly hallucinatory English landscapes of all three films (most memorably *Rebecca*'s Manderley) are governed by the same social riddle of territorial and sexual betrayal and loyalty that binds together, against an American landscape, the factory worker and advertising model of *Saboteur*.

Hitchcock's use of Josephine Tey's mystery, *A Shilling for Candles*, as the basis for the screenplay of the movie after *Sabotage*, *Young and Innocent*, likely stems in part from Tey's own fascination with cinematic form (something Tey's work shares with Du Maurier's). Full of allusions to cinema, *A Shilling for Candles* is premised on the fact that the murder victim is the famous American film star, Christine Clay. In the introductory revelation of the murder victim, Tey weaves into the fabric of the story's suspense a set of references to film production and direction, beginning with the humming of "a bar of 'Sing to me sometimes'" which inaugurates the conversation between the sergeant and the songwriter Jay Harmer:

> "Perhaps you haven't seen *Bars of Iron* yet?"
> "No, I can't say I have."
> "That's the worst of wireless and gramophone records and what not: they take all the pep out a film. Probably by the time you hear Chris sing that song you'll be so sick of the sound of it that you'll retch at the ad lib. It's not fair to a film. All right for songwriters and that sort of cattle, but rough on a film, very rough. There ought to be some sort of agreement."[69]

Related media—radio, gramophone, and cinematography—are here configured as rival elements in a labor process whose idealized hegemonic form is the film industry. Jay Harmer's film metaphors are sustained—along with the ambiguity of his own place in the murder plot—when, unwittingly revealing the murder victim's identity, he confesses that he is planning to leave the famous film star, "for treating me like bits on the cutting-room floor."[70]

As with the relocation of Conrad's Brett Street stationery into the Bijou cinema of *Sabotage*, Hitchcock's use of Tey's *A Shilling for Candles* as the basis for *Young and Innocent* reveals a dialectical interplay of complicitous knowledge and innocent ignorance of the film industry. While Tey condenses the cinematic labor process in the suspicious (but ultimately innocent) figure of the Jewish songwriter Jay Harmer, Hitchcock's film displaces that figure entirely, reframing the plot around the relatively minor character of the young Erica Burgoyne. There is a deliberate irony in the fact that Hitchcock enlarges the role of the only two characters from Tey's book (the young Erica and the innocent murder suspect) who seem to know the least about movies. If Jay Harmer's complicitous knowledge of film gets displaced by Hitchcock's screenplay, ignorance of the film industry is translated as the "innocent" motif of the title's *Young and Innocent*. The equation is all the more striking by contrast to the everyday familiarity with cinema that casts so sinister a shadow over *Sabotage*.

The dialectic of this screenplay involves the coordination of a range of media—primarily gramophone, radio, and cinematography, as Tey's mystery conceives it—into the coherent fiction of a "Hitchcock picture." The famous concluding sequence to *Young and Innocent* offers a classic example of such coordination in Hitchcock's manipulation of the long tracking shot that begins with the camera's sweeping panorama of a crowded Brighton restaurant and ends with a close-up of the nervous twitching of eyes that identifies the murderer disguised as the blackface band's drummer. According to Žižek, this tracking shot illustrates one of the two principal forms of the "Hitchcockian blot": specifically, when "the blot" or "terminal point of the tracking shot" forms "the gaze of the other insofar as our position as spectator is already inscribed within the film—i.e. the point from which the picture itself gazes at us."[71]

What identifies the blackface drummer is not only the camera's manipulation of the viewer's gaze as it is directed inexorably toward the guilty man's involuntary blinking. As part of the film's overall condensation and displacement of film, the virtuoso effect of the scene depends on a particular coordination of background music, words, and narrative. The number the band plays—"No one can like the drummer man"—not only adumbrates the concluding close-up. It also takes up the theme used in the film's opening title sequence and thus, in text and sound, invokes the murderous twitching of eyes with which the movie begins, producing an unconscious optics of cinematic production. Recalling Josephine Tey's film analogies in establishing the murder victim's identity, the virtuosity of Hitchcock's concluding revelation of the murderer's identity depends on a corresponding anatomy of the different media of voice, image, and text. As with the scene of Mrs. Verloc's viewing the Walt Disney cartoon, this scene constitutes a complex reframing of the culture industry which itself inscribes the cinematic labor process in a kind of blindspot (following the elementary grammar of what Rothman baptized the "murderous gaze").[72]

The blindspot, in each case, is the emergence of an impossible cinematic subject, an impossible coincidence of mass and individual audience, of consuming and producing social agents. This impossibility emerges in *Young and Innocent* through a double masquerade—of class position (the aristocratic Champneis passing as band member) and race (the blackface). Such masquerade produces an ethnographic hallucination of white racial identity through which the film registers, even as it renders unconscious, the cinematic labor process. The blackface of the blinking drummer in *Young and Innocent*, and the Southern white belle pose of the cartoon's Cock Robin in *Sabotage* each constitute complex ethnographic masquerades. To be sure, there is something different going on in the transatlantic fantasy of the Walt Disney cartoon and the affixing of guilt through blackface entertainment. The two are sharply differentiated as an older to a newer form of entertainment. While the Disney cartoon frames a hallucination of Victorian culture, blackface entertainment itself constitutes Victorian culture framed: not as the truth of ethnic identity unveiled, but as the remotivation of another regime of ethnic and international masquerade—the geopolitical fiction of a white atlantic.[73]

The location of this fiction is revealed in *Sabotage* to be the cinema screen itself, a logic reiterated in *Saboteur* as the split scene of cinematic production and consumption. This emerges at the narrative turning point in the flight of hero and heroine across America. Arriving in Soda City after their adventurous concealment from the police by a train of circus performers, the hero and heroine encounter a deserted factory town. The uncannily desolate industrial scene seems part of a cynical joke-work at the expense of the very American heartland threatened with sabotage. The point, as it turns out, is that hero, heroine, and viewer misrecognize the industrial significance of the scene. The narrative effect of this, the second of the movie's three sabotage sites, depends on leading characters and viewers alike from the uncanny scene of a ghost town for a deserted factory to the industrial apparatus of a hydroelectric dam, the target of the movie's Nazi saboteurs. In order to recognize the connection between the deserted workyard and the hydroelectric dam, the couple must together reconstruct the one as a site for making the other a target of sabotage. It is in this passage from ignorance to knowledge that the movie makes almost explicit the parallels between the methods of the filmmaker and the methods of the saboteur.

Drawn to a peculiarly bright circle of light, then to the aperture that lets the sunlight in, hero and heroine gradually reconstruct the saboteurs' apparatus of surveillance. The heroine discovers first the tripod, and then (pausing long enough to suggest the camera which the heroine in fact almost locates) the telescope that reveals the hydroelectric dam. Only by recognizing the conspiratorial system of surveillance and communication, can hero, heroine, and viewer make the connection between different kinds of industry—from the soda factory to the hydroelectric dam. The circular patch of sunlight is, for *Saboteur*, what Žižek calls the "Hitchcockian blot." Only after it is recognized as that rudimentary physiological principle of cinematography—the projection of light through an aperture—does it signal the conspiratorial complex of organized sabotage. Prefigured by the auditory blot of a telephone ringing, the visual clue of the blot of sunlight is already part of a hidden logic of social relations coordinating the most rudimentary forms of harnessing natural energy (sunlight, minerals, water) with the work of big-scale industrialism (the hydroelectric dam)—and mapping in turn the political geography of the heartland, the metropolis, and the world.

If the image of the sunblot precipitates a knowledge of the saboteur's methods, it does so by calling attention to an elementary reversibility of the optical image. The reversibility of the image functions in a number of ways to organize the scene: enhancing the suspense of the basic chase plot in which the one pursued as saboteur is himself in pursuit of the saboteur, the opportunity simultaneously to discover or be discovered also confirms the ambiguity of the saboteur motif. Indeed, it is only in this central moment in the plot that the title assumes the full ambiguity of its meaning: in order to sabotage sabotage, the hero must himself become a saboteur (which is what happens, with the result that this is the only one of the three intended acts of sabotage that is foiled).

This problem of loyalty, inherent in sabotage, is redoubled in the heroine's relation to the hero. The blot of sunlight organizes a fundamentally ambiguous narrative perspective on the conflicted loyalties with which she is made to attend the hero's journey. All at once consolidating her complicitous involvement in the hero's flight, the knowledge each shares about the apparatus of sabotage ultimately confirms her prior suspicion that he has "a saboteur's disposition." In one of those seemingly gratuitous examples of Hitchcockian misogyny, the hero's impersonation of a saboteur, once discovered by the real saboteurs, rises to an almost hysterical pitch when a sound betrays the presence of the concealed heroine not only to the real saboteurs but also to our hero, who seems unaccountably clueless as to how to incorporate her into his saboteur act. The hero's moment of forgetfulness—repeated many frames later when he unexpectedly rediscovers the heroine held captive by the Nazi saboteurs in New

York—in fact serves all the more to emphasize the impossible position of women that defines the geopolitics of Hitchcock's screenplays.

In much the same way that the auditory afterimage of the final explosion in *Sabotage* works to psychologize as Mrs. Verloc's trauma the shock-effect of big-scale industrialism, the blot of sunlight organizes a reversible narrative and temporal logic. Prefiguring the heroine's knowledge and complicity in the saboteur plot, it also serves as the entoptical afterimage of her own face caught in the light of the policemen's flashlight during the search of the circus train in the previous sequence. The look of her face in that moment of symbolic capture by a whole series of paternal figures (her blind uncle, the police, and the bearded lady of the circus) brings together in a single subjectified image the dialectic of objectified advertising images that attend the hero on his journey through the American heartland. Having been identified by Esmeralda, the bearded circus lady, as one of the "good people in the world," she is bound to uphold the masquerade of the circus actors' democratic vote to protect the couple from the police. The impossible double-bind of her position, having somehow to avoid betraying herself as the "good-looking ... dame" the police are looking for, subjects her look to a complex miniature study in the meaning of "good looks." The afterimage of this look, the blot of sunlight psychologizes the apparatus of industrial wartime sabotage as the impossibility of her own loyalties and identifications.

This impossibility of either loyalty or betrayal is what is projected across the American landscape of *Saboteur* in the form of the three consecutive advertising images of the heroine that attend the hero's journey. Organizing the comic screenplay of text and image in the witty exchange between the hero's gaze and the heroine's advertising images, the logic of "good looks" produces an hallucinatory identification with a look caught between the masquerade of circus freaks and the celebrity of an advertising model.

The double-bind of the heroine's "good" looks in *Saboteur*, the Disney cartoon in *Sabotage*, and the eye-twitching of the blackface drummer of *Young and Innocent* each constitutes a different side of the same underlying fantasy motivating the sequence of transatlantic movies: the utopian fantasy of coordinating the different media of the film industry into what Adorno and Horkheimer characterized as the dystopia of the Culture Industry. The riddle of subjectivity and representation in each delineates the impossible ideal of cinema, the industrialized management and direction of social relations. To realize this ideal Hitchcock consistently returns to the motif of sabotage, in order to imply the hidden coordination of a whole complex of organized industry, international labor, and world politics.

The mirage of subjectivity and ethnographic hallucination of whiteness in all the movies of Hitchcock's transatlantic crossover is a product of the same classic problem of international labor and sabotage. This is already suggested by the text of Josephine Tey's novel, whose plot resolution is significantly altered by Hitchcock's *Young and Innocent*. In order to frame the coming-of-age story of the "innocent" young star, actress Nova Pilbeam, the screenplay eliminates an elaborate subplot in the mystery novel. The change of subjects appears a deliberate reframing of the novel's and film's shared concern with sabotage. In Tey's novel, Jay Harmer belongs to an elaborate conspiracy that casts suspicion on Christine Clay's estranged husband, the aristocratic Champneis, who champions the cause of Galeria, an obscure, invented country "east of Europe."[74] Recasting this geopolitical plot, Hitchcock's screenplay fixes guilt on the Champneis figure after all—not, however, to eliminate entirely the string of ethnic and racial stereotypes that constitute suspense in Tey's mystery, but all the more effectively to form cinematic narrative around the production of a geopolitical unconscious.

In *Young and Innocent* Hitchcock does not need the sensational fiction of geopolitics announced in the title motifs of *Sabotage* and *Saboteur*. It is already embedded in the cinematographic effects that go toward the making of the movie's "Hitchcockian blot." Once the camera has identified the murderer as the drummer man, all that is needed to finish the movie is, literally, to break up entertainment. To do this, the film does not provide the spectacle of blowing up the cinema house, which concludes *Sabotage*. Nor does it stage the kind of spectacular disruption of cinema evoked by the giant image of the screaming woman on screen in *Saboteur*—which presides over the saboteur Frei's anarchic intrusion into a movie theater, in the final chase scene of that film, and which constitutes a hystericized moving afterimagining of the heroine's "good" looks. *Young and Innocent*, however, ends in a way that corresponds in some respects more closely to the real meaning of sabotage. Between the involuntary nervous twitching of his eyes and the drugs taken to soothe his nerves, the drummer man cannot but confess his guilt by destroying the coordination of music, text, and image on which entertainment depends ("I pay someone else to make the orchestration," the conductor explains to him in between numbers). Destroying the music, the drummer man disrupts the culture industry of entertainment. In its allusive reference to a historical complex of overlapping systems of culture, industry, and labor, this symptomatic form of involuntary sabotage unravels the fiction of geopolitics sensationalized in the titles of *Sabotage* and *Saboteur*.

Coda

Sabotage thus organizes the series of movies from the period of Hitchcock's transatlantic crossing. Hitchcock's celebrated mastery of narrative cinema, and of Hollywood, constitutes an extended and systematic attempt to screen industrial political relations. In the process, and by way of coordinating the cinematographic labor process itself, these films symptomatically reenact the historical polemic over sabotage from the 1890s to the 1940s, revealing "sabotage" as the contradictory principle of organization for modern industrial society. This is the contradiction rehearsed in the first full scene of *Sabotage*, when the blackout caused by Verloc's act of sabotage produces a restive theater crowd angry at not being able to view the film. In the sudden shift from the machinery of industry to the entertainment industry, the inner connection between the two is exposed as the contradictory working and breakdown of modern industrial society.

Hitchcock's films replay the prehistory of the term "sabotage"—both in its anarchist and syndicalist meaning, and in the ideological containment of that meaning. The sensational charge of the term as a keyword in the formation of geopolitical discourses in the 1940s draws from that complex of contested meanings whereby the old nineteenth-century Specter of international communism gets reconfigured into the world war-time threat of sabotage. As Hitchcock's movies thus suggest, the work of geopolitical thinking takes place not so much as the labor of those geographers and geography books classified as "geopolitical." Geopolitics rather, is the work—and play—of fiction; the twentieth-century attempt to coordinate audio, visual, and textual media to imagine the fiction of an organized coherence of world political relations

REFERENCE MATTER

Notes

Introduction

1. See, in particular, O Tuathail, *Critical Geopolitics*, Agnew, *Geopolitics*, and O Tuathail, Dalby, and Routledge, *The Geopolitics Reader*.
2. Agnew, *Geopolitics*, 2.
3. GoGwilt, *The Invention of the West*.
4. Anderson adapts the phrase from Seton-Watson. See Anderson, *Imagined Communities*, 86.
5. For the relevance of this term both for the nineteenth-century culture-complex and for the twentieth-century power-complex of geopolitics, see the recent anthology of essays edited by Cheah and Robbins, *Cosmopolitics*. See, in particular, Cheah's Introduction (20–41) and his essay, "Given Culture: Rethinking Cosmopolitical Freedom in Transnationalism" (290–328).
6. Hobsbawm, *The Age of Empire*, 119.
7. Laclau and Mouffe, *Hegemony and Socialist Strategy*.
8. See the definition in the *Oxford English Dictionary*: "Leadership, predominance, preponderance; esp. the leadership or predominant authority of one state of ancient Greece, whence transferred to German states, and in other modern applications." See also the O.E.D. citation from the London *Times* (5 May 1860): "No doubt it is a glorious ambition which drives Prussia to assert her claim to the leadership, or as that land of professors phrases it, the 'hegemony' of the German Confederation." For Bismarck's formulation, "a Union- or Hegemony-politics," see Bismarck, *Gedanken und Erinnerungen*, 2:20.

Somerset Maugham's short story, "The Traitor" (one of the two stories used as the basis for the screenplay of Hitchcock's *The Secret Agent*) offers a concise illustration of the word's meaning for the fiction of geopolitics. Of the wife of the "traitor," Ashenden explains: "Her ideal was a German world in which the rest of the nations under a hegemony greater than that of Rome should enjoy the benefits of

German science and German art and German culture." See Maugham, *Collected Short Stories*, 3, 139.

9. One of the most interesting of the many contributions to this topic, which I do not directly take up in discussion here, is Derrida's *Specters of Marx*. This work, along with related considerations on "what has been promised under the name of Europe" (in, for example, *The Other Heading*, *The Gift of Death*, and *Aporias*) constitute an extended meditation on what I'm calling the fiction of geopolitics. It is in *Specters of Marx* that Derrida argues, about the "specter" of communism heralded at the beginning of *The Communist Manifesto*, that the communism announced there inaugurated geopolitics: "No organized political movement in the history of humanity had ever yet presented itself as *geo-political*, thereby inaugurating the space that is now ours and that today is reaching its limits, the limits of the earth and the limits of the political" (38).

10. Lyotard, *The Postmodern Condition*.

11. Kittler, *Discourse Networks, 1800/1900*.

12. O Tuathail, *Critical Geopolitics*, 24.

13. See Derek Gregory's discussion of the "ocularcentrism" of geography in *Geographical Imaginations*.

14. See the chronology by Meda Mladek and Margit Rowell in Kupka, *Frantisek Kupka, 1871-1957*, 311.

15. Rowell, "Frantisek Kupka," in Kupka, *Frantisek Kupka 1871-1957*, 73.

16. Crary, *Techniques of the Observer*, 16.

17. Žižek, *Looking Awry*, 88–106.

18. Truffaut, *Hitchcock*, 138.

19. Ibid.

20. Ibid.

21. Richards, *The Imperial Archive*. Richards explores "what it means to think the fictive thought of imperial control" (2) through a range of novels—Kipling's *Kim*, Stoker's *Dracula*, Wells's *Tono-Bungay*, and Childers's *Riddle of the Sands*.

22. Nadel, *Containment Culture*.

23. For the idea of the "world-system," see Immanuel Wallerstein's entry on the topic in Bottomore, *Dictionary of Marxist Thought*, 590–91. For a survey of world-systems analysis, see Hopkins and Wallerstein, *World-Systems Analysis*. See also Wallerstein, *The Politics of the World-Economy* and *Geopolitics and Geoculture*.

Chapter 1

1. Joyce, *Portrait of the Artist*, 7.

2. Joyce, *Portrait of the Artist*, 12–13.

3. Joyce, *Portrait of the Artist*, 15.

4. The most recent surveys are to be found in O Tuathail, *Critical Geopolitics*, Agnew, *Geopolitics*, and O Tuathail, Dalby, and Routledge, *The Geopolitics Reader*. For earlier book-length surveys, see Parker, *Western Geopolitical Thought in the*

Twentieth Century, and O'Sullivan, *Geopolitics*. See also Kern, *The Culture of Time and Space*, Smith, *Uneven Development*, and Soja, *Postmodern Geographies*.

5. Although this is not a diagnosis of the current state of cultural studies, the parallels are particularly interesting, given that geopolitical problems occupy something of a central position in cultural studies today. Some indications include, generally, the prominence of geography and geographers in recent debates within cultural studies (see, in particular, Gregory, *Geographical Imaginations*); and the intersection of these concerns with directions in postcolonial studies (see, for example, Said, *Culture and Imperialism*, Pratt, *Imperial Eyes*, and Mitchell, *Colonising Egypt*).

6. Joyce, *Portrait of the Artist*, 17.

7. See, in particular, O Tuathail, *Critical Geopolitics*.

8. For accounts of the German concept of "Bildung," see Mücke, *Virtue and the Veil of Illusion*, especially chapter 4. See also Richter, *Der Wandel des Bildungsgedankens*. For more general discussions of the idea of "Bildung" throughout the nineteenth century, see note 27 below. For some of the numerous discussions of the "Bildungsroman," see note 17 to Chapter 2.

9. Arnold translates Wilhelm Humboldt's ideal of "Bildung" in the epigraph for his report on education, *Schools and Universities on the Continent*. The idea of "Bildung," discussed in that work (177), also shapes the spirit and title of *Culture and Anarchy*. As Raymond Williams suggests, this blurring of the senses of "culture" is by no means merely an English "Bildung"-effect (see Williams, *Keywords*, 91, and his *Culture and Society*). Nor is it only the European and North American "Bildung"-effect Lyotard describes. As Gauri Viswanathan has shown, the colonial shaping of educational ideals opens the translation-effect of "culture" to a great many more inflections (see *Masks of Conquest*).

10. Mackinder, *The Scope and Methods of Geography*, 194.

11. "Geography must be a continuous argument, and the test of whether a given point is to be included or not must be this:—Is it pertinent to the main line of argument?" (ibid., 24).

12. Ibid., 16.

13. In his survey, "Recent Discussion on the Scope and Educational Applications of Geography," the Scottish geographer A. J. Herbertson, another champion of the "new geography" in education who collaborated with Mackinder in setting up the Geographical Institute at Oxford, provides an indication of the variety of competing terminologies for Mackinder's distinction between "physical geography" and "political geography." In addition to those mentioned, although with an emphasis on discussing Ratzel, he also refers to the American geographer W. M. Davis, whose term "ontography" is contrasted to "physical geography" (4).

14. Ratzel, *Anthropo-Geographie oder Grundzüge der Anwendung der Erdkunde auf die Geschichte*, 1:20 [hereafter cited as *Anthropogeographie* I]. All translations from Ratzel's work are my own unless otherwise noted.

15. Ratzel, *Anthropogeographie* I, 22.

16. This is the story Woodruff Smith takes up in *Politics and the Sciences of Culture in Germany*. It is notable that Friedrich Ratzel is the main figure in that story. For accounts of Ratzel's work, see also Buttmann, *Friedrich Ratzel*, and Hunter, *Perspectives on Ratzel's Political Geography*. For selected extracts of Ratzel's work in English translation, see Dorpalen, *The World of General Haushofer*.

17. Besides the studies of geopolitics listed above, see also the volume of essays edited by Godlewska and Smith, *Geography and Empire*, especially their Introduction, 2–3; and Sandner and Rössler, "Geography and Empire in Germany," 115–27.

18. Mackinder, *Democratic Ideals and Reality*, 26 (Mackinder's emphasis).

19. I use the term "official nationalism" in the sense developed by Benedict Anderson's adaptation from Seton-Watson. See Anderson, *Imagined Communities*, 86.

20. "Germany may be taken as the model which all the other Continental countries are following" (Keltie, *Geographical Education*, 37). It should be noted that Keltie presents Germany as a model for education at both the primary and the university levels.

21. The "Instruction" is included, Keltie writes, to counter objections "to the recognition of geography by the Universities that it is not a 'manly' subject, but one fit only for elementary classes" (Keltie, *Geographical Education*, 30).

22. Ibid., 111.

23. Ibid.

24. See Dorpalen, *The World of General Haushofer*, 16.

25. Reclus, *L'Homme et la Terre*, 2:622, cited in the Introduction (1:64) to Béatrice Giblin's 1982 edition [hereafter cited as Reclus, *L'Homme et la Terre*, ed. Giblin]. All translations from Reclus's work are my own unless otherwise stated.

26. For this point and on Reclus generally, see Fleming, *The Anarchist Way to Socialism*.

27. Lyotard, *The Postmodern Condition*, 31. Lyotard's argument traces two major versions of this narrative—the first, "more political" one, whose subject is "humanity as the hero of liberty," is associated with the politics of French primary education; the second, "more philosophical" version, Lyotard traces back to the ideals of German "Bildung" (education/culture) as instituted with Wilhelm Humboldt's founding of the University of Berlin. What Lyotard suggestively calls the "Bildung"-effect of the second higher-educational ideal of "the disinterested pursuit of learning" (32) has a particular bearing on what I call here the hypothesis of culture in the most general sense. It is a "Bildung"-effect, for example, that shapes Matthew Arnold's notion of culture in *Culture and Anarchy*. Already evident in Arnold's translation of the ideal of German "Bildung" is the attempted combination of the politics of primary education and the political contradictions of higher-educational ideals. If Reclus's unwavering insistence on the quest for liberty suggests Lyotard's first "narrative of freedom," Reclus (a student of Carl Ritter at Berlin) also held to the ideals of that second, "more philosophical" narrative associated with the model of German higher education. The hero, for Reclus, was *both* science *and* liberty.

28. Reclus, *The Universal Geography*, 1:3. Translation from the English edition edited by Ravenstein.
29. Cited in Williams, *Keywords*, 89; see Herder, *Ideen*, 8, 335. All further translations from Herder, unless otherwise stated, are my own.
30. Herder, *Ideen*, 20, 897.
31. Ibid., 47.
32. Ibid., 47–48.
33. Cf. Pheng Cheah's argument in "Given Culture," in Cheah and Robbins, *Cosmopolitics*, 290–328. Cheah argues that the unresolved problem of nineteenth-century cosmopolitics turns on what he calls the "given"-ness of culture. While the canonical culture-concept posits culture as the realm of human freedom over nature, the "objective dimension" of culture, of our cultural activity in the most general sense, paradoxically presents culture as the given, natural world over which we would exercise our freedom (see p. 308). To the extent that Herder's argument here reproduces just this aporia, we might adapt Cheah's formulation to characterize the nineteenth-century culture-concept as premised on the problematic "given"-ness of Europe and European culture.
34. Buckle's *History of Civilization in England*, noted for its emphasis on the influence of geography on human history, provides a useful point of reference for the geographical formulation of Eurocentrism: "looking at the history of the world, as a whole, the tendency has been, in Europe, to subordinate nature to man; out of Europe to subordinate man to nature. . . . The great division, therefore, between European civilization and non-European civilization, is the basis of the philosophy of history" (1:115). The formulation is a particularly useful point of reference for a great many liberal versions of the hypothesis of culture—perhaps especially in that it suggests the highly unstable, imaginary anchor of Eurocentrism for nineteenth-century narratives.
35. Mackinder's respect for Reclus's work is indicated, albeit ambiguously, by the inclusion of Reclus in a series he was editing. The title of the series—The Regions of the World—already suggests Mackinder's own abbreviation of the encyclopedic reach of an earlier geography. In the prospectus, Elisée Reclus himself is listed as a contributor, entrusted with the region *Western Europe and the Mediterranean*. In the end, Reclus's work—and that of his fellow anarchist geographer Kropotkin—never appeared. It is nonetheless revealing that, at the time Mackinder published his own contribution, *Britain and the British Seas*, in 1902, Reclus—at that time both well known as a geographer and notorious as an anarchist—figured so prominently in Mackinder's editorial vision. It points to the shaping presence (albeit edited) of an anarchist geography and politics in the reactive formation of geopolitics.
36. Mackinder, *The Development of Geographical Teaching out of Nature-Study*, 7.
37. The "problematic of visualization" in geography is taken up at length in Derek Gregory's *Geographical Imaginations*, especially in chapter 1; O Tuathail takes this up in the first chapter of *Critical Geopolitics*, especially p. 35. Gregory's arguments

also underpin John Agnew's formulation of what he calls, more generally than O Tuathail, the "geopolitical imagination."

38. The link between primary and university education in Mackinder's vision is summed up by the nickname given to the courses Mackinder organized, at the request of R. B. Haldane, Secretary of State for War, for senior army officers at the London School of Economics. Taught from 1906 until 1914, the years in which Mackinder produced his school textbooks, they came to be known as "Haldane's Mackindergarten" (see Parker, *Mackinder*, 35).

39. Joyce, *Portrait of the Artist*, 16.

40. Mackinder, *The Development of Geographical Teaching out of Nature-Study*, 1.

41. Mackinder, *Britain and the British Seas*, 1.

42. I have rearranged the sequence of Mackinder's maps slightly in order to emphasize the correspondence Mackinder sets up between the two pairs of Greek and medieval maps. Although he refers, in the passage cited, to all four of the figures here reproduced in sequence, Mackinder places his key to the thirteenth-century map at the end of the chapter, side by side with the map of the world according to Ptolemy (where the maps [Figures 4b and 5b] serve to illustrate the supplementary note on the word "world" to which I turn in the following section).

43. Mackinder, *Britain*, 1.

44. Ibid., 13.

45. Ibid., 5.

46. Ibid., 1–4.

47. Mackinder's work for that committee—the eight lectures on India published in 1908—helpfully sums up the sort of use of media Mackinder had begun to make already in the 1890s, possibly following from the work of Patrick Geddes and his student A. J. Herbertson. Those lectures were accompanied by a set of 480 slides, 60 for each lecture. Much of the style of the lectures suggests that the aim was to make the text appear as mere captions to the visual image. Perhaps the most striking example is provided in comments accompanying the concluding slide to Lecture IV on "The United Provinces: The Mutiny": "Finally, we look at the bronze monument of the Queen-Empress Victoria, whose direct government displaced that of the East India Company after the quelling of the Mutiny in 1858. Hindu gardeners are at work in the foreground. No Briton can visit Lucknow and Cawnpore without being moved. We may well be proud of the heroic deeds of those of our race who in 1857 suffered and fought and died to save the British Raj in India" (*India: Eight Lectures*, 67).

One recalls Walter Benjamin's comment on the example of the *Kaiserpanorama* in the "dialectic of development" of the movies: "Shortly before the movie turned the reception of pictures into a collective one, the individual viewing of pictures in these swiftly outmoded establishments came into play" ("The Work of Art in the Age of Mechanical Reproduction," in *Illuminations*, 250). What is notable about Mackinder's educational experiments in this regard is the light they shed on the importance of the *educational* audience in the development of the moving picture, an audience that is neither "collective" nor "individual" in the sense Benjamin discusses—whose "establishment" (whether the classroom or the lecture hall) was not, moreover, "swiftly outmoded."

48. See O Tuathail, *Critical Geopolitics*, 35.
49. Jameson, *The Political Unconscious*, 230–32; Krauss, *The Optical Unconscious*, especially chapter 1, 1–27.
50. Conrad, *Youth and Two Other Stories*, 52.
51. Mackinder, *Our Own Islands*, 298.
52. The phrase is intended to echo Walter Benjamin's argument that "the camera introduces us to unconscious optics as does psychology to unconscious impulses" (*Illuminations*, 237). It also provides an abbreviated point of reference not only to the work of Fredric Jameson (*The Political Unconscious* and *The Geopolitical Aesthetic*), but also to that of Rosalind Krauss (*The Optical Unconscious*).
53. Mackinder, *Britain and the British Seas*, 11.
54. Mackinder, *The Scope and Methods of Geography*, 30.
55. "The period forming the introduction to Modern History is characterized by three broad or general facts; the first intellectual and emotional, the second geopolitical, and the third political proper. . . . The second great fact was the immense widening of the geographical horizon and of the possible area for political activity by means of the vast discoveries made likewise by Italians and by the Portuguese and the Spanish. At once the centre of gravity which had hitherto been the Mediterranean was shifted to the eastern shores of the Atlantic; and *England from having been almost outside the large currents of European politics, suddenly found herself in their very centre*" (Reich, "Recent Historical Methods," 129–30; emphasis added).
56. Reich, *Handbook of Geography*, 1:vi.
57. Ibid., 1:3. Reich's codification of the geopolitical image of Britain is enacted with a formalist gesture toward the sciences of mathematics, physics, and astronomy: "England has now become the centre of the political and commercial world. Herschel has well proved, that she occupies the geometrical centre of all the great continental masses of the globe" (ibid., 4); this claim is reiterated in the Mathematical part of the *Handbook of Geography*, (2:102).
58. It is worth specifying the hyphenated form of this inaugural English usage, since it stands in interesting relation to O Tuathail's efforts to problematize and displace geopolitics as "geo-politics": "In hyphenating geopolitics . . . I seek to place the putative stability and unity of geopolitics in question. It is a means of problematizing geopolitics, a way of putting it under erasure so the hidden logocentric infrastructures that make it possible are exposed to view. Geo-politics does not mark a fixed presence but an unstable and indeterminate problematic; it is not an 'is' but a question. The hyphen ruptures the givenness of geopolitics and opens up the seal of the bonding of the 'geo' and 'politics' to critical thought" (*Critical Geopolitics*, 67).
59. Kjellén, *Grundriss zu einem System der Politik*, 40 (my translation).
60. Reich, "Recent Historical Methods," 124.

61. Ibid., 124–25.
62. See Reich, *Handbook of Geography*, 2:xvi, where he repeats his reformulation of Horace's "est modus in rebus."
63. Mackinder, *Britain and the British Seas*, 12–13.
64. In this, Mackinder nonetheless pinpoints the significance of Ratzel's work generally for a genealogy of geopolitics. In miniature, Mackinder rehearses the shift from Ratzel's two-volume *Anthropogeographie* (1882–1891) to the later *Politische Geographie* (1897), where Ratzel takes up, with rather different implications from those in *Anthropogeographie*, "the political significance of the OEkumene" (*Politische Geographie*, 266–68).
65. Ratzel, *Anthropogeographie. Zweiter Teil: Die Geographische Verbreitung des Menschen*, 2:614 [hereafter cited as *Anthropogeographie* II].
66. Ratzel, *Anthropogeographie* I, 431.
67. Clifford, *The Predicament of Culture*, 93. For Ratzel's influence on twentieth-century anthropologists, see Bloch, *Marxism and Anthropology*, 106–7 and 126–27. Between the publication of volume 1 and volume 2 of *Anthropogeographie*, Ratzel wrote his *Völkerkunde* (1885–1888), translated into English in 1896 as *The History of Mankind*. In E. B. Tylor's introduction to that translation, it is interesting to trace the beginnings of a new, relativist conception of culture in the "special mention" Tylor makes of the 1,160 illustrations, which offer "in a way which no verbal description can attain to, an introduction and guide to the use of the museum collections on which the Science of Man comes more and more to depend on working out the theory of human development" (v). One of the "two different ways" in which such illustrations (in the book and in museums) serve "the student of culture," according to Tylor, is in presenting "all the objects which go to furnish the life of a people" (vi). Tylor remains attached to what I have called the hypothesis of culture, praising Ratzel, above all, for providing the basis for "understanding the likeness which pervades the culture of all mankind" (ix).
68. Ratzel, *Anthropogeographie* I, 470–71.
69. Robert J. C. Young's *Colonial Desire* provides an illuminating account of the complexity of this moment. Offering a crucial corrective to Williams's account in *Keywords*, Young calls attention to the late-nineteenth-century reconfiguration of Herder's concept of culture into an opposition between culture and civilization. "It was only at the end of the century, when civilization itself had become so identified with colonialism and the project of imperialism, and could no longer even be used in its relativistic comparative sense, that liberal anthropology sought to discriminate between culture and civilization, and to use the former to describe the 'savage' and 'barbarian' cultures that civilization had come to destroy" (43).
70. Ratzel, *Völkerkunde*, 1:11.
71. Ibid., 14–15.
72. Ibid., 16.
73. Ratzel, *Politische Geographie*, 194.
74. Ratzel, *Kleine Schriften*, 2:118.

75. Ibid.
76. Herder, *Ideen*, 339–40.
77. Ratzel, *Kleine Schriften*, 2:141.
78. Reclus, *L'Homme et la Terre*, 6:1.
79. Reclus's *L'Homme et la Terre* is throughout illustrated not only with maps, but also with illustrations by the Czech painter Frantisek Kupka. For other examples of these illustrations, see the cover illustration and part-opening illustrations of the present volume. For further discussion of Kupka (1871–1957), a Czech painter who moved from Prague to Paris in 1895, see the Introduction.
80. Reclus, *L'Homme et la Terre*, 6:1–2.
81. Ibid., 4:460.
82. Kjellén, *Der Staat als Lebensform*, 46.
83. Ratzel, *Anthropogeographie* I, 43.
84. Ratzel's *Politische Geographie* opens with the claim, "For Biogeography, the human State is a form of the expansion of life across the earth's surface" (3).
85. John Clark draws attention to the ecological scope of Reclus's work in this regard. See his "The Dialectical Social Geography of Elisée Reclus."
86. As Reclus puts it in the preface to *The Universal Geography*, "Our arbitrary political divisions . . . possess but a transitory value" (21; Ravenstein translation).
87. Reclus, *The Universal Geography*, 21.
88. Reclus, *L'Homme et la Terre*, 1:iii.
89. Kant, *Political Writings*, 217–18. This counter-argument was made in the third of his reviews of Herder's *Ideen*.
90. Ibid., 50. This point is made in the eighth proposition of Kant's "Idea for a Universal History with a Cosmopolitical Purpose" (1784).
91. Ibid., 108.
92. Hegel, *Philosophy of Right*. See, in particular, p. 160. See also Hegel, *Phenomenology of Spirit*, the section on "Self-alienated Spirit. Culture [Bildung]," 294–363. Here, Hegel develops the argument that "through culture . . . the individual acquires standing and actuality" (298), which he then relates to the conception of "state power": "As state power is the simple *substance*, so too is it the universal '*work*'—the absolute 'heart of the matter' itself in which individuals find their *essential* nature expressed, and where their separate individuality is merely a consciousness of their *universality*" (301).
93. Marx, "Critique of Hegel's Doctrine of the State," in *Early Writings*, 57–198, (quotes on pp. 107, 62). Marx's spirited critique, an early elaboration of his later theories, is particularly interesting for the insistence with which Marx returns to Hegel's use of "the forming processes of education" as a premise for arguing for the unity of the state. As part of his critique of Hegel's "bureaucracy" and "state formalism" (education conceived as an agency for training civil servants), Marx also attacks the abstract formalism of Hegel's defense of constitutional monarchy (crucial for his notion of state sovereignty). As part of his spirited satire, Marx hits upon an amusing caricature of Hegel's argument that anticipates the terms of our next

chapter's discussion: "and so we have *His Majesty the Accident*. Accident is accordingly the *real unity* of the state" (94).

94. For lengthy discussion of this, see Lloyd and Thomas, *Culture and the State*.

95. Lacoste, "The Geographical and the Geopolitical," 14. Lacoste adds that, in its "analysis of imperialist rivalries, their methods of conquest and territorial control," the work remains unsurpassed. We might also note that Reclus's work anticipates something of the reach of Immanuel Wallerstein's world-systems theory.

96. *L'Homme et la Terre*, 1:iv.

97. Ibid., 1:ii.

98. Kristin Ross argues that Reclus's "social geography" "had to be repressed" for the field of French academic geography "to take institutional shape" (*The Emergence of Social Space*, 19; see also 90–94).

99. The liberal-sounding term "equilibrium" and Reclus's quotation marks around "class struggle" might well have aroused Marxists' suspicions. A notable example of the active neglect of Reclus in Marxist debates is provided by Plekhanov's 1906 review of Metchnikoff's analysis of the geographical causes of oriental despotism, in which Plekhanov uncovers an anarchist tendency in Metchnikoff's reference to Reclus (see Bailey and Llobera, *The Asiatic Mode of Production*, 66.) For an extensive discussion of the differences between Reclus's anarchism and Marxism, see Marie Fleming, *The Anarchist Way to Socialism* (especially p. 131), where she argues that the point I make here is the defining difference.

100. Reclus, *The Universal Geography*, 4 (Ravenstein translation).

101. Cited in Fleming, *The Anarchist Way to Socialism*, 240.

102. Reclus, *L'Homme et la Terre*, ed. Giblin, 2:139.

103. Gramsci, *Selections from the Prison Notebooks*, 416–18. Gramsci's Eurocentrism is also made clear in this section: "European culture . . . is the only historically and concretely universal culture" (416).

104. The work of Stuart Hall in this regard is perhaps decisive. See, in particular, "Cultural Studies and the Centre," and "Notes on Deconstructing 'the Popular.'" I am thinking, too, of the use to which the Subaltern Studies group has put Gramscian ideas (see Guha and Spivak, *Selected Subaltern Studies*). The significance of Reclus's turning to the use of the term "hegemony" in the mid-1890s is suggested by the genealogy of the concept offered by Laclau and Mouffe, whose *Hegemony and Socialist Strategy* has also shaped the conceptual use of the term today.

105. Cited in Fleming, *The Anarchist Way to Socialism*, 242.

106. Mackinder, *Britain and the British Seas*, vi.

107. Proust, *Selected Letters*, 86.

108. See O Tuathail, *Critical Geopolitics*, 111–40, 114.

109. "Dream monument" is a translation of Reclus's own description of the design as "ce monument rêvé" ("Project de Construction d'un Globe Terrestre," 630).

110. Mitchell, *Colonising Egypt*, 13.

111. Derek Gregory uses Reclus's Great Globe as just such an illustration, drawing on Timothy Mitchell's argument, in *Geographical Imaginations* (38). An inter-

esting problem with this illustration emerges in Reclus's account of the scaffolding needed to exhibit the Globe. In his project for the Great Globe, presented at the Sixth International Geographical Congress of 1895, held in London, Reclus conceived of a *second* globe, framing the scientific globe, in order to protect it from the weather (Reclus, "Project de Construction d'un Globe Terrestre"). We might thus note that Gregory's reproduction of the 1897 illustration for the Paris World Exhibition of 1900 in fact represents only one part of the extraordinary utopian project—and, notably, the form imagined for exhibition: a form that *leaves out* the actual globe, not only in its display of the outer model, but also in conceiving the inner vault as the screen for the projection of a vast panorama.

112. Reclus, "Project de Construction d'un Globe Terrestre," 627.

113. See Gregory, *Geographical Imaginations*, 65.

114. It also stands at the center of another imagined "National Institute of Geography," a proposal presented by J. G. Bartholomew, head of the well-established, Edinburgh-based map printers of the same name, in *The Scottish Geographical Magazine* of March 1902. The orchestrator of this proposed Institute, Patrick Geddes, the Scottish sociologist, geographer, and father-figure (via Lewis Mumford) of American urban studies, imagined Reclus's Great Globe as the central feature of a "complex collaboration" of disciplines, political perspectives, commercial, civic, and educational aims—a sort of amalgam of University and Museum: the "galleries of Industry and Commerce" leading "naturally" on one side to that of "Education" and, on the other, "and less naturally, to space for a Peace Museum." Despite the eminently imperial rationale offered in Bartholomew's "Plea" for a National Institute, the Royal Geographical Society supported an English proposal instead—despite the fact that, as Helen Meller points out, geography "had only a lowly status" at Oxford, where the rival Institute was set up, whereas in Edinburgh, "Scottish scientists and explorers had not only an honourable record in geographical exploration, research and cartography, but had also pioneered related subjects" (Meller, *Patrick Geddes*, 132). The rival Institute was H. J. Mackinder's Geographical Institute at Oxford.

115. Cited in Gregory, *Geographical Imaginations*, 36. Note, however, the sense of "image" as well as "picture" in the German term "Bild" (see Heidegger, *Holzwege*, 73–110, especially 87).

116. Mitchell, *Colonising Egypt*, 13.

Chapter 2

1. The quotation is from Arnold, *Culture and Anarchy*, 70.

2. See, in particular, Hall, "Rethinking Imperial Histories"; and Suleri, *The Rhetoric of English India*, and notably her comments on Viswanathan's *Masks of Conquest* (22).

3. Young, *Colonial Desire*, 57.

4. Arnold, "The Popular Education of France," in *Selected Prose*, 108.

5. Žižek, *For They Know Not What They Do*, 267.

6. Following the Jacobin logic of Lefort, as it were, what Arnold calls "Jacobinism"—the institution of middle-class reforming ideas—comes to be figured in the place of the sovereign: "culture, just because it resists this tendency of Jacobinism to impose on us a man with limitations and errors of his own along with the true ideas of which he is the organ, really does the world and Jacobinism itself a service" (*Culture and Anarchy*, 68). Here is an odd return of Burke upon Arnold indeed: culture *in the service* of Burke's "blot of a continual usurpation."

7. Williams, *Culture and Society*, 136; Said, *Culture and Imperialism*, xiii.

8. See Collins, "The Unknown Public," in *My Miscellanies*.

9. See, for example, *Cornhill Magazine*—where *Armadale* was serialized between November 1864 and June 1866, where Arnold published the essay "My Countrymen" (in February 1866) and the prelude to *Culture and Anarchy* (made up of the series of essays published in *Cornhill* from 1867 to 1868), and where an anonymous essay entitled "The Modern Doctrine of Culture" appeared in April 1866.

10. The only other discussion I know of that addresses the relation between Wilkie's painting and Collins's novel is Jaya Mehta's essay, "English Romance: Indian Violence" (see, especially, 619–20).

11. Collins, *The Moonstone*, 63 (hereafter cited in the text).

12. Of the many critics who discuss the possible sexual meanings (and for the further examples they cite), see, for example, Ian Duncan, Tamar Heller, Mark Hennelly, and Ashish Roy (all cited below).

13. Williams, *The Country and the City*, 248–49.

14. For an extensive discussion of the relation between the sensational novel and Marx's *Capital*, see Cvetkovich, *Mixed Feelings*.

15. Williams, *The Country and the City*, 249.

16. Ibid.

17. Raymond Williams's use of the term "blurred" to describe the distortion of class perspective (*The Country and the City*, 166) recalls a similar, and similarly influential, formulation by E. P. Thompson, whose discussion of the Waltham Black Act of 1723 drew attention to the way the authorities lumped together a whole range of rural disturbances "within one common blur, as outrages by the Blacks" (*Whigs and Hunters*, 145).

18. Williams, *The Country and the City*, 249.

19. For discussions of the relation between "Bildung" and the genre of the novel, see the special issue of *Genre* on "Education, Identity, and Constructions of the Novel" edited by Richard A. Barney. As Barney notes in his introduction (359), the defining twentieth-century formulation of the relation between "Bildung" and the genre of the novel is Wilhelm Dilthey's *Das Erlebnis und die Dichtung* (1905). See also Abel, Hirsch, and Langland, *The Voyage In*; Fraiman, *Unbecoming Women*; Moretti, *The Way of the World*; and Mücke, *Virtue and the Veil of Illusion*.

20. Arnold, *Culture and Anarchy*, 6.

21. In the character of Mr. Wragge in *No Name* (1862), Wilkie Collins provided a brilliant parody of the debates over "culture" in the 1860s in such magazines as *Cornhill*—debates that have yet, to my knowledge, to be fully documented. Captain Wragge offers a definition of himself as a "moral agriculturist": "Definition: A moral agriculturalist; a man who cultivates the field of human sympathy. I am that moral agriculturalist, that cultivating man. Narrow-minded mediocrity, envious of my success in my profession, calls me a Swindler. What of that? The same low tone of mind assails men in other professions in a similar manner—calls great writers, scribblers—great generals, butchers—and so on. It entirely depends on the point of view" (*No Name*, 153).

22. This ambiguity is dissected by John Kucich in *The Power of Lies*.

23. It is also worth noting that the figure of the art collector (Mr. Fairlie in *The Woman in White*, Noel Vanstone in *No Name*) embodies the ambiguity of middle-class respectability by associating a fetishization of cultural treasures with the function of misguided paternal duties.

24. Watt, *The Rise of the Novel*, 20. Collins's manipulation of proper names constitutes, however, more than a mid-Victorian variation on Watt's "formal realism." In organizing these plots around the struggle over the proper name alluded to in the titles (*No Name*, *Armadale*), Collins's plots to acquire or retain the proper name look back on those problems of gender and class perspective that had long shaped the genre of the novel, and according to which Watt's "formal realism" might be rethought in terms of what Fraser Easton has called "perspectival realism" (s.v. "*Moll Flanders*," in Schellinger, *Encyclopedia of the Novel*, 2:862).

25. Ranajit Guha has adapted E. P. Thompson's usage of the term "blur" discussed above to theorize peasant insurgency against British rule, by suggesting that what Thompson calls "blurring," viewed from the peasant's perspective "operates in reverse"—i.e., lumping "all forms of defiance of the law" "as perfectly justifiable—even honourable—acts of social protest" (*Elementary Aspects of Peasant Insurgency*, 89).

26. The precedent for such allusive transcoding of political references from the East to the West Indies is to be found in the collaborative work of Collins and Dickens, whose "The Perils of Certain English Prisoners," though set in the East Indies, was clearly a response to the Indian Mutiny. The story was begun by Dickens, in the Christmas number of *Household Words* for 1857—a vitriolic and racist response, which Collins sought to modulate and moderate with a more ironic and comic grasp of the plight of the "English prisoners." For accounts of the collaboration, see Robinson, *Wilkie Collins*, and Peters, *The King of Inventors*; for discussion of its relation to responses to the Indian Mutiny in general, see Brantlinger, *Rule of Darkness*. Collins's own immediate response to the events of 1857–1858 is best represented by "A Sermon for Sepoys," published in *Household Words* in February 1858. Attempting to moderate the plethora of sermonizing in the press, Collins's "sermon" proposed "to preach to the people of India, in the first instance, out of their own books" (*Household Words*, 27 February 1858, p. 244). By contrast to Dickens's re-

sponse, and general reaction in Britain, this is a moderate response indeed, harking back to an older Orientalism of European regard for "Oriental literature."

27. Mehta, "English Romance: Indian Violence," 620.

28. Ibid., 621.

29. Forrest, *Tiger of Mysore*, 2.

30. According to Pratapaditya Pal and Vidya Dehejia, "British obsession with Tipu Sultan . . . continued for generations and was evident in both literature and the visual arts" (see Pal and Dehejia, *From Merchants to Emperors*, 51–52).

31. According to Allan Cunningham's *Life of Sir David Wilkie*, Wilkie Collins visited his godfather's house just as the painting was being completed (254). Even if Collins had no memories to speak of concerning the visit, he might have read of the visit in Cunningham's *Life* which, in turn, provides an additional source for the fascination in Tipu's treasures.

32. Mehta, "English Romance: Indian Violence," 619.

33. Ibid., 620.

34. Reed, "English Imperialism and the Unacknowledged Crime of *The Moonstone*," 286.

35. Miller, "From *Roman Policier* to *Roman-Police*: Wilkie Collins's *The Moonstone*," chapter 2 of *The Novel and the Police*.

36. Roy, "The Fabulous Imperialist Semiotic of Wilkie Collins's *The Moonstone*," 657.

37. Duncan, "*The Moonstone*, the Victorian Novel, and Imperialist Panic," 297.

38. Mehta, "English Romance: Indian Violence," 619.

39. Forrest, *Tiger of Mysore*, 299. For further details on the squabbling, see Ramaswami, "Tippu's Golden Sword." As Ramaswami points out, some of the squabbling was over the valuation of the "legitimate" loot divvied out to the military leaders. Of Baird, Ramaswami notes, "General Baird, an unlucky man, found his large ruby ring only a lump of coloured glass" (11). One reason for emphasizing that the squabbling controversy concerned the valuation of the spoils of victory is that, as we see in the Prologue to *The Moonstone*, Baird's reputation may have been secured, in part, by displacing this aspect of the military conquest onto the story of looting by ordinary soldiers—what Baird is credited with having at least attempted to police.

40. See "The Royal Academy. The Seventy-First Exhibition. 1839," *Art-Union* 1 (May 1839): 65–71, reprinted in Olmsted, *Victorian Painting*, 1:276.

41. "Royal Academy," *Athenaeum* (11 May 1839), reprinted in Olmsted, *Victorian Painting*, 1:288.

42. Thackeray, "A Second Lecture on the Fine Arts, by Michael Angelo Titmarsh, Esq."; see also Olmsted, *Victorian Painting*, 1:297.

43. This iconography of victor and vanquished is still more evident in an early sketch for the portrait. Its significance for Wilkie himself is clear in his own account of the painting, cited in Cunningham's *Life of Sir David Wilkie*: "In considering the taking of Seringapatam as a subject for art, one of its greatest recommendations I

conceive to be, the bringing the leaders of each side in the moment of victory, to the same spot" (264–67).

44. Armstrong, *Desire and Domestic Fiction*, 213.

45. *The Moonstone* itself offers a number of interesting examples of this crossing of aesthetic media—and notably in Betteredge's initial descriptions of character: "There you have the portrait of the man before you, as in a picture: a character that braved everything; and a face, handsome as it was, that looked possessed by the devil" (*Moonstone*, 64); "and there behold the portrait of her, to the best of my painting, as large as life!" (*Moonstone*, 87). These examples—character sketches of the wicked uncle Herncastle and his victim Rachel Verinder, respectively—already suggest how Wilkie's iconography of military victory gets transfigured into that "iconography of subjectivity" Armstrong finds so characteristic of Victorian narrative.

46. Foucault, *The History of Sexuality*, 103–4.

47. Heller, *Dead Secrets*, 146. It is an argument that also points to the specific historical contours of complicity in imperialism reenacted in the process: "Blake's fears, reminiscent of the paranoia about female chastity whipped into hysterical fury by the Mutiny, also reveal how his 'innocence' is a social and rhetorical construct."

48. Ibid., 11.

49. Heller discusses this crisis in terms of Gaye Tuchman's formulation (in *Edging Women Out*) of the "edging out" of women in the professionalization of literature. Still more significant for the current argument is Mary Poovey's examination, in *Uneven Developments*, of Dickens's *David Copperfield* and the process by which it constructs "the reader as a particular kind of subject—a psychologized, classed, developmental individual" around the contradictory effect of an effort to "construct and maintain the separate spheres of the home and literary labor" (90), whose *failure* is marked by "the 'stain' of sexuality, the 'blight' of class, the 'degradation' of work" (123).

50. Heller, *Dead Secrets*, 11–12.

51. Lacan, *The Four Fundamental Concepts of Psycho-Analysis*, 88.

52. Archer, *Sovereignty and Intelligence*, 10.

53. The most conventional of formulations for "blind love" comes, in fact, in the posthumous *Blind Love*: "The one unassailable vital force in this world is the force of love. It may submit to the hard necessities of life; it may acknowledge the imperative claims of duty; it may be silent under reproach, and submissive to privation—but, suffer what it may, it is the master-passion still; subject to no artificial influences, owning no supremacy but the law of its own being" (*Blind Love*, 25). Earlier formulations, however, are more revealing—for example, in *Poor Miss Finch*, where the figurative expression is literalized in the title-character's perverse attachment to her blindness.

54. Foucault, *The History of Sexuality*, 155.

55. Collins, *The Woman in White*, 89–90.

56. Smiles, *Self-Help*, 26.

57. In the context of the current argument, it is worth mentioning that, among Smiles's "illustrations" of good "character," is a sequence of references to generals and officers in India who were able to *resist* gifts of money and treasures accruing from military campaigns and Company service (see 433–34).

58. What gets repudiated, with Blake's blindness to Rosanna's love, is a story of urban working-class experience that has explicitly rejected the principles of middle-class respectability, reform, and improvement ("My life was not a very hard life to bear, while I was a thief. It was only when they had taught me at the reformatory to feel my own degradation, and to try for better things" [*Moonstone*, 363]). It is a story, moreover, explicitly linked to a vision of rural and working-class revolution, as articulated by Rosanna's friend Limping Lucy ("The day is not far off when the poor will rise against the rich" [*Moonstone*, 227]), and attached to that prototypically nineteenth-century utopian plan, the women's collective ("I had a plan for our going to London together like sisters, and living by our needles" [*Moonstone*, 227]).

59. Žižek, *Looking Awry*, 95.

60. Among the more intriguing complexities of the moonstone's figurative meanings is its relation to the trope of the "jewel in the crown." This figure of speech for Britain's territorial possession of India gets grafted onto the famous image of the Koh-i-Noor, and then, as Jenny Sharpe explores it, becomes something like a central geopolitical image for allegorizing Empire. See Sharpe's discussion of Paul Scott's *The Jewel in the Crown* in *Allegories of Empire*, especially 149–52.

61. Duncan, "*The Moonstone*, the Victorian Novel, and Imperialist Panic," 310.

62. Pierre Bourdieu develops the idea of cultural capital in *Outline of a Theory of Practice*, where he offers the following, concise formula: "Academic qualifications are to cultural capital what money is to economic capital" (187). The "social history of all forms of *distinction*" projected in that study (236, n. 42) is then elaborated in *Distinction*. See also Ian Duncan's comments on the moonstone as cultural capital ("*The Moonstone*, the Victorian Novel, and Imperialist Panic," 311).

63. Walter Benjamin, "Eduard Fuchs: Collector and Historian," in Arato and Gebhardt, *The Essential Frankfurt School Reader*, 233.

64. An interesting example is found in the figure of the mediocre artist Valentine Blyth in the early novel *Hide and Seek*, who is caught between the conflicting claims of "High Art and Classical Landscape" on the one hand, and "cheap portrait-painting, cheap copying, and cheap studies of Still Life" on the other (39), but in whom the novel invests a sort of consolatory self-satisfaction: "Let him work, though ever so obscurely, . . . and he shall find the labour itself its own exceeding great reward. . . . Thus it was with Valentine. He had sacrificed a fortune to his Art; and his Art—in the world's eye at least—had given to him nothing in return" (33). Besides suggesting a root formula for Collins's lifelong attachment to an ideal of Art, his own distinctive term for what Arnold, with a rather different emphasis, sought to articulate with the word "culture," the passage is interesting because Collins quotes from it in the 1871 preface to *The Moonstone*, though without acknowledging he is quoting from himself: "The Art which had been always the pride and the pleasure

of my life, became now more than ever 'its own exceeding great reward'" (*Moonstone*, 29).

65. Mitchell, *Picture Theory*, 156. William Collins's *Memoirs of a Picture*, too, belongs to this shared "genre"—perhaps still more strikingly, not only in the organizing fiction of the title, but also in its hybrid mixture of biography (the second volume is a serious biography of George Morland), novel writing, and art criticism and history. Anticipating the problem of portraiture and world history on display in Wilkie's painting, the book is, more significantly, a sort of primal model for the young Collins's own art, as indicated in his description of the book at the beginning of his own first published book, the biography of his father, William Collins (see *Memoirs of the Life of William Collins, R.A.*, 9).

66. Wilkie's excitement on receiving these treasures (from all over Britain) is reported in Allan Cunningham's *Life of Sir David Wilkie*. On 20 August 1837, for instance, he reported to Lady Baird that "Mrs. Parker . . . has since brought me a dress, consisting of pelisse and trowsers, *actually worn by Tippoo Saib himself*!!" He goes on to write, "Mr. Charles Russell has also sent me a coach-load of turbans, pelisses, trowsers of the richest stuffs, with matchlocks, scymitars, and a superb shield. These, with what your Ladyship is pleased to send me from Fern Tower, will supply completely the Indian part of the picture" (225). A year later, he reported that, "Amongst other details, the charmed amulet has been painted on the right arm of Tippoo, and the real charm itself has been returned to Mrs. Young at Aberdeen" (255).

67. Cohn, "Representing Authority in Victorian India," 178.

68. Cohn, *Colonialism and Its Forms of Knowledge*, 80.

69. Hook's description (which is an account of one Major Allan recorded in Alexander Beatson's *A View of the Origin and Conduct of the War with Tippoo Sultan* [1800]) provided the script for a long and dramatic description that accompanied its exhibition at the Royal Academy in 1839 (reproduced in Archer, *India and British Portraiture*, 435). Since the quotation (and caption) almost exactly fits the moment of Wilkie's portrait, it provides an inversion of the narrow definition of ekphrasis by offering a visual representation of verbal representation.

70. Cohn, "Representing Authority in Victorian India," 171.

71. Ibid., 168.

72. The significance of this stereotype is revealed by Sara Suleri, *The Rhetoric of English India* (see, especially, p. 45), who shows its central role in Burke's contribution to the "rhetoric of English India"—that rhetoric in which, as Suleri argues, "'India' becomes the absent point toward which nineteenth-century Anglo-Indian narrative may lean but which it may never possess, causing both national and cultural identities to disappear in the emptiness of a representational mirage" (11).

73. Cohn, "Representing Authority in Victorian India," 171.

74. For discussions of Kantorowicz's thesis, see John M. Archer (*Sovereignty and Intelligence*, 2–3), who cites Claude Lefort, whose criticism of Kantorowicz is also the basis for Slavoj Žižek's discussion in *They Know Not What They Do* (253–73).

75. Barrell, *The Infection of Thomas de Quincey*, 50.

76. Suleri, *The Rhetoric of English India*, 24–48.
77. Reed, "English Imperialism and the Unacknowledged Crime of *The Moonstone*," 287.
78. See Roy, "The Fabulous Imperialist Semiotic of Wilkie Collins's *The Moonstone*," especially p. 674, and see also, p. 679 n. 12.

Chapter 3

1. Nietzsche, *Will to Power*, 9.
2. Schreiner, *The Story of an African Farm*, 135 (hereafter abbreviated as *The Story* in the text).
3. Nietzsche, *Will to Power*, 3.
4. "I shall probe these things more thoroughly and severely in another connection (under the title 'On the History of European Nihilism'; it will be contained in a work in progress: The Will to Power: Attempt at a Revaluation of All Values)." Nietzsche, *On the Genealogy of Morals*, 159–60.
5. Nancy, "Nietzsche's Thesis on Teleology," 59.
6. Nietzsche, *Will to Power*, 3.
7. Nietzsche, *Ecce Homo*, 326–27.
8. Nietzsche, *Will to Power*, 3–4.
9. Ibid., 544.
10. See, for example, Edmund Walsh's "Geopolitics and International Morals" in Weigert and Stefansson, *Compass of the World*, 30.
11. Heidegger, *Nietzsche*, 1.
12. "'I am a man who believes nothing, hopes nothing, fears nothing, feels nothing. I am beyond the pale of humanity; no criterion of what you should be who lives here among your ostriches and bushes'" (*The Story*, 159).
13. Peter Kropotkin's *Memoirs of a Revolutionist* also makes Herbert Spencer a touchstone of the nineteenth-century meaning of nihilism. In his attempt to dissociate Russian nihilism from its later confusion with terrorism, he points out that the typical nihilist of the 1860s was "a positivist, an agnostic, a Spencerian evolutionist, or scientific materialist" (195).
14. Heidegger, *Nietzsche*, 2.
15. GoGwilt, *The Invention of the West*.
16. Nietzsche, *Genealogy of Morals*, 79.
17. Ibid., 157.
18. Ibid., 15.
19. The phrase Nietzsche used to advertise the "common goal" of the series of books from *Human, All Too Human* (1878) to *The Gay Science* (1882).
20. Nietzsche, *Thus Spoke Zarathustra*, 41. (Unless otherwise stated, citations are from the Hollingdale translation.)
21. Kahane, *Passions of the Voice*, 81–82.
22. Förster-Nietzsche, Introduction to *Thus Spake Zarathustra*, trans. Common, 15.

23. Nietzsche used the term in a letter to Salomé in 1882, which Salomé cites at the beginning of her Nietzsche study "in place of a preface" (Salomé, *Friedrich Nietzsche*, 3). As Biddy Martin points out, citing the letter, "The juxtaposition of the letter to the epigraph establishes a particular convergence between them, figures her as his sister or brother brain, his confidante, and if not the origin, then at least the affirmation and enactment of his ideas" (Martin, *Woman and Modernity*, 95).

24. Förster-Nietzsche, Introduction to *Thus Spake Zarathustra*, trans. Common, 9.

25. Ibid., 10–11.

26. See Salomé, *Friedrich Nietzsche*, 89–90.

27. Dilthey, *Das Erlebnis und die Dichtung*, 396.

28. Salomé, *Friedrich Nietzsche*, 89.

29. See Livingstone, *Salomé*, 44.

30. Salomé reprinted part of the photograph to illustrate her Nietzsche book, adding as a caption a quotation from a letter Nietzsche had written to Paul Rée in 1879: "Friedrich Nietzsche, *formerly* professor and now a wandering fugitive." Nietzsche's photograph was "mischievously snipped and transposed," Siegfried Mandel argues, to give graphic support to Salomé's "provocative diagnosis" that "Nietzsche's madness [was] the inevitable result of psychophysical factors ostensibly mirrored in his writings" (see Mandel's Introduction to Salomé, *Friedrich Nietzsche*, ix). As for Förster-Nietzsche, according to Biddy Martin, "When Salomé apparently unveiled the Lucerne photograph in Bayreuth, Förster-Nietzsche took it as proof that Salomé was blatantly misrepresenting her brother's character and intentions" (Martin, *Woman and Modernity*, 75). Martin reproduces the photograph on p. 74.

31. Martin, *Woman and Modernity*, 78.

32. Förster-Nietzsche, *Life of Nietzsche*, 2:144, 2:143; originally published as *Der einsame Nietzsche*.

33. Förster-Nietzsche, *Life of Nietzsche*, 2:139.

34. Ibid., 2:122.

35. Ibid., 2:131.

36. Kittler, *Discourse Networks, 1800/1900*, 200.

37. Nietzsche, *Beyond Good and Evil*, xv.

38. Salomé, *Friedrich Nietzsche*, 78.

39. Ibid., 56.

40. Ibid.

41. In Förster-Nietzsche's account of the "Lou affair," the repeated insistence on Salomé's inability to appreciate Nietzsche's "greatness" symptomatically demonstrates her effort to repudiate Salomé's Nietzsche book.

42. Nietzsche, *Thus Spoke Zarathustra*, 142.

43. Hardy, *Jude the Obscure*, 287.

44. 1912 Postscript to the Preface to the first edition of ibid., 42.

45. Showalter, *A Literature of Their Own*, 199.

46. Mill, *Utilitarianism, On Liberty, Representative Government*, 63.

47. Nietzsche, *The Gay Science*, 128.

48. Ibid., 127–28.
49. Responses to Nietzsche's anti-feminism constitute something of an extended tradition of feminist readings of Nietzsche, beginning with Lou Salomé. For a glimpse of something of the reach of this central tradition within philosophical, literary, and cultural studies, see Burgard, *Nietzsche and the Feminine*.
50. Salomé, *Friedrich Nietzsche*, 111–12.
51. Nietzsche, *The Gay Science*, 253.
52. Spencer, *First Principles*, vi. The quotation is from the 1862 preface outlining the entire "system of philosophy" to follow from "First Principles."
53. Of the many discussions of the role of the culture-concept in Nietzsche's work, see, in particular, Blondel, *Nietzsche: The Body and Culture*, particularly chapter 3. Blondel claims "the central problem posed by Nietzsche's enigmatic thought concerns an obscure, polysemic and perhaps contestable notion, that of culture" (42). He goes on to offer a particularly illuminating discussion of the relation between the German senses of "Bildung," "Kultur," and "Zivilisation."
54. See also Thatcher, *Nietzsche in England*, 53.
55. Showalter, *A Literature of Their Own*, 210, 214.
56. Elaine Showalter has examined this issue at great length, notably in *The Female Malady*, but also in *Sexual Anarchy: Gender and Culture in the Fin de Siècle*.
57. Nietzsche, *Ecce Homo*, 219.
58. See, in particular, Salomé, *Friedrich Nietzsche*, 123–24. See also Martin, *Woman and Modernity*, 107.
59. Nietzsche, *Thus Spake Zarathustra*, trans. Common, 38; for the German, see Nietzsche, *Also Sprach Zarathustra*, 17. Cf. Nietzsche, *Thus Spoke Zarathustra*, trans. Hollingdale, 52.
60. Nietzsche, *The Gay Science*, 274. Increasing the allegory of the Zarathustra fiction, Nietzsche alters the geographical specification of "Lake Urmi" to "the lake of his home" when he transposes it, otherwise word for word, to provide the introduction to *Thus Spoke Zarathustra*.
61. As noted by Hollingdale in Nietzsche, *Thus Spoke Zarathustra*, 339.
62. Salomé, *Friedrich Nietzsche*, 89–90.
63. Förster-Nietzsche, *Life of Nietzsche*, 2:21–22; Nietzsche, *Ecce Homo*, 327–28.
64. Salomé, *Friedrich Nietzsche*, 123.
65. Ibid., 139. Salomé's characterization is all the more revealing in that she is describing the difficulty of evaluating the position from which to imagine the narrator of "his unpublished and partially completed major work *The Will to Power*."
66. Nietzsche, *Thus Spoke Zarathustra*, 142.
67. Ibid.
68. Browning, *The Poems*, 2:1096.
69. Zimmern, *The Epic of Kings*, xx–xxi.
70. Salomé, *Friedrich Nietzsche*, 158.
71. See Blondel, *Nietzsche: The Body and Culture*, 10–11.
72. Kittler, *Discourse Networks, 1800/1900*, 205.

73. Nietzsche, *Thus Spoke Zarathustra*, 319.
74. Nietzsche, *Ecce Homo*, 263.
75. Ibid., 262–63.
76. "Olive Schreiner: The Limits of Colonial Feminism," chapter 7 of McClintock, *Imperial Leather*, 258–95.
77. Nietzsche, *Genealogy of Morals*, 24.
78. First and Scott, *Olive Schreiner*, 82.
79. McClintock, *Imperial Leather*, 283. On Schreiner and Darwinism, see also Barash, "Virile Womanhood," 269–81.
80. First and Scott, *Olive Schreiner*, 115.
81. Nietzsche, *Genealogy of Morals*, 17.
82. First and Scott, *Olive Schreiner*, 121.
83. Ibid., 119.
84. Horton, *Difficult Women, Artful Lives*, 22–23; 72–73. Horton's is the only study I know that explores the striking correspondences between Nietzsche and Schreiner. Guided mostly by the more evident correspondence between Nietzsche and Isak Dineson, she nonetheless offers revealing insights into Schreiner's "nihilism"—almost all of which are informed by her extraordinary and unique reading of Schreiner's landscape.
85. For a discussion of the epigraph, see Walter Kaufmann's translator's introduction to *The Gay Science*, 7–8.
86. See ibid., 8, 10.
87. In Nietzsche, *The Gay Science*, 181–82.
88. For more on this, see McClintock, *Imperial Leather*.
89. Nietzsche, *Twilight of the Idols*, 93–94.
90. Nietzsche, *Will to Power*, 255.
91. Dan Jacobson, introduction to *The Story of an African Farm* by Olive Schreiner, 7.
92. See, in particular, Bhabha, *The Location of Culture*, 131–32.
93. Ibid., 113.
94. Ibid., 117.
95. Ibid., 113. The Bible is split according to a hybridity of Anglo–Dutch historical and linguistic entanglement whose implications for worldwide culture systems are suggested by the historic rivalry between the Dutch and British East India Companies—a rivalry described as *mimicry* by Karl Marx, in an extraordinary passage full of the problematic echo-effects of colonial mimicry in translation across, indeed undermining European languages. Marx is discussing British rule in India and explaining his use of Stamford Raffles as an authoritative reference:

> I do not allude to European despotism, planted upon Asiatic despotism, by the British East India Company, forming a more monstrous combination than any of the divine monsters startling us in the Temple of Salsette. This is no distinctive feature of British colonial rule, but only an imitation of the

Dutch, and so much so that in order to characterize the working of the British East India Company, it is sufficient to literally repeat what Sir Stamford Raffles, the *English* Governor of Java said of the Dutch East India Company. (Marx, *Surveys from Exile*, 302)

96. Bhabha, *The Location of Culture*, 102.

97. When the title crops up in Waldo's unfinished letter to Lyndall, it is casually classified as "Sunday school prize" material, by contrast to the racy "Black-eyed Creole." The juxtaposition of titles signals a difference of much more than reading preferences between Waldo and this last in a series of friends who abandon him. The complex confusion of racial, sexual, and class identifications constitutes an extreme splitting of the idealized text of colonial authority, leaving Waldo with the feeling "as if I were having a bad dream, and I wanted to be far away" (Schreiner, *The Story*, 253).

98. It is Olive Schreiner's autobiographical account in her letters that confirms the book is Spencer's *First Principles*: "The book that the Stranger gives to Waldo was intended to be Spencer's 'First Principles.' When I was up in Basuto Land with an old Aunt & cousin, one stormy, rainy night, there was a knock at the door; they were afraid to go & open it so I went. There was a stranger there like Waldos [*sic*] Stranger exactly. There was no house within fifty miles so he slept there: the next morning he talked with me for a little while & after that I saw him twice for half an hour: & then I never saw him again. He lent me Spencer's 'First Principles.' I always think that when Christianity burst on the dark Roman world it was what that book was to me. I was in such complete, blank atheism. I did not even believe in my own nature, in any right or wrong, or certainty. I can still feel myself lying before the fire to read it. I had only three days." (Draznin, "My Other Self," 39)

99. Showalter, *A Literature of Their Own*, 197.

100. Spivak, "Three Women's Texts and a Critique of Imperialism."

101. Kahane, *Passions of the Voice*, 84.

102. Salomé, *Friedrich Nietzsche*, 158.

103. Schreiner's description (pseudonymously as R. Iron) in the preface to *The Story of an African Farm*, 27.

104. Nietzsche, *The Case of Wagner*, 170.

105. Ibid., 165.

106. Nietzsche, *Will to Power*, 3.

107. Ibid., 438.

108. Said, *Culture and Imperialism*, 130. Referring explicitly to Timothy Mitchell's *Colonising Egypt*, at the beginning of his discussion, Said places Verdi's opera within the same context as the world exhibitions that form the basis for Mitchell's formulation of "the world-as-exhibition" discussed at the end of Chapter 1.

109. Nietzsche, *The Birth of Tragedy*, 180.

110. Nietzsche, *The Case of Wagner*, 186.

111. Nietzsche, *The Gay Science*, 142; for the German, see Nietzsche, *Werke*, vol. 5, bk. 2, p. 120.

112. Nietzsche, *The Case of Wagner*, 169.
113. Nietzsche, *Will to Power*, 255.
114. Nietzsche, *Will to Power*, 255; for the German, see Nietzsche, *Nachgelassene Werke*, 486–87.
115. Nietzsche, *Will to Power*, 255.
116. Kittler, *Discourse Networks, 1800/1900*, 185.
117. Nietzsche, *Birth of Tragedy*, 67.
118. Kittler, *Discourse Networks, 1800/1900*, 188.
119. Salomé, *Friedrich Nietzsche*, 158.
120. Nietzsche, *Genealogy of Morals*, 19; for the German, see Nietzsche, *Werke*, vol. 6, bk. 2, p. 264.

Chapter 4

1. Tucker, *The Marx-Engels Reader*, 497–99.
2. Ibid., 693–94.
3. Cited in Marin, *Utopics*, 278.
4. Marx's utopian, anti-utopian trope is itself an allusion to Goethe's formulation of the trope of emigration to America, in *Wilhelm Meister's Apprenticeship*—"America is here or nowhere" (284). Already with Goethe, this is a complex reformulation of Herder's specifically geographical formulation of the hypothesis of culture, as discussed in Chapter 1. Marx's materialist version of this hypothesis ("Europe has all the elements to set up communal wealth") is reiterated in a number of important places—in "The Eighteenth Brumaire," for example, as I discuss in *The Invention of the West* (203–11).
5. In *Cunninghame Graham: A Critical Biography*, Cedric Watts and Laurence Davies offer the best account of Cunninghame Graham in historical context.
6. Chesterton, *Autobiography*, 269.
7. The dating of the portrait is from Walter Shaw-Sparrow, *John Lavery and his Work*, 98. The quotation is from Lavery's autobiography, *The Life of a Painter*, 89. The comparison to Whistler is discussed by Kenneth McConkey in *Sir John Lavery, R.A. 1856-1941*, 43–44. I thank Raquel DaRosa for tracking down this reference.
8. Graham was much sought after as an artistic "model"—by Lavery, Will Rothenstein, Jacob Epstein, and William Strang (who used Don Roberto as a model for his etchings of Don Quixote); and also, notably, by G. B. Shaw, whose Captain Brassbound is the dramatic portrait (one of a number) most explicitly modeled on Cunninghame Graham.
9. Lavery, *The Life of a Painter*, 89.
10. Ibid., 92.
11. Shaw-Sparrow, *John Lavery and His Work*, xxiii. In the typescript of this introduction, located in the National Library of Scotland, this passage is spliced into the text (with the single variation of "stuff" for "raw material") (NLS, Deposit 205).
12. For discussion of the relation between "high" and "low" cultural forms, from a variety of disparate perspectives, see the volume in which an earlier version of

the current chapter originally appeared: DiBattista and McDiarmid, *High and Low Moderns*.

13. Tsuzuki, *Tom Mann*, 23.
14. Thompson, *William Morris*, 482–503.
15. Watts and Davies, *Cunninghame Graham*, 69.
16. Cited in Tsuzuki, *Tom Mann*, 24.
17. Tsuzuki, *Tom Mann*, 70.
18. Cunninghame Graham, *Selected Writings*, 42.
19. Ibid., 43–44.
20. Ibid., 44.
21. Ibid., 39.
22. Ibid., 40.
23. Ibid., 44.
24. Cited in Watts and Davies, *Cunninghame Graham*, 66–67.
25. Watts and Davies, *Cunninghame Graham*, 88.
26. Cited in Watts and Davies, *Cunninghame Graham*, 94.
27. Ibid., 63.
28. Watts and Davies, *Cunninghame Graham*, 64.
29. Cunninghame Graham to John Burns, 22 October 1891, Add. MSS. 46,284, British Library.
30. Laclau and Mouffe, *Hegemony and Socialist Strategy*, 7–8.
31. Cunninghame Graham, *Success*, 86.
32. Watts and Davies, *Cunninghame Graham*, 108.
33. See Cunninghame Graham's letter to Edward Garnett, 31 October 1904, in Stape and Knowles, *A Portrait in Letters*, 46.
34. Hobsbawm, *The Age of Empire*, 119.
35. After *Father Archangel of Scotland and Other Essays* (1895), a volume of tales and essays by himself and Gabriela Cunninghame Graham, his wife.
36. A choice whose importance is underscored by the fact that, together with the prospectus, it was designed to broadcast the news of the series throughout the world: "Of course the First Vol should be scattered very widely & sent to all parts of the Colonies on sale" (Garnett to Unwin, n.d., Berg Collection of English and American Literature, the New York Public Library, Astor, Lenox and Tilden Foundations).
37. For discussion of the series see Watts, *Joseph Conrad's Letters to R. B. Cunninghame Graham*; and Watts and Davies, *Cunninghame Graham*, 169–70. Further information on the *Over-Seas Library* is from Garnett's correspondence with T. Fisher Unwin, at the Berg Collection of English and American Literature, the New York Public Library, Astor, Lenox and Tilden Foundations.
38. Cunninghame Graham, *The Ipané*, flyleaf.
39. Garnett to Cunninghame Graham, 2 January 1898, National Library of Scotland, Deposit 205.
40. As Michael Taussig begins to discuss, Roger Casement is an especially interesting figure for sorting out the complexity of this sort of fantasy in the produc-

tion of what Taussig calls "the attraction and repulsion of colonial mythology" (*Shamanism, Colonialism, and the Wild Man*, 15). Casement's experiences as colonial agent (Conrad knew him from the Belgian Congo), his maligned homosexuality, and his involvement in the Irish Easter Rebellion of 1916 (for which he was hanged), made him "a traitor not only to his country but to his 'manhood'" (14). This sort of betrayal is inscribed, too, in the afterimages of Don Roberto, constituting, indeed, whatever glamour or utopian appeal they also possess.

41. Garnett to Cunninghame Graham, 17 February 1899, National Library of Scotland, Deposit 205.

42. Garnett to Cunninghame Graham, 31 July 1898, National Library of Scotland, Deposit 205.

43. The implications of this adjustment for Conrad's literary work I examine at length in *The Invention of the West*.

44. Orwell, *Dickens, Dali, and Others*, 153.

45. Garnett to Cunninghame Graham, 26 January 1899, National Library of Scotland, Deposit 205.

46. Cunninghame Graham, *The Ipané*, flyleaf.

47. Garnett to Cunninghame Graham, 22 May 1898, National Library of Scotland, Deposit 205.

48. Ibid.

49. Watts and Davies, *Cunninghame Graham*, 162; see also 161–64.

50. Garnett to Cunninghame Graham, 23 June 1898, National Library of Scotland, Deposit 205.

51. Cunninghame Graham, *Selected Writings*, 66.

52. Letter dated 6 April 1897, National Library of Scotland, Deposit 205. For details about Harriette Colenso, see Marks, "Harriette Colenso and the Zulus."

53. Upon receiving the sketches, he praised them for their variety in portraying "everyday, commonplace, exceptional, or vanishing human figures, the Gaucho on the plains, Mistress Campbell in Gart-na-Cloich, Heather Jock, or the Bristol Steamer, all remote from each other, all part of the great ridiculous common Human Family" (Garnett to Cunninghame Graham, 22 May 1898, National Library of Scotland, Deposit 205).

54. Garnett to Cunninghame Graham, 22 May 1898, National Library of Scotland, Deposit 205.

55. Garnett to Cunninghame Graham, 9 August 1898, National Library of Scotland, Deposit 205.

56. Watts and Davies, *Cunninghame Graham*, 162.

57. Garnett to Cunninghame Graham, 16 May 1901, National Library of Scotland, Deposit 205.

58. Cunninghame Graham, *Success*, 99.

59. Ibid., 98.

60. Ibid., 88.

61. Hobsbawm, *The Age of Empire*, 119.

62. E. P. Thompson has emphasized the significance of the role of newspapers in guiding Morris's response to "Bloody Sunday": "Bloody Sunday showed him not so much the weakness of the people as the true face of reaction. He saw not only the mounted police and the batons; he also saw the complicity of almost the entire capitalist Press, the treachery of the professed advocates of freedom in Parliament and public life" (*William Morris*, 502).

63. Bellamy, *Looking Backward*, 61.

64. "The huge ears of a phonographic mechanism gaped in a battery for his words, the black eyes of great photographic cameras awaited his beginning, beyond metal rods and coils glittered dimly, and something whirled about with a droning hum. He walked into the centre of the light, and his shadow drew together black and sharp to a little blot at his feet." (Wells, *When the Sleeper Wakes*, 205–6)

65. Cunninghame Graham, *The Ipané*, 187. "Heather Jock" originally appeared in *The Saturday Review*, 30 January 1897, pp. 110–12.

66. See Introduction n. 8.

67. "Heather Jock," published in January of 1897, bears an interesting relation to Conrad's "Karain: A Memory," published later that year and a forerunner of the Marlow tales. Cf., also, Aniela Kowalska, *Conrad 1896-1900*, listed in John Walker's "R. B. Cunninghame Graham: An Annotated Bibliography of Writings About Him," 115.

68. Cunninghame Graham, "Heather Jock," 112.

69. The force of the parable remains, even though Graham discarded this line from the version that appears in *The Ipané*.

70. Cunninghame Graham, *The Ipané*, 179.

71. Conrad, *The Collected Letters of Joseph Conrad*, 2:124.

72. The subtitle of Fredric Jameson's *The Political Unconscious*.

73. Cunninghame Graham, *The Ipané*, 181.

74. Conrad, *Youth and Two Other Stories*, 157.

75. In the author's note to *Youth and Two Other Stories*, Conrad writes: "'Heart of Darkness' is experience, too; but it is experience pushed a little (and only a very little) beyond the actual facts of the case for the perfectly legitimate, I believe, purpose of bringing it home to the minds and bosoms of the readers" (xi).

76. Conrad, *Youth and Two Other Stories*, 189, 238.

77. Cunninghame Graham, *The Ipané*, 182.

78. Ibid., 181–82.

79. Cunninghame Graham, *Notes on the District of Menteith*, 6.

80. See Watts and Davies, *Cunninghame Graham*, 173, 174.

81. Cited in Watts and Davies, *Cunninghame Graham*, 174.

82. Watts and Davies, *Cunninghame Graham*, 175–76.

83. Ibid., 176.

84. Cunninghame Graham and Cunninghame Graham, *Father Archangel of Scotland and Other Essays*, 167.

85. Cunninghame Graham, *The Ipané*, 186.

86. Fredric Jameson, "Of Islands and Trenches: Neutralization and the Production of Utopian Discourse," in *The Ideologies of Theory*, 82.
87. Cunninghame Graham, *The Ipané*, 24.
88. See Peralta and Osuna, *Diccionario Guaraní–Español y Español–Guaraní*.

Chapter 5

1. Jameson, *The Geopolitical Aesthetic*, 4.
2. Ibid., 3.
3. O Tuathail, *Critical Geopolitics*, chapter 4, 111–40. O Tuathail cites from a 1943 review of books on geopolitics written by Robert Strausz-Hupé, "It's Smart to be Geopolitical": "The awakening of the American public to global consciousness created a ready market for 'systems' of global politics . . . [and] in the absence of any similar product, geopolitics became the raging fashion" (cited on p. 112).
4. O Tuathail, *Critical Geopolitics*, 133.
5. Tucker, *The Marx-Engels Reader*, 473.
6. Orwell, *The Lost Writings*, 81.
7. Ibid., 81–82.
8. Ibid., 83.
9. Cited in Brissenden, *The I.W.W.: A Study in American Syndicalism*, 385. Consider also the wording of the Minnesota statute: "Criminal syndicalism is hereby defined as the doctrine which advocates crime, sabotage (*this word as used in this bill meaning malicious damage or injury to the property of an employer by an employee*), violence or other unlawful methods of terrorism as a means of accomplishing industrial or political ends" (381).
10. Orwell, *The Lost Writings*, 81.
11. Brown, *Sabotage*, xii.
12. Russell, *Proposed Roads to Freedom*, 66.
13. Ibid., 66–67.
14. Veblen, *The Engineers and the Price System*, 1–2. The essay was originally published in the *Dial* in 1919.
15. Brown, *Sabotage*, 43.
16. Veblen, *The Engineers and the Price System*, 6–7.
17. Ibid., 18.
18. The style of "debunking" in Veblen's cultural criticism rests, according to Adorno, on "a moment of buffoonery" ("ein Moment der Clownerie") (*Prisms*, 84). Adorno's critique of Veblen's *The Theory of the Leisure Class* is relevant to the current discussion, since Adorno finds in Veblen's "amalgam of positivism and historical materialism" (78) an uncritical acceptance of industrial and technological progress. That uncritical element in Veblen's "attack on culture" makes Veblen unable to grasp dialectically the true significance of "leisure" in modern industrial society—what Adorno himself (writing in 1941) was engaged in doing, in the celebrated collaboration with Horkheimer in their critique of the Culture Industry.

Veblen's "scorn" for "conspicuous consumption," according to Adorno, leads him to misdiagnose the function of pleasure in modern society. Adorno's diagnosis, a kind of miniature rehearsal for the argument of *The Dialectic of Enlightenment*, turns on the dialectical interrelation between utopia and sabotage:

> Kein Glück, das nicht dem gesellshaftlich konstituierten Wunsch Erfüllung verhieße, aber auch keines, das nicht in dieser Erfüllung das Andere verspräche. Die abstrakte Utopie, die darüber sich täuscht, wird zur Sabotage am Glück die gesellschaftlichen Male zu tilgen unternimmt, muss sie zur Leugnung jeglichen konkreten Glücksanspruchs schreiten und den Menschen zur blossen Funktion seiner eigenen Arbeit reduzieren. (Adorno, *Prismen*, 100–101)
>
> [There is no happiness which does not promise to fulfill a socially constituted desire, but there is also none which does not promise something qualitatively different in this fulfillment. Abstract utopian thinking which deludes itself about this, sabotages happiness and plays into the hands of that which it seeks to negate. For, although it strives to purge happiness of the social stigma, it is forced to renounce every concrete claim to happiness and to reduce human beings to a mere function of their own work. (Adorno, *Prisms*, 87)]

19. Conrad, *The Collected Letters of Joseph Conrad*, 3:333.

20. Pouget, *Le Syndicat*, 19. Since this is the earliest trace of the word "sabotage" I have found, it is interesting to note that the German translation of this pamphlet, which appeared the same year, reproduces the list of syndicalist tactics as follows: "Je nach der Lage benutzen sie *Streik, Sabot, Boykott, Label*" (Depending on the situation they make use of *strike, sabotage, boycott, label*) (*Die Gewerkschaft*, 25).

21. As described by Louis Adamic in his 1934 reflections *Dynamite*, 374.

22. Pouget, *Le Sabotage*, 3 (my translation). Cf. Giovannitti's translation: "Up to fifteen years ago the term SABOTAGE was nothing but a slang word, not meaning 'to make wooden shoes' as it may be imagined but, in a figurative way, TO WORK CLUMSILY AS IF BY SABOT BLOWS" (Pouget, *Sabotage*, 37). Pouget adds the footnote: "*Sabot* means a wooden shoe."

23. Pouget, *Le Sabotage*, 3. Cf. Giovannitti's translation: "The new term was not at first accepted by the working class with the warmest enthusiasm—some even saw it with mistrust, reproaching it not only for its humble origin but also its—immorality" (Pouget, *Sabotage*, 37–38).

24. Pouget, *Le Sabotage*, 3. Cf. Giovannitti's translation: "Nevertheless, despite all these prejudices which seemed almost hostilities, SABOTAGE went steadily on its way around the world. It has now the full sympathy of the workers. More still, it has secured its rights of citizenship in the Larousse and there is no doubt that the Academy (unless it is itself 'saboted' before arriving at the letter S of its dictionary) will have to bow to the word SABOTAGE its most ceremonious curtsey and open to it the pages of its official sanctum" (Pouget, *Sabotage*, 38). Giovannitti adds in a footnote explaining that the Larousse is the "standard dictionary of the French lan-

guage": "The word is not registered in any English dictionary, but it surely will be in the near future."

25. Pouget, *Le Sabotage*, 3–4. Cf. Giovannitti's translation: "However, it would be a mistake to believe that the working class waited to apply sabotage until this new weapon of economic action had been consecrated by the confederation congress. Sabotage as a form of revolt is as old as human exploitation" (Pouget, *Sabotage*, 38).

26. The cartoon appeared in the 26 May 1917 issue of *Solidarity* under the caption "The Sphinx: 'How Little you Look to Me Mr. Exploiter.'" See Salerno, *Red November, Black November*, where the cartoon is reproduced (23).

27. See Adamic, *Dynamite*; Brown, *Sabotage*; and Salerno, *Red November, Black November*.

28. Brown, *Sabotage*, 25.

29. Ibid., 29.

30. Pouget, *Le Sabotage*, 5. Cf. Giovannitti's translation: "Neither must it be believed that sabotage is a product with a Parisian trade mark. It is, indeed, if anything, a theory of English importation and it has been practiced across the Channel for a long time under the name of 'Go cannie'—a Scotch expression which means literally "Go slow" (Pouget, *Sabotage*, 41).

31. Pouget's variant spelling of "ca' canny" as "go canny" suggests the kind of anti-Scots, Anglicized polemic registered in the Webbs' anxiety about the effects on the "personal character" of workers that might result from what they termed "the doctrine of 'go'canny'" (cited in Brown, *Sabotage*, 8).

32. Orwell, *The Lost Writings*, 81.

33. Cunninghame Graham, "Ca Canny," 6.

34. As Watts and Davies explain: "Graham did not involve himself in organizing strikes; all too often, he felt, they focused on particular grievances to the point of losing sight of the general picture. There were other means available. In the short term, there was the policy of 'Ca' canny': 'Reduce your output; for poor wages, give a poor day's work.' In the long term, there was labour representation: 'The strike is dear and drains the union funds, but legislation does not cost a penny.'" (Watts and Davies, *Cunninghame Graham*, 87)

35. Pouget, *Le Sabotage*, 7–8.

36. Sorel, *Reflections on Violence*, 137.

37. Laclau and Mouffe, *Hegemony and Socialist Strategy*, 41. The passage I quote from Sorel is also the key passage cited by Laclau and Mouffe (40).

38. Lenin, in 1914, wrote: "Only the waves of mass strikes that swept over the whole country, strikes connected with the severe lessons of the imperialist Russo-Japanese War, roused the broad masses of peasants from their lethargy. The word 'striker' acquired an entirely new meaning among the peasants: it signified rebel, a revolutionary, a term previously expressed by the word 'student'" (Tucker, *The Lenin Anthology*, 283–84).

39. Conrad, *The Secret Agent*, xxxvii (hereafter cited as *TSA* in the text).

40. Conrad's account of the origins of the novel lays notable emphasis on dia-

logic exchange: he claims he himself came upon the topic in "casual conversation [with a friend] about anarchists or rather anarchist activities" (*TSA*, xxxiii); and discussing his use of "the rather summary recollections of an Assistant Commissioner of Police" (Anderson's *Sidelights on the Home Rule Movement*), he claims to have been "arrested" by "a little passage of about seven lines, in which the author . . . reproduced a short dialogue held in the Lobby of the House of Commons after some unexpected anarchist outrage, with the Home Secretary" (*TSA*, xxxv).

41. Pataud and Pouget, *How We Shall Bring About the Revolution*, xxxviii.

42. "Hier soir je me suis echappé du navire pour le pélérinage de la gare. J'ai mon colis 4 mille et quelque chose. Voyez un peu une oeuvre d'art appelée: colis No: 4000 etc!! J'ai dit a l'individu au guichet: 'Monsieur votre lettre d'avis est une infamie'—'Plait-il?'—'Une infamie; vous êtes des scélérats des bourgeois. Comprenez-Vous?—Non—repondit-il—mais Vous êtes un anarchiste, Vous! Ou est Votre bombe? La-dessus comme il criait 'au secours!' je m'enfuis et je me precipite dans un fiacre. 'Cocher'—dis-je—'je suis pressé, detelez votre cheval; la voiture roulera plus vite.'—'Fameuse idée. s'ecriat-il.—Et voilà comment j'ai echappé aux agents de police altérés de mon sang." (Yesterday evening, I escaped from the ship for the pilgrimage to the station. I have my parcel No. 4000 and something. Just imagine a work of art called Parcel No. 4000, etc. etc.!! I said to the person at the window: "Sir, your letter is an outrage." "I beg your pardon?" "An outrage. You are bourgeois scoundrels. Do you understand?" "No," he replied, "but you are an anarchist, that's what you are! Where is your bomb?" Thereupon, while he was shouting, "Help!" I fled, throwing myself into a cab. "Driver," I said, "I am in a hurry, unharness your horses; the cab will go faster." "Fine idea," he cried. And that is how I escaped the police officers who were thirsting for my blood.) (Conrad, *The Collected Letters of Joseph Conrad*, 1:142–43; translation from the same source). Karl and Davies date the letter 7 January 1894, noting that the Greenwich explosion occurred "soon after" on 15 February.

43. For discussion of the relation of modernism to anarchism, see, inter alia, Weir, *Anarchy and Culture*, and compare his discussion of *The Secret Agent*, in particular.

44. English, *Comic Transactions*, 39, 52.

45. Conrad, indeed, seems deliberately to follow the psychological disorders Bergson offers as examples throughout *Matter and Memory*—thus, testing his hypothesis of a motor-mechanism coordinating perception-images and memory-images, Bergson considers a case of "word deafness," in which the patient retains the memory of words and the ability to hear, but cannot recognize the spoken word: "there must therefore be in consciousness itself a gap, a solution of continuity, something, whatever it is, which hinders the perception from joining the memories" (115). It is worth noting the odd resonance between this and a passage in *The Secret Agent*: "In the close-woven stuff of relations between conspirator and police there occur unexpected solutions of continuity, sudden holes in space and time" (*TSA*, 85). Whether or not the odd phrase "solutions of continuity" is deliberately

lifted from Bergson, the consequence is the same: Conrad's novel dwells on the "gap" in consciousness; his concern is not the working mechanism of "consciousness" but rather its breakdown.

46. Watt claims that the narrative device "takes us directly into the observer's consciousness at the very moment of the perception, before it has been translated into its cause" (cited in Lothe, *Conrad's Narrative Method*, 40).

47. Watts, *The Deceptive Text*, 43.

48. Lothe, *Conrad's Narrative Method*, 30.

49. See my *The Invention of the West*, 180.

50. Bergson, *Oeuvres*, 483.

51. Benjamin, *Illuminations*, 157. Benjamin goes on to argue that Bergson's philosophy "thus indirectly furnishes a clue to the experience which presented itself to Baudelaire's eyes in its undistorted version in the figure of the reader." One might say, following this train of thought, that the question of readership with Conrad furnishes a further clue to the problem Benjamin seeks to address here; for with Conrad the "figure of the reader" is ultimately eclipsed altogether—not so much in the gesture of hostility against mass readership sometimes ascribed to Conrad's texts, but rather in the premise that mass, popular readership is itself a product of the new technologies of "big-scale industrialism."

52. Conrad, *Youth and Two Other Stories*, 157.

53. See Buck-Morss, *The Dialectics of Seeing*, especially 66–67.

54. See Aumont, *Montage Eisenstein*; see also Mark Wollaeger's comments in "Killing Stevie," 349.

55. Wollaeger, "Killing Stevie," 326.

56. Deleuze, *Cinema* 1, 1–11, and passim.

57. Bergson, *Matter and Memory*, 103.

58. Put another way, if the network of things represented by Conrad's London stationery anticipates the social function of the movie theater, Hitchcock's movie theater serves as a kind of nostalgic reconstruction of the London shop. For us, the movie theater may *seem* a more perfect location, because the function of a stationery shop appears to have been replaced by the function of cinema. The historical significance of the stationery, embedded in the hieroglyph of its name, is relevant here: connected to the archaic meaning of bookseller and publisher, the Company of Stationers controlled the circulation of printed matter up until the passing of the Copyright Act of 1842. For Dickens, this plays a significant part in the literary representation of London as a nexus of literary commerce. Conrad replays the Dickensian literary scene of London as a nightmare of commercial letters disfigured through mass (re)production—in Kittler's terms, transposing the lettered discourse network of 1800 into the multimedia discourse network of 1900.

59. Truffaut, *Hitchcock*, 138. See also the discussion in the Introduction to the present volume.

60. This coordination of a relation between work and leisure is what enables the movie to name "sabotage" more effectively than, for example, Charlie Chaplin's

Modern Times, which otherwise offers a clearer *representation* of sabotage, and in which, moreover, the disruption of industrial machinery is linked to the apparatus of the movie industry, as Mark Wollaeger points out, comparing Verloc's tragic end to Chaplin's miraculous survival: "One thinks of Verloc's death in *The Secret Agent*, in which the clock trope describing his dripping blood evokes the body's subordination to mechanical time, and of a film precisely contemporaneous with *Sabotage*, Charlie Chaplin's *Modern Times* (1936), in which the little tramp is wound through the massive cogs of an industrial machine that also resembles the film apparatus" (346).

61. For extensive discussion of this important context for Hitchcock's movies, see Ryall, *Alfred Hitchcock and the British Cinema*.

62. Gilroy, *The Black Atlantic*.

63. Hitchcock himself suggests the linking of these three movies: "*North by Northwest* can be seen as a remake of *Saboteur*. The approach to both pictures was a desire to cover various parts of America in the same way that *The Thirty-Nine Steps* travelled across England and Scotland" (Truffaut, *Hitchcock*, 150).

64. Truffaut, *Hitchcock*, 125.

65. In a 1939 interview, "What I'd Do to the Stars," Hitchcock rehearsed this fantasy in terms of what he would do with Gary Cooper: "I would have him mixed up in a big studio swindle in which thugs and professional strikers are brought in by one big producer to sabotage the property of another—or something along those lines" (Gottlieb, *Hitchcock on Hitchcock*, 91).

66. Truffaut, *Hitchcock*, 151.

67. Ibid., 127.

68. Laura Mulvey, "Visual Pleasure and Narrative Cinema," in Penley, *Feminism and Film Theory*, 57–68.

69. Tey, *A Shilling for Candles*, 19.

70. Ibid.

71. Žižek, *Looking Awry*, 96.

72. Rothman, *Hitchcock*. What I consider here as the most interesting and productive point of reference in Hitchcock's movies, their "blindspots," Rothman considers as problems requiring solutions—and, with *Sabotage* particularly in mind, as problems of "hold[ing] his audience while acknowledging its capacity to acknowledge him" (175). Wollaeger considers this problem extensively in terms of "mastery." As with Conrad's "delayed decoding," however, the effects of mastery may always be more delayed than our critical perspectives like to believe.

73. The effect seems to me analogous to the manner in which, according to Rey Chow, Zhang Yimou's films produce a "collective, hallucinatory signification of 'ethnicity'" (see Chow, *Primitive Passions*, 144).

74. Tey, *A Shilling for Candles*, 76.

Bibliography

Abel, Elizabeth, Marianne Hirsch, and Elizabeth Langland, eds. *The Voyage In: Fictions of Female Development*. Hanover, N.H.: University Press of New England, 1983.
Adamic, Louis. *Dynamite: The Story of Class Violence in America*. New York: Viking, 1934.
Adorno, Theodor. *Prisms*. Translated by Samuel Weber and Shierry Weber. Cambridge, Mass.: MIT Press, 1981. Originally published as *Prismen* (Frankfurt: Suhrkamp, 1976).
Agnew, John. *Geopolitics: Re-Visioning World Politics*. London: Routledge, 1998.
Anderson, Benedict. *Imagined Communities: Reflections on the Origin and Spread of Nationalism*. Rev. ed. New York: Verso, 1991.
Anderson, Robert. *Sidelights on the Home Rule Movement*. London: John Murray, 1906.
Arato, Andrew, and Eike Gebhardt, eds. *The Essential Frankfurt School Reader*. New York: Continuum, 1990.
Archer, John Michael. *Sovereignty and Intelligence: Spying and Court Culture in the English Renaissance*. Stanford, Calif.: Stanford University Press, 1993.
Archer, Mildred. *India and British Portraiture: 1770-1825*. London: Sotheby Parke Bernet, 1979.
Armstrong, Nancy. *Desire and Domestic Fiction: A Political History of the Novel*. Oxford: Oxford University Press, 1987.
Arnold, Matthew. *Culture and Anarchy*. 1869. Reprint, Cambridge: Cambridge University Press, 1960.
———. *Schools and Universities on the Continent*. London: Macmillan & Co., 1868.
———. *Selected Prose*. Harmondsworth, U.K.: Penguin, 1970.
Aumont, Jacques. *Montage Eisenstein*. Bloomington: Indiana University Press, 1987.

Bailey, Anne, and Josep R. Llobera. *The Asiatic Mode of Production: Science and Politics.* London: Routledge & Kegan Paul, 1981.
Barash, Carol. "Virile Womanhood: Olive Schreiner's Narratives of a Master Race." In *Speaking of Gender*, edited by Elaine Showalter. New York: Routledge, 1989.
Barnard, Frederick M., ed. and trans. *J. G. Herder on Social and Political Culture.* Cambridge: Cambridge University Press, 1969.
Barney, Richard A., ed. Special issue on "Education, Identity, and Constructions of the Novel." *Genre* 26, no. 4 (1993).
Barrell, John. *The Infection of Thomas de Quincey: A Psychopathology of Imperialism.* New Haven, Conn.: Yale University Press, 1991.
Bartholomew, John George. "A Plea for a National Institute of Geography." Reprint from *The Scottish Geographical Magazine* 18, no. 3 (March 1902): 144–48.
Bellamy, Edward. *Looking Backward: 2000-1887.* 1887. Reprint, New York: Penguin, 1982.
Benjamin, Walter. *Illuminations.* Translated by Harry Zohn. New York: Schocken Books, 1978.
———. *Reflections: Essays, Aphorisms, Autobiographical Writings.* Translated by Edmund Jephcott. New York: Schocken Books, 1978.
Bergson, Henri. *Matter and Memory.* Translated by Nancy Margaret Paul and W. Scott Palmer. New York: Zone Books, 1991. Originally published as *Matière et Mémoire* (Paris: Presses Universitaires de France, 1896).
———. *Oeuvres.* Édition du Centenaire. Paris: Presses Universitaires de France, 1972.
Bhabha, Homi. *The Location of Culture.* London: Routledge, 1994.
Bismarck, Otto Fürst von. *Gedanken und Erinnerungen.* 2 vols. 1898. Reprint, Stuttgart: J. C. Cotta, 1915.
Bloch, Maurice. *Marxism and Anthropology.* Oxford: Oxford University Press, 1983.
Blondel, Eric. *Nietzsche: The Body and Culture; Philosophy as a Philological Genealogy.* Translated by Seán Hand. Stanford, Calif.: Stanford University Press, 1991.
Bottomore, Tom, ed. *A Dictionary of Marxist Thought.* Cambridge, Mass.: Blackwell, 1995.
Bourdieu, Pierre. *Distinction: A Social Critique of the Judgement of Taste.* Translated by Richard Nice. Cambridge, Mass.: Harvard University Press, 1984. Originally published as *La Distinction: Critique sociale du jugement* (Paris: Les Éditions de Minuit, 1979).
———. *Outline of a Theory of Practice.* Translated by Richard Nice. Cambridge: Cambridge University Press, 1977. Originally published as *Esquisse d'une théorie de la pratique, précédé de trois études d'ethnologie kabyle* (Switzerland: Librairie Droz, 1972).

Brantlinger, Patrick. *Rule of Darkness: British Literature and Imperialism, 1830-1914.* Ithaca, N.Y.: Cornell University Press, 1980.
Brissenden, Paul. *The I.W.W.: A Study in American Syndicalism.* New York: Longmans, 1920.
Brown, Geoff. *Sabotage: A Study in Industrial Conflict.* Bristol, U.K.: Spokesman Books, 1977.
Browning, Robert. *The Poems.* Edited by John Pettigrew. 2 vols. New Haven, Conn.: Yale University Press, 1981.
Buck-Morss, Susan. *The Dialectics of Seeing: Walter Benjamin and the Arcades Project.* Cambridge, Mass.: MIT Press, 1989.
Buckle, Henry Thomas. *History of Civilization in England.* 3 vols. 1857–1861. Reprint, London: Oxford University Press, 1911.
Burgard, Peter, ed. *Nietzsche and the Feminine.* Charlottesville: University Press of Virginia, 1994.
Buttmann, Günther. *Friedrich Ratzel: Leben und Werk eines Deutschen Geographen, 1844-1904.* Stuttgart: Wissenschaftliche Verlagsgesellschaft MBH, 1977.
Cheah, Pheng. "Given Culture: Rethinking Cosmopolitical Freedom in Transnationalism." In *Cosmopolitics: Thinking and Feeling Beyond the Nation,* ed. Pheng Cheah and Bruce Robbins. Minneapolis: University of Minnesota Press, 1998.
Cheah, Pheng, and Bruce Robbins, eds. *Cosmopolitics: Thinking and Feeling Beyond the Nation.* Minneapolis: University of Minnesota Press, 1998.
Chesterton, G. K. *Autobiography.* London: Hutchinson, 1936.
Chow, Rey. *Primitive Passions: Visuality, Sexuality, Ethnography, and Contemporary Chinese Cinema.* New York: Columbia University Press, 1995.
Clark, John. "The Dialectical Social Geography of Elisée Reclus." *Philosophy and Geography.* Vol. 1, *Space, Place, and Environmental Ethics.* Lanham, Md.: Rowman and Littlefield, 1997.
Clifford, James. *The Predicament of Culture: Twentieth-Century Ethnography, Literature, and Art.* Cambridge, Mass.: Harvard University Press, 1988.
Cohn, Bernard S. *Colonialism and Its Forms of Knowledge: The British in India.* Princeton: Princeton University Press, 1996.
———. "Representing Authority in Victorian India." In *The Invention of Tradition,* edited by Eric Hobsbawm and Terence Ranger. Cambridge: Cambridge University Press, 1983.
Collins, Wilkie. *Armadale.* 1866. Reprint, Oxford: Oxford University Press, 1989.
———. *Blind Love.* 1890. Reprint, New York: Dover, 1986.
———. *Hide and Seek.* 1854. Reprint, Oxford: Oxford University Press, 1993.
———. *Memoirs of the Life of William Collins, R.A.* London: Longman, 1848.
———. *The Moonstone.* 1868. Reprint, Harmondsworth, U.K.: Penguin, 1987.
———. *My Miscellanies.* London: Sampson Low, 1863.
———. *No Name.* 1862. Reprint, Oxford: Oxford University Press, 1986.
———. *Poor Miss Finch.* 1872. Reprint, Oxford: Oxford University Press, 1995.
———. *The Woman in White.* 1860. Reprint, Harmondsworth, U.K.: Penguin, 1979.

Collins, William. *Memoirs of a Picture: Containing the Adventures of Many Conspicuous Characters, and Interspersed with a Variety of Amusing Anecdotes of Several Very Extraordinary Personages Connected with the Arts; Including a Genuine Biographical Record of that Celebrated Original and Eccentric Genius, the Late Mr. George Morland.* 3 vols. London: C. Stower, 1805.

Conrad, Joseph. *The Collected Letters of Joseph Conrad.* Edited by Frederick Karl and Laurence Davies. 5 vols. to date. Cambridge: Cambridge University Press, 1983–.

———. *The Secret Agent: A Simple Tale.* Oxford: Oxford University Press, 1996.

———. *Youth and Two Other Stories.* New York: Doubleday, 1926.

Copjec, Joan, ed. *Supposing the Subject.* London: Verso, 1994.

Crary, Jonathan. *Techniques of the Observer: On Vision and Modernity in the Nineteenth Century.* Cambridge, Mass.: MIT Press, 1996.

Cunningham, Allan. *The Life of Sir David Wilkie.* London, 1843.

Cunninghame Graham, Robert Bontine. "Ca Canny." *The People's Press,* 29 November 1890, 6–7.

———. "Heather Jock." *The Saturday Review,* 30 January 1897, 110–12.

———. *The Ipané.* The Overseas Library. London: T. Fisher Unwin, 1899.

———. *Mogreb-el-Acksa: A Journey to Morocco.* London: Heinemann, 1898.

———. *Notes on the District of Menteith for Tourists and Others.* London: Adam & Charles Black, 1895.

———. *Selected Writings of Cunninghame Graham.* Edited by Cedric Watts. London: Associated University Presses, 1981.

———. *Success.* London: Duckworth, 1902.

———. *Thirteen Stories.* London: Heinemann, 1900.

———. *A Vanished Arcadia: Being Some Account of the Jesuits in Paraguay, 1607 to 1767.* London: Heinemann, 1901.

Cunninghame Graham, R. B., and Gabriela Cunninghame Graham. *Father Archangel of Scotland and Other Essays.* London: Adam & Charles Black, 1896.

Cvetkovich, Ann. *Mixed Feelings: Feminism, Mass Culture, and Victorian Sensationalism.* New Brunswick, N.J.: Rutgers University Press, 1992.

Deleuze, Gilles. *Cinema 1: The Movement-Image.* Translated by Hugh Tomlinson and B. Habberjam. Minneapolis: University of Minnesota Press, 1986.

———. *Cinema 2: The Time-Image.* Translated by Hugh Tomlinson. Minneapolis: University of Minnesota Press, 1989.

———. *Nietzsche and Philosophy.* Translated by Hugh Tomlinson. New York: Columbia University Press, 1983.

Derrida, Jacques. *Aporias.* Translated by Thomas Dutoit. Stanford, Calif.: Stanford University Press, 1993.

———. *The Gift of Death.* Translated by David Wills. Chicago: University of Chicago Press, 1995.

———. *Specters of Marx: The State of the Debt, the Work of Mourning, and the New International.* Translated by Peggy Kamuf. London: Routledge, 1994.

Devi, Mahasweta. *Imaginary Maps*. Translated by Gayatri Chakravorty Spivak. London: Routledge, 1995.
DiBattista, Maria, and Lucy McDiarmid, eds. *High and Low Moderns: Literature and Culture, 1889-1939*. New York: Oxford University Press, 1996.
Dilthey, Wilhelm. *Das Erlebnis und die Dichtung*. 1905. 4th revised edition, Leipzig: Teubner, 1913.
Dorpalen, Andreas. *The World of General Haushofer: Geopolitics in Action*. Port Washington, Wis.: Kennikat Press, 1942.
Draznin, Yaffa Claire. *"My Other Self": The Letters of Olive Schreiner and Havelock Ellis, 1884–1920*. New York: Peter Lang, 1992.
Duncan, Ian. "*The Moonstone*, the Victorian Novel, and Imperialist Panic." *Modern Language Quarterly* 55, no. 3 (September 1994): 297–319.
English, James F. *Comic Transactions: Literature, Humor, and the Politics of Community in Twentieth-Century Britain*. Ithaca, N.Y.: Cornell University Press, 1994.
Fassbender, Peter. *Kupka, Balla, Delaunay/Ferk: Eine Untersuchung zu den Anfängen der Gegenstandslosen Malerei bis 1914*. Kastellaun: A. Henn, 1979.
First, Ruth, and Ann Scott. *Olive Schreiner*. New York: Schocken, 1980.
Fleming, Marie. *The Anarchist Way to Socialism: Elisée Reclus and Nineteenth-Century European Anarchism*. London: Croom Helm, 1979.
Flynn, Elizabeth Gurley. *Sabotage: The Conscious Withdrawal of Workers' Industrial Efficiency*. Cleveland: I.W.W. Publishing Bureau, 1916.
Forrest, Denys. *Tiger of Mysore: The Life and Death of Tipu Sultan*. London: Chatto & Windus, 1970.
Förster-Nietzsche, Elisabeth. *The Life of Nietzsche*. Translated by Paul V. Cohn. 2 vols. New York: Sturgis and Walton Company, 1915. Volume 1 originally published as *Der junge Nietzsche* (Leipzig: Alfred Kröner, 1912); volume 2 originally published as *Der einsame Nietzsche* (Leipzig: Alfred Kröner, 1914).
———. Introduction to *Thus Spake Zarathustra* by Friedrich Nietzsche (trans. Thomas Common). New York: The Modern Library, n.d.
Foucault, Michel. *The History of Sexuality*. Vol. 1: *An Introduction*. New York: Vintage, 1980.
Fraiman, Susan. *Unbecoming Women: British Women Writers and the Novel of Development*. New York: Columbia University Press, 1993.
Geddes, Patrick. *City Development: A Study of Parks, Gardens, and Culture-Institutes*. Birmingham: St. George's Press, 1904.
———. "A Great Geographer: Elisée Reclus, 1830–1905." Parts 1 and 2. *The Scottish Geographical Magazine* 21, no. 9 (September 1905): 490–96; 21, no. 10 (October 1905): 548–55.
———. "Nature Study and Geographical Education." *The Scottish Geographical Magazine* 18, no. 10 (October 1902): 525–36.
Gilroy, Paul. *The Black Atlantic: Modernity and Double Consciousness*. Cambridge, Mass.: Harvard University Press, 1993.

Godlewska, Anne, and Neil Smith. *Geography and Empire*. Oxford: Blackwell, 1994.
Goethe, Johann Wolfgang von. *Wilhelm Meister's Apprenticeship*. Edited and translated by Eric A. Blackall. New York: Suhrkamp, 1989.
———. *Wilhelm Meisters Lehrjahre*. 1796. Reprint, Frankfurt am Main: Insel, 1980.
GoGwilt, Christopher. *The Invention of the West: Joseph Conrad and the Double Mapping of Europe and Empire*. Stanford, Calif.: Stanford University Press, 1995.
Gottlieb, Sidney, ed. *Hitchcock on Hitchcock: Selected Writings and Interviews*. Berkeley: University of California Press, 1997.
Goudsblom, Johann. *Nihilism and Culture*. London: Blackwell, 1980.
Gramsci, Antonio. *Selections from the Prison Notebooks*. Edited and translated by Quintin Hoare and Geoffrey Nowell Smith. New York: International Publishers, 1971.
Gregory, Derek. *Geographical Imaginations*. Cambridge, Mass.: Blackwell, 1994.
Guha, Ranajit. *Elementary Aspects of Peasant Insurgency*. Delhi: Oxford University Press, 1983.
Guha, Ranajit, and Gayatri Spivak, eds. *Selected Subaltern Studies*. Oxford: Oxford University Press, 1988.
Hall, Catherine. "Rethinking Imperial Histories: The Reform Act of 1867." *New Left Review* 208 (November/December 1994): 3–29.
Hall, Stuart. "Cultural Studies and the Centre: Some Problematics and Problems." In *Culture, Media, Language: Working Papers in Cultural Studies*, edited by D. Hobson Hall, A. Lowe, and P. Wills. Hutchinson: CCCS, 1980.
———. "Notes on Deconstructing 'the Popular.'" In *People's History and Socialist Theory*. London: Routledge, 1981.
Hardy, Thomas. *Jude the Obscure*. 1896. Reprint, Harmondsworth, U.K.: Penguin, 1978.
Hegel, Georg Wilhelm Friedrich. *Phenomenology of Spirit*. Translated by A. V. Miller. Oxford: Oxford University Press, 1977.
———. *Philosophy of Right*. Translated by T. M. Knox. Oxford: Oxford University Press, 1967.
Heidegger, Martin. *Holzwege*. Frankfurt am Main: Klostermann, 1980.
———. *Nietzsche: Der Europäische Nihilismus*. Frankfurt: Klostermann, 1986.
Heller, Tamar. *Dead Secrets: Wilkie Collins and the Female Gothic*. New Haven, Conn.: Yale University Press, 1992.
Hennelly, Mark. "Detecting Collins' Diamond: From Serpentstone to Moonstone." *Nineteenth-Century Fiction* 39, no. 1 (1984): 25–47.
Herbertson, A. J. "Recent Discussion on the Scope and Educational Applications of Geography." *The Geographical Journal* 24, no. 4 (October 1904): 417–27.
Herder, Johann Gottfried. *Ideen zur Philosophie der Geschichte der Menschheit*. 1784–1791. Reprint, Frankfurt am Main: Deutscher Klassiker Verlag, 1989.

———. *Outlines of a Philosophy of the History of Man.* Translated by T. Churchill. New York: Bergman Publishers, [1800?].

———. *Reflections on the Philosophy of the History of Mankind.* Abridged by Frank E. Manuel [based on the Churchill translation]. Chicago: University of Chicago Press, 1968.

Hobsbawm, Eric J. *The Age of Empire, 1875-1914.* New York: Vintage, 1989.

Hopkins, Terence K., and Immanuel Wallerstein. *World-Systems Analysis: Theory and Methodology.* Beverly Hills: Sage Publications, 1982.

Horkheimer, Max, and Theodor W. Adorno. *Dialectic of Enlightenment.* Translated by John Cumming. New York: Seabury Press, 1972. Originally published as *Dialektik der Aufklärung* (New York: Social Studies Association, 1944).

Horton, Susan. *Difficult Women, Artful Lives: Olive Schreiner and Isak Dinesen, In and Out of Africa.* Baltimore: Johns Hopkins University Press, 1995.

Hunter, James. *Perspectives on Ratzel's Political Geography.* Lanham, Md.: University Press of America, 1983.

Husserl, Edmund. *Phenomenology and the Crisis of Philosophy: Philosophy as Rigorous Science and Philosophy and the Crisis of European Man.* Translated by Quentin Lauer. New York: Harper and Row, 1965.

Jameson, Fredric. "Cognitive Mapping." In *Marxism and the Interpretation of Culture*, edited by Cary Nelson and Lawrence Grossberg. Urbana: University of Illinois Press, 1988.

———. *The Geopolitical Aesthetic: Cinema and Space in the World System.* Bloomington: Indiana University Press, 1992.

———. *The Ideologies of Theory: Essays 1971-1986.* 2 vols. Minneapolis: University of Minnesota Press, 1988.

———. *The Political Unconscious: Narrative as a Socially Symbolic Act.* Ithaca, N.Y.: Cornell University Press, 1981.

———. *Postmodernism, or, The Cultural Logic of Late Capitalism.* Durham, N.C.: Duke University Press, 1991.

Jenkins, Edward. *Blot on the Queen's Head: or, How Little Ben, the waiter, changed the sign of the "Queen's inn" to "Empress Hotel, limited," and the consequences thereof.* London: Strahan, 1876.

Joyce, James. *A Portrait of the Artist as a Young Man.* 1916. Reprint, Harmondsworth, U.K.: Penguin, 1985.

Kahane, Claire. *Passions of the Voice: Hysteria, Narrative, and the Figure of the Speaking Woman, 1850-1915.* Baltimore: Johns Hopkins University Press, 1995.

Kant, Immanuel. *Political Writings.* Edited by Hans Reiss, translated by H. B. Nisbet. 2d, enlarged ed. Cambridge: Cambridge University Press, 1991.

Keltie, J. Scott. *Geographical Education: Report to the Council of the Royal Geographical Society.* London: John Murray, 1885.

Kern, Stephen. *The Culture of Time and Space, 1880-1918.* Cambridge, Mass.: Harvard University Press, 1983.

Kittler, Friedrich. *Discourse Networks, 1800/1900*. Stanford, Calif.: Stanford University Press, 1990.
Kjellén, Rudolf. *Grundriss zu einem System der Politik*. Leipzig: S. Hirzel, 1920.
———. *Der Staat als Lebensform*. Leipzig: S. Hirzel, 1917.
Krauss, Rosalind. *The Optical Unconscious*. Cambridge, Mass.: MIT Press, 1993.
Kropotkin, Peter. *Memoirs of a Revolutionist*. 1899. Reprint, London: Cresset, 1962.
Kucich, John. *The Power of Lies: Transgression in Victorian Fiction*. Ithaca, N.Y.: Cornell University Press, 1994.
Kupka, Frantisek. *Frantisek Kupka, 1871-1957: A Retrospective*. New York: Solomon R. Guggenheim Foundation, 1975.
Lacan, Jacques. *The Four Fundamental Concepts of Psycho-Analysis*. New York: Norton, 1981.
Laclau, Ernesto, and Chantal Mouffe. *Hegemony and Socialist Strategy: Towards a Radical Democratic Politics*. London: Verso, 1985.
Lacoste, Yves. "The Geographical and the Geopolitical." In *Geopolitical Analysis: A Selection from Hérodote*, edited by Pascal Girot and Eleonore Kofman. London: Croom Helm, 1987.
Lavery, John. *The Life of a Painter*. London: Cassell, 1940.
Livingstone, Angela. *Salomé: Her Life and Work*. Mt. Kisko, N.Y.: Moyer Bell, 1984.
Lloyd, David, and Paul Thomas. *Culture and the State*. New York: Routledge, 1998.
Lothe, Jakob. *Conrad's Narrative Method*. Oxford: Clarendon Press, 1989.
Lyotard, Jean-François. *The Postmodern Condition: A Report on Knowledge*. Minneapolis: University of Minnesota Press, 1985.
Mackinder, Halford J. *Britain and the British Seas*. Oxford: Clarendon Press, 1902.
———. *Democratic Ideals and Reality: A Study in the Politics of Reconstruction*. London: Constable & Co., 1919.
———. *The Development of Geographical Teaching out of Nature-Study*. London: George Philip, 1908.
———. *Distant Lands: An Elementary Study in Geography*. London: George Philip, [1910].
———. *India: Eight Lectures*. London: George Philip, 1910.
———. *Lands Beyond the Channel: An Elementary Study in Geography*. London: George Philip, [1908].
———. *The Modern British State: An Introduction to the Study of Civics*. London: George Philip, 1914.
———. *The Nations of the Modern World*. London: George Philip, 1911.
———. *Our Island History: An Elementary Study in History*. London: George Philip, [1914].
———. *Our Own Islands: An Elementary Study in Geography*. London: George Philip, 1906.
———. *The Scope and Methods of Geography and The Geographical Pivot of History*. London: The Royal Geographical Society, 1951. First published as two separate articles, "The Scope and Methods of Geography," in *Proceedings of the*

Royal Geographical Society 9 [1887]: 141–60; and "The Geographical Pivot of History," *Geographical Journal* 23 [1904]: 421–44.
———. *The Teaching of Geography and History.* London: George Philip, 1914.
Marin, Louis. *Utopics: Spatial Play.* Translated by Robert A. Vollrath. London: Macmillan, 1984.
Marks, Shula. "Harriette Colenso and the Zulus, 1874–1913." *Journal of African History* 4, no. 3 (1963): 403–11.
Martin, Biddy. *Woman and Modernity: The (Life)Styles of Lou Andreas-Salomé.* Ithaca, N.Y.: Cornell University Press, 1991.
Marx, Karl. *Capital: A Critique of Political Economy.* Vol. 1. 1867. Reprint, translated by Ben Fowkes. Harmondsworth, U.K.: Penguin, 1990.
———. *Early Writings.* Translated by Rodney Livingstone and Gregor Benton. New York: Vintage, 1975.
———. *Surveys from Exile.* Translated by David Fernbach. New York: Vintage, 1974.
Maugham, W. Somerset. *Collected Short Stories.* Vol. 3. New York: Penguin, 1977.
McClintock, Anne. *Imperial Leather: Race, Gender, and Sexuality in the Colonial Contest.* New York: Routledge, 1995.
McConkey, Kenneth. *Sir John Lavery, R.A., 1856-1941.* Exhibition catalogue for the Ulster Museum, Belfast and the Fine Arts Society, 1984–1985.
Mehta, Jaya. "English Romance: Indian Violence." *Centennial Review* 39, no. 3 (1995): 611–57.
Meller, Helen. *Patrick Geddes: Social Evolutionist and City Planner.* London: Routledge, 1990.
Mill, John Stuart. *Utilitarianism, On Liberty, Representative Government.* London: Dent, 1976.
Miller, D. A. *The Novel and the Police.* Berkeley: University of California Press, 1988.
Mitchell, Timothy. *Colonising Egypt.* Berkeley: University of California Press, 1991.
Mitchell, W. J. T. *Picture Theory.* Chicago: University of Chicago Press, 1994.
Mladek, Meda, and Margit Rowell. "Chronology." In Frantisek Kupka, *Frantisek Kupka, 1871-1957: A Retrospective.* New York: Solomon R. Guggenheim Foundation, 1975.
Moretti, Franco. *The Way of the World: The Bildungsroman in European Culture.* London: Verso, 1987.
Morris, William. *News From Nowhere or An Epoch of Rest.* 1891. Reprint, edited by James Redmond, London: Routledge & Kegan Paul, 1970.
Moszynska, Anna. *Abstract Art.* London: Thames and Hudson, 1990.
Mücke, Dorothea E. von. *Virtue and the Veil of Illusion: Generic Innovation and the Pedagogical Project in Eighteenth-Century Literature.* Stanford, Calif.: Stanford University Press, 1991.
Nadel, Alan. *Containment Culture: American Narratives, Postmodernism, and the Atomic Age.* Durham: Duke University Press, 1995.

Nancy, Jean-Luc. "Nietzsche's Thesis on Teleology." In *Looking After Nietzsche*, edited by Laurence A. Rickels. Buffalo: State University of New York Press, 1990.

Nietzsche, Friedrich. *Beyond Good and Evil*. Translated by Helen Zimmern. 1886. Reprint, New York: Modern Library, n.d.

———. *The Birth of Tragedy* and *The Case of Wagner*. Translated by Walter Kaufmann. 1872/1888. Reprint (2 vols. as 1), New York: Vintage, 1967.

———. *The Gay Science*. Translated by Walter Kaufmann. 1887. Reprint, New York: Vintage, 1974.

———. *Nachgelassene Werke*. Leipzig: Alfred Kröner, 1911.

———. *On the Genealogy of Morals* and *Ecce Homo*. Translated by Walter Kaufmann and R. J. Hollingdale. 1887/1908. Reprint (2 vols. as 1), New York: Vintage, 1969.

———. *Thus Spake Zarathustra*. Translated by Thomas Common. 1883–1885. Reprint, New York: Modern Library, n.d. Originally published as *Also Sprach Zarathustra*. 1883–1885. Reprint (as one volume), Stuttgart: Reclam, 1980.

———. *Thus Spoke Zarathustra*. Translated by R. J. Hollingdale. 1883–1885. Reprint (as one volume), Harmondsworth, U.K.: Penguin, 1987. Originally published as *Also Sprach Zarathustra*. 1883–1885. Reprint (as one volume), Stuttgart: Reclam, 1980.

———. *Twilight of the Idols* and *The Anti-Christ*. Translated by R. J. Hollingdale. 1889/1895. Reprint (2 vols. as 1), Harmondsworth, U.K.: Penguin, 1968.

———. *Werke*. Vol. 5, bk. 2: *Die fröhliche Wissenschaft*. Berlin: Walter de Gruyter, 1973.

———. *Werke*. Vol. 6, bk. 2: *Jenseits von Gut und Böse* and *Zur Genealogie der Moral*. Berlin: Walter de Gruyter, 1968.

———. *Werke*. Vol. 6, bk. 3: *Der Fall Wagner*; *Götzen-Dämmerung*; *Der Antichrist*; *Ecce Homo*; *Dionysos-Dithyramben*; and *Nietzsche contra Wagner*. Berlin: Walter de Gruyter, 1969.

———. *The Will to Power*. Translated by Walter Kaufmann and R. J. Holingdale. New York: Vintage, 1968.

O Tuathail, Gearóid. *Critical Geopolitics: The Politics of Writing Global Space*. Minneapolis: University of Minnesota Press, 1996.

O Tuathail, Gearóid, Simon Dalby, and Paul Routledge, eds. *The Geopolitics Reader*. London: Routledge, 1998.

Olmsted, John Charles, ed. *Victorian Painting: Essays and Reviews*. Vol. 1, 1832–1848. New York: Garland Publishing, 1980.

Orwell, George. *Dickens, Dali, and Others*. New York: Harcourt Brace Jovanovich, 1946.

———. *The Lost Writings*. Edited by W. J. West. New York: Avon, 1985.

O'Sullivan, Patrick. *Geopolitics*. London: Croom Helm, 1986.

Pal, Pratapaditya, and Vidya Dehejia. *From Merchants to Emperors: British Artists and India, 1757-1930*. Ithaca, N.Y.: Cornell University Press, 1986.

Parker, Geoffrey. *Western Geopolitical Thought in the Twentieth Century*. London: Croom Helm, 1985.
Parker, W. H. *Mackinder: Geography as an Aid to Statecraft*. Oxford: Clarendon, 1982.
Pataud, Emile, and Emile Pouget. *How We Shall Bring About the Revolution: Syndicalism and the Co-operative Commonwealth*. 1913. Reprint, London: Pluto Press, 1990. Originally published as *Comment nous ferons la révolution* (Paris: J. Tallandier, 1909).
Penley, Constance, ed. *Feminism and Film Theory*. New York: Routledge, 1988.
Peralta, A. Jover, and T. Osuna, eds. *Diccionario Guaraní–Español y Español–Guaraní*. Buenos Aires: Editore Litocolor, 1984.
Peters, Catherine. *The King of Inventors: A Life of Wilkie Collins*. London: Secker & Warburg, 1991.
Poovey, Mary. *Uneven Developments: The Ideological Work of Gender in Mid-Victorian England*. Chicago: University of Chicago Press, 1988.
Pouget, Emile. *Le Sabotage*. Bibliothèque du Mouvement Prolétarien XIII. Paris: Librairie des Sciences Politiques et Sociales, Marcel Rivière et Cie, [1910].

———. *Sabotage*. Translated by Arturo M. Giovannitti. Chicago: Charles H. Kerr, 1913.

———. *Le Syndicat*. Paris: Bibliothèque Syndicaliste, 1907. Published in German as *Die Gewerkschaft* (Zürich: Aeschbacher Verlag, 1907).

Pratt, Mary Louise. *Imperial Eyes: Travel Writing and Transculturation*. London: Routledge, 1992.
Proust, Marcel. *Selected Letters: 1880-1903*. Edited by Philip Kolb, translated by Ralph Manheim. London: Collins, 1983.
Ramaswami, N. S. "Tippu's Golden Sword." *Sultan* [annual journal of the Tipu Sultan Research Institute and Museum] 4 (1986): 10–12.
Ratzel, Friedrich. *Anthropo-Geographie oder Grundzüge der Anwendung der Erdkunde auf die Geschichte*. [Vol. 1]. Stuttgart: Engelhorn, 1882.

———. *Anthropogeographie. Zweiter Teil: Die Geographische Verbreitung des Menschen*. [Vol. 2]. Stuttgart: Engelhorn, 1891.

———. *The History of Mankind* (Völkerkunde). Translated by A. J. Butler, with an introduction by E. B. Tylor. 3 vols. London: Macmillan, 1896–1898. (This translation is based on the 2d. revised edition of the original German work: *Völkerkunde*, 2d rev. ed., 2 vols. [Leipzig: Bibliographisches Institut, 1894– 1895]).

———. *Kleine Schriften*. 2 vols. München: Oldenbourg, 1906.

———. *Politische Geographie*. München: Oldenbourg, 1897.

———. *Völkerkunde*. 3 vols. Leipzig: Verlag des Bibliographischen Instituts, 1885–1888.

Reclus, Elisée. "Anarchy: By an Anarchist." *The Contemporary Review* 45 (May 1884) 627–41.

———. *Evolution and Revolution*. London: International Publishing Company, 1885.

———. *L'Homme et la Terre*. 6 vols. Paris: Librairie Universelle, 1905–1908.

———. *L'Homme et la Terre*. [Selections.] Edited by Béatrice Giblin. 2 vols. Paris: François Maspero, 1982.

———. "Project de Construction d'un Globe Terrestre à l'Echelle du 100,000e." In *Report of the Sixth International Geographical Congress*. London: John Murray, 1896.

———. *The Universal Geography: The Earth and Its Inhabitants*. Edited by E. G. Ravenstein. 19 vols. London: Virtue & Co., 1882–1895. Originally published as *La Nouvelle Géographie Universelle* (Paris: Hachette, 1876–1894).

Reed, John R. "English Imperialism and the Unacknowledged Crime of *The Moonstone*." *Clio* 2 (1973): 281–90.

Reich, Emil. *Foundations of Modern Europe: Twelve Lectures Delivered in the University of London*. London: George Bell, 1904.

———. *Handbook of Geography: Descriptive and Mathematical*. 2 vols. London: Duckworth, 1908.

———. "Recent Historical Methods and the Cambridge Modern History." *The Monthly Review* 9 (November 1902): 117–32.

Reid, Fred. *Keir Hardie: The Making of a Socialist*. London: Croom Helm, 1978.

Richards, Thomas. *The Imperial Archive: Knowledge and the Fantasy of Empire*. London: Verso, 1993.

Richter, Wilhelm. *Der Wandel des Bildungsgedankens: die Brüder von Humboldt, das Zeitalter der Bildung und die Gegenwart*. Berlin: Colloquium Verlag, 1971.

Rickels, Laurence, ed. *Looking After Nietzsche*. Albany: State University of New York Press, 1990.

Robinson, Kenneth. *Wilkie Collins: A Biography*. New York: Macmillan, 1952.

Ross, Kristin. *The Emergence of Social Space: Rimbaud and the Paris Commune*. Minneapolis: University of Minnesota Press, 1988.

Rothman, William. *Hitchcock: The Murderous Gaze*. Cambridge, Mass.: Harvard University Press, 1982.

Rowell, Margit. "Frantisek Kupka: A Metaphysics of Abstraction." In Frantisek Kupka, *Frantisek Kupka, 1871-1957: A Retrospective*. New York: Solomon R. Guggenheim Foundation, 1975.

Roy, Ashish. "The Fabulous Imperialist Semiotic of Wilkie Collins's *The Moonstone*." *New Literary History* 24 (1993): 657–81.

Russell, Bertrand. *Proposed Roads to Freedom: Socialism, Anarchism, and Syndicalism*. New York: Henry Holt, 1919.

Ryall, Tom. *Alfred Hitchcock and the British Cinema*. Atlantic Highlands, N.J.: Athlone Press, 1996.

Said, Edward. *Culture and Imperialism*. New York: Vintage, 1994.

———. *Orientalism*. New York: Vintage, 1979.

Salerno, Salvatore. *Red November, Black November: Culture and Community in the Industrial Workers of the World*. Albany: State University of New York Press, 1989.

Salomé, Lou Andreas. *Friedrich Nietzsche: The Man in His Works.* Translated by Siegfried Mandel. 1894. Reprint, Redding Ridge, Conn.: Black Swan Books, 1988.

Sandner, Gerhard, and Mechtild Rössler. "Geography and Empire in Germany, 1871–1945." In *Geography and Empire*, edited by Anne Godlewska and Neil Smith. Oxford: Blackwell, 1994.

Sayers, Dorothy L. *Wilkie Collins: A Critical and Biographical Study.* Edited by E. R. Gregory. Toledo: Friends of University of Toledo Library, 1977.

Schellinger, Paul, ed. *Encyclopedia of the Novel.* 2 vols. Chicago: Fitzroy Dearborn, 1998.

Schreiner, Olive. *The Letters of Olive Schreiner, 1876-1920.* Edited by S. C. Cronwright-Schreiner. 1924. Reprint, New York: Hyperion, 1976.

———. *The Story of an African Farm.* 2 vols. 1883. Reprint (2 vols. in 1), Harmondsworth, U.K.: Penguin, 1982.

Sharpe, Jenny. *Allegories of Empire: The Figure of Woman in the Colonial Text.* Minneapolis: University of Minnesota Press, 1993.

Shaw-Sparrow, Walter. *John Lavery and his Work.* London: Kegan Paul, 1912.

Showalter, Elaine. *The Female Malady: Women, Madness, and English Culture, 1830-1980.* New York: Viking Penguin, 1987.

———. *A Literature of Their Own.* Princeton: Princeton University Press, 1977.

———. *Sexual Anarchy: Gender and Culture in the Fin de Siècle.* New York: Viking Penguin, 1990.

Smiles, Samuel. *Self-Help.* New York: Harper Brothers, [1859].

Smith, Neil. *Uneven Development: Nature, Capital, and the Production of Space.* Oxford: Blackwell, 1984.

Smith, Woodruff. *Politics and the Sciences of Culture in Germany, 1840-1920.* New York: Oxford University Press, 1991.

Soja, Edward. *Postmodern Geographies: The Reassertion of Space in Critical Social Theory.* London: Verso, 1989.

Sorel, Georges. *Reflections on Violence.* Translated by T. E. Hulme. 1915. Reprint, New York: Peter Smith, 1941.

Spencer, Herbert. *First Principles.* New York: Burt, 1880.

Spivak, Gayatri. "Three Women's Texts and a Critique of Imperialism." In *"Race," Writing, and Difference*, edited by Henry Louis Gates, Jr. Chicago: University of Chicago Press, 1986.

Stape, J. H., and Owen Knowles, eds. *A Portrait in Letters: Correspondence to and about Conrad.* Amsterdam: Rodopi, 1996.

Suleri, Sara. *The Rhetoric of English India.* Chicago: University of Chicago Press, 1992.

Taussig, Michael. *Shamanism, Colonialism, and the Wild Man: A Study in Terror and Healing.* Chicago: University of Chicago Press, 1987.

Tey, Josephine. *The Man in the Queue.* 1929. Reprint, New York: Collier, 1993.

———. *A Shilling for Candles.* 1936. Reprint, New York: Collier, 1988.

Thackeray, W. M. "A Second Lecture on the Fine Arts, by Michael Angelo Titmarsh, Esq." *Fraser's Magazine* 19 (June 1839): 743–50.
Thatcher, David. *Nietzsche in England: 1890-1914*. Toronto: University of Toronto Press, 1970.
Thompson, Edward P. *William Morris: Romantic to Revolutionary*. London: Merlin Press, 1976; Stanford, Calif.: Stanford University Press, 1988.
———. *Whigs and Hunters*. London, 1975.
Truffaut, François. *Hitchcock*. Revised ed. New York: Simon & Schuster, 1985.
Tsuzuki, Chushuchi. *Tom Mann, 1856-1941: The Challenges of Labour*. Oxford: Clarendon Press, 1991.
Tuchman, Gaye. *Edging Women Out*. New Haven: Yale University Press, 1989.
Tucker, Robert C., ed. *The Lenin Anthology*. New York: Norton, 1975.
———. *The Marx-Engels Reader*. New York: Norton, 1972.
Veblen, Thorstein. *The Engineers and the Price System*. 1921. Reprint, New York: Viking Press, 1947.
Viswanathan, Gauri. *Masks of Conquest: Literary Study and British Rule in India*. New York: Columbia University Press, 1989.
———. "Raymond Williams and British Colonialism." *Yale Journal of Criticism* 4, no. 2 (1991): 47–66.
Walker, John. "R. B. Cunninghame Graham: An Annotated Bibliography of Writings About Him." *English Literature in Transition* 22, no. 2 (1979): 78–156.
Wallerstein, Immanuel. *Geopolitics and Geoculture: Essays on the Changing World-System*. Cambridge: Cambridge University Press, 1991.
———. *The Politics of the World-Economy*. Cambridge: Cambridge University Press, 1984.
Watt, Ian. *The Rise of the Novel: Studies in Defoe, Richardson, and Fielding*. Berkeley: University of California Press, 1957.
Watts, Cedric. *The Deceptive Text: An Introduction to Covert Plots*. Sussex: The Harvester Press, 1984.
———. *Joseph Conrad's Letters to R. B. Cunninghame Graham*. Cambridge: Cambridge University Press, 1969.
Watts, Cedric, and Laurence Davies. *Cunninghame Graham: A Critical Biography*. Cambridge: Cambridge University Press, 1979.
Weigert, Hans W., and Vilhjalmur Stefansson, eds. *Compass of the World: A Symposium on Political Geography*. New York: The Macmillan Company, 1947.
Weir, David. *Anarchy and Culture: The Aesthetic Politics of Modernism*. Amherst: University of Massachusetts Press, 1997.
Wells, H. G. *The Time Machine*. 1895. Reprint, New York: Bantam, 1982.
———. *When the Sleeper Wakes*. 1899. Reprint, London: Everyman, 1994.
Williams, Raymond. *The Country and the City*. Oxford: Oxford University Press, 1973.
———. *Culture and Society: 1750-1950*. Harmondsworth, U.K.: Penguin, 1963.

———. *Keywords: A Vocabulary of Culture and Society.* New York: Oxford University Press, 1983.
Wollaeger, Mark. "Killing Stevie: Modernity, Modernism, and Mastery in Conrad and Hitchcock." *Modern Language Quarterly* 58, no. 3 (September 1997): 323–50.
Young, Robert J. C. *Colonial Desire: Hybridity in Theory, Culture, and Race.* London: Routledge, 1995.
Zimmern, Helen. *Arthur Schopenhauer: His Life and His Philosophy.* London: Longmans, Green & Co., 1876.
———. *The Epic of Kings: Stories Retold from Firdusi.* London: T. Fisher Unwin, 1883.
Žižek, Slavoj. *For They Know Not What They Do.* London: Verso, 1991.
———. *Looking Awry: An Introduction to Jacques Lacan Through Popular Culture.* Cambridge, Mass.: MIT Press, 1991.

Index

In this index an "f" after a number indicates a separate reference on the next page, and an "ff" indicates separate references on the next two pages. A continuous discussion over two or more pages is indicated by a span of page numbers, e.g., "57–59." *Passim* is used for a cluster of references in close but not consecutive sequence.

Adamic, Lous   is, 168
Adorno, Theodor, 166, 196, 227f
Advertising, 190f, 196
Aesthetics, 4, 19, 39f, 70f; and Nietzsche, 101–6, 119-23. *See also* Anamorphosis; Art; Ekphrasis; Media; Narrative form; Novel form; Painting; Perspective
Africa, 34, 90, 92, 146, 154. *See also* South Africa
Afterimage: retinal afterimage, 7–10, 122f, 188, 196; and Nietzsche, 8, 88, 93f, 122f; and Bergson, 8, 180f, 183, 188; and Benjamin, 8, 180f, 183, 188; and cinematography, 8, 180–84 *passim*, 190, 195f; of country house, 67, 79; of loot, 84f; of utopia, 128,and Conradian narrative, 180f, 183; of Cunninghame Graham, 129–33 *passim*, 159, 224f; of sabotage, 173
Agency, 160, 165, 176f, 180, 184; social agency, 160, 172, 176, 193
Agnew, John, 1f, 206
Aida (Verdi), 120f

A la recherche du temps perdu (Proust), 181
Allen, E. J. B., 170
Ambassadors, The (Holbein), 74, 77
America: cinema, 6, 13, 188; emigration to, utopian trope of, 127f, 223n4; Spanish-American war, 156-9; setting for *Saboteur*, 162, 173, 190, 194, 196; war machine, 163f, 165; labor and industry, 163–73 *passim*, immigrant politics, 170. *See also* Hollywood; New World; South America
American Federation of Labor (A.F.L.), 170
Amorpha, Fugue in Two Colours (Kupka), 8–11 *passim*
Amorpha, Warm Chromatics (Kupka), 8, 11
Analepsis, 180
Anamorphosis, 11, 74f, 77. *See also* Hitchcockian blot
Anarchism: and geography, 3, 9, 11, 18, 46, 49ff, 205n35; anarchist geopolitics, 46;

250 INDEX

and propaganda, 50, 173, 177; and Conrad, 167, 173–80 *passim*, 230n42; and modernism, 178–81. *See also* Anarcho-syndicalism
Anarcho-syndicalism, 3, 161, 163, 167, 172–78 *passim*, 181. *See also* Criminal syndicalism statutes; Utopian narratives
Anderson, Benedict, 4, 204n19
Anthropogeography, 21f, 37–42, 45; Ratzel's coinage, 22; Kulturgeographie as synonym, 40. *See also under* Ratzel
Anthropology, 2, 18, 22, 180, 208; and Ratzel, 38–43, 208n67. *See also* Ethnography
Anti-colonial struggle, 12, 49, 181
Aphorism, 91, 102, 104
Archer, John M., 74
Argentina, 130, 133, 150
Arms and the Man (Shaw), 139
Armstrong, Nancy, 71, 215n45
Arnold, Matthew: on culture, 4, 20, 47f, 57–60, 77f, 100f, 204n27, 212, 216n64; translates "Bildung" as culture, 4, 20, 203n9, 204n27; on the State, 47f; and Nietzsche, 100f. Works: *Culture and Anarchy*, 4, 48, 57–60 *passim*, 203n5, 204n27; *Schools and Universities on the Continent*, 203n5
Art, 34, 57f, 80, 216f; abstract, 34; collectors, 80, 213n23; objects, 80. *See also* Aesthetics; Cultural capital; Modernism
Assassination, 160, 167f
Atlantic: North Atlantic, 33; trading routes, 78; Black Atlantic, 190; White Atlantic, 190, 194
Auditory image, 17, 188
Austen, Jane, 59, 64, 66, 79; *Mansfield Park*, 66

Baird, Lady, 68
Baird, Sir David, 60f, 68–71, 81–84, 214
Barney, Richard A., 212n19
Barrell, John, 84

Bartholomew, J. G., 211
Battle of Trafalgar Square. *See* Bloody Sunday
Bellamy, Edward, 128f, 134, 149, 153; *Looking Backward*, 128, 149
Benjamin, Walter: and afterimage, 8, 180f, 183, 188; dialectical image, 52, 183; "Paris, Capital of the Nineteenth Century," 52; on culture, 80f; critique of Bergson, 180, 188, 231n51; on cinema, 206n47, 207n52
Bergson, Henri: and afterimage, 8, 180f, 183, 188, 231; and "global knowledge," 171f, 188. Works: *L'Evolution créatrice* [*Creative Evolution*], 177; *Matière et mémoire* [*Matter and Memory*], 177, 180, 230n45; *Le Rire* [*Laughter*], 178f
Berlin, University of, 23, 204n27; War Academy Instruction, 25f, 204n21
Betrayal, 140f, 172f, 190, 196, 225n40
Bhabha, Homi, 115f
Bible, 109f, 115f, 221n95
Bijou cinema house (*Sabotage*), 165, 184–92 *passim*, 197, 231n58
Bild (image/picture), 39, 42, 53, 211n115
Bildung: German idealist notion of education, 4, 19, 204n27; and Mill, 4f, 99; Arnold's translation as culture, 5, 19f, 100, 203n9, 204n27; and Humboldt (Wilhelm), 4, 19, 27, 96, 99, 203n9, 204n27; and middle-class consciousness, 6, 100f; and Herder, 19, 26f, 42f, 47; and Ratzel, 42f; relation to "Kultur," 43, 47f; and Hegel, 48, 209; Nietzsche's critique of, 96, 103, 122; and nihilism, 100, 115; Lyotard on, 203n9, 204n27; and novel form, 212n19. *See also* Bildungsroman
Bildungsroman, 19, 91, 93, 115, 180; Dilthey on, 93, 180, 212n19; and *Thus Spoke Zarathustra*, 93; and *The Story of an African Farm*, 91, 115. *See also* Bildung; Narrative form; Novel form
Biogeography (Ratzel), 22, 209n84
Bismarck, Otto Fürst von, 6

Black Atlantic, 190
Blackface entertainment, 193f, 196
Black Hole of Calcutta (1756), 67
Blind love (formula for Collins' novels), 75f, 215n53
Blondel, Eric, 220n53
Bloody Sunday (13 November 1887), 135–40 passim, 148f, 226n62; Cunninghame Graham on, 137–40; Morris on, 135f, 137
Blot: and Plot, 11, 57, 75; definition, 57, 59; "blot of the Diamond" (*Moonstone*), 62f, 73, 77, 84; on the family name, 62–5 passim; and metonymy of stain, 72, 75; of sunlight, 194ff; auditory blot, 195. See also Hitchcockian blot; Victorian blot
Blot on the Queen's Head (Jenkins), 57, 59
Boer War: First (1880–1881), 114; Second (1899–1902), 106
Bonaparte, Napoleon, 84, 91, 113f
Bourdieu, Pierre, 80, 216n62
Bourgeois. See Middle class
Boycott, 168
Brett Street shop (*The Secret Agent*), 168, 176, 184, 190, 192, 231n58
Brissenden, Paul, 227n9
Britain: schools, 20; position of, 29–33, 43–46 passim, 53, 207; relation to India, 58ff, 68–71, 79–85, 213f, 221n95; Schreiner's arrival in, 106; labor and industry in, 135–41, 148–51, 168–72 passim; and film industry, 184–90. See also British Empire; England; India; Scotland
British Empire, 5, 9, 12, 44, 46, 69; formalization of, 5, 58–60; 79–85. See also Britain; British Raj; India; Victoria
British Labour Party, 136
British Raj, 85, 206n47. See also British Empire; India
Brown, Geoff, 164, 166, 170
Browning, Robert, 103f
Buckle, Henry Thomas, 27, 205
Burke, Edmund, 57, 59, 84, 212n6, 217n72

Burns, John, 135f, 139ff

Ca' Canny, 170f, 229
Capital, 63, 79
Capra, Frank, 161
Carlyle, Thomas, 104
Cartesian perspectivalism, 7, 28, 33, 74
Casement, Roger, 224f
Cawnpore Massacre (1856), 67
Chaplin, Charlie, 231f
Cheah, Pheng, 201, 205
Chernyshevsky, N. G., 97
Chesterton, G. K., 129f, 132, 146
Chicago, 138, 160, 181
Chow, Rey, 232n73
Christianity, 73, 109f, 115f, 134, 148, 154f, 158, 222n98; evangelical, 73; Lutheran, 109; missionary, 109f, 115f; Jesuit missions, 134; Anglican mass, 148, 155
Cinema: narrative form of, 6f, 77, 163, 183–89, 195, 197f; and afterimage, 8, 180–84 passim, 190, 195ff; early development of, 33, 161, 183f, 206f; American industry, 7, 13, 161, 164, 188–91, 198; and geopolitics, 159–62, 186f; screenplay, 167, 191f, 196f, 201n8; distribution, 189f; cinematic labor process of, 185–93 passim. See also Hitchcock; Hitchcockian blot; Montage
Cinematic labor process. See under Cinema
Cinematograph Films Act (1927), 189
Citizenship, 83f
Civilization, 47, 208n69. See also Culture
Class. See Class struggle; Middle class; Working class
Class struggle, 48, 137, 149f; and world war, 162, 172f, 198. See also Anarchosyndicalism; Demonstrations; Labor movement; Sabotage; Strikes
Clifford, James, 40
Clifford, Sir Hugh, 146
Coal Mines Regulation Bill, 139
Cohn, Bernard S., 81ff
Colenso, Harriette Emily, 145

Collins, Wilkie, 3f, 59–85 *passim*, 123, 213f; and culture-concept, 59f, 65, 76, 78f, 85; divided critical response to, 64, 68f; blind love motif, 75f, 215n53. Works: *Armadale*, 60–66 *passim*; *Blind Love*, 64, 75f; *Hide and Seek*, 216f; *No Name*, 60–66 *passim*; "Perils of Certain English Prisoners," 213f; *Poor Miss Finch*, 215n53; "A Sermon for Sepoys," 213; *The Woman in White*, 60–64 *passim*, 75f
——*The Moonstone*: 60–85 *passim*; and Wilkie's portrait of Baird, 60, 67–71, 80–84; and middle-class perspective, 60, 63–69 *passim*; Shivering Sands topos, 66f, 71f; Blake's self-incrimination, 73ff, 78, 83; and scandal of narrative form, 74; geopolitical image of moonstone, 85
Collins, William, 80, 217n65
Colonialism: and culture, 4, 13, 78f, 203n9; governance, 12, 50, 58, 67, 81ff; anti-colonialism, 12, 58, 67ff, 181, 206n47, 213n26, 215f; ideology of, 34f, 111f, 134, 142, 145f; and class perspective, 65f, 77, 83f, 153, 181f, 213n25; estate-cultivation, 66, 79, 111; and *The Story of an African Farm*, 90, 109ff, 119; missionary, 109f, 115f; phantom subject, 112–19, 123. *See also* East India Company; Imperialism
Commonweal, The, 137, 140
Communism, 128, 135, 162, 198, 202n9
Communist Manifesto (Marx and Engels), 162, 202n9
Confederal Congress of Toulouse (1897), 168
Confessions of an English Opium Eater (De Quincey), 78
Conrad, Joseph, 6; and maps, 34, 51; friendship and collaboration with Cunninghame Graham, 129f, 134f, 141–44 *passim*, 151f, 156f; and anarchism, 160, 167f, 173f, 176–81, 230n42. Works: *Almayer's Folly*, 178; *Heart of Darkness*, 34, 151–54 *passim*, 181; *Lord Jim*, 151; *Nostromo*, 130, 140, 158
——*The Secret Agent*, 6, 171–90 *passim*; relation to Hitchcock's *Sabotage*, 160, 163, 167, 174, 183–90 *passim*; Brett Street shop, 168, 176, 184, 187, 190, 192, 231n58; disruption of narrative form, 173–78 *passim*, 183; Stevie's fireworks, 176, 179, 181, 187, 189; and cinematography, 183f
Consciousness, elision of, 177, 179, 231. *See also* Middle class; Working class
Consumption, 13, 50, 167f, 176; and production, 187f, 190, 194; women and, 189. *See also* Culture systems; Industry; Production
Cooper, Gary, 232n65
Cornhill Magazine, 212n9, 213n21
Cosmopolitanism, 3ff, 159, 201; as against geopolitics, 3, 5, 58, 60, 85; and culture-hypothesis, 3, 26f, 47f, 58, 205; and Kant, 26f, 47; and middle-class education, 78, 83, 95. *See also* Culture; Culture-hypothesis; Kant
Country estate, 62–67 *passim*, 72
Country-house novel, 63–66 *passim*, 74, 79. *See also* Country estate; Novel form
Crary, Jonathan, 8–11
Criminal syndicalism statutes, 163f, 167f, 227n9
Critical geopolitics, 2, 7
Cultural capital, 79ff, 84, 216n62
Cultural studies, 18, 203n5. *See also* Kulturwissenschaften
Culture: and geopolitics, 1, 4, 13, 19, 23, 40, 43, 58, 79, 85; and cosmopolitanism, 3, 5, 26f, 47f, 58, 85, 201n5, 205n33; definitional confusion of, 4, 26, 41f, 57–60, 77, 100, 107, 203n9; and civilization, 47, 208n69; and drugs, 78, 122, 198; and capital, 79ff, 121; and nihilism, 90, 99ff, 115. *See also* Anthropology; Arnold; Bildung; Culture-

complex; Culture-hypothesis; Culture industry; Kultur; Self-culture; Victorian blot
Culture-complex, 20; and power-complex, 122, 201
Culture-hypothesis: eclipse of geopolitics with, 2f, 19, 41f, 46ff, 58, 85; and Arnold, 5, 19, 58, 100; and Bildung, 5, 19, 99; and Humboldt, 19, 27; phenomenological condition of, 11, 177; and culture systems, 13, 79; Herder's geographical condition of, 26, 27, 115, 205, 223n4; and Hegel, Buckle, and Marx, 27; and the nation-state, 46ff; Nietzsche's nihilist hypothesis, 99ff; feminist challenge to, 116f; Victorian translations of, 107, 204n27, 205n34. *See also* Cosmopolitanism; Culture; Culture-complex
Culture industry, 167, 193, 196, 198, 227–28
Culture systems, 13f, 78f, 198, 221n95
Cunninghame Graham, Gabriela (Caroline Horsfall), 224n35
Cunninghame Graham, Robert Bontine, 5f, 127–59, 170f, 223–26; sketch-artistry of, 5, 130–34 *passim*, 141, 144–54 *passim*, 158; and impressionism, 129, 134, 152, 156f; as labor activist, 129, 135–38 *passim*; and Parliament, 129, 135–40 *passim*; portraits of, by Lavery, 130–33, 143, 156, 158; use of word "hegemonist," 132, 141, 151, 155; and Garnett's *Over-Seas Library*, 141–50; South American settings of, 156–59. Works: "Bloody Niggers," 145, 147; "Bloody Sunday," 137–40; "Ca' Canny," 170f, 229; "The Gualichu Tree," 147; "Heather Jock," 150–58, 226; "A Hegira" 158; *The Ipané*, 130, 133, 141–47, 150, "The Ipané," 159; *Mogreb-el-Acksa*, 134, 152; *Notes on the District of Menteith*, 133, 155; *Success*, 147; "Sursum Corda," 140, 147f; *A Vanished Arcadia*, 134; "A Vanishing Race," 158; "Victory," 157f

Darwinism, 90, 107
Davies, Laurence, 136–39 *passim*, 145, 147, 156f
Defoe, Daniel, 78
Deleuze, Gilles, 183, 188
Democracy, 57–60 *passim*, 130, 139. *See also* Reform; Revolution; Socialism
Demonstrations, 135f, 140, 148f, 172. *See also* Bloody Sunday
De Quincey, Thomas, 78, 84
Derrida, Jacques, 202n9
Detective fiction: and novel form, 59, 63, 67, 69, 79; and cinema, 182, 197
Dickens, Charles, 184, 213f, 215n49, 231n58
Dilthey, Wilhelm, 93, 180, 212n19
Direct action, 167f, 177
Disks of Newton (Kupka), 8
Disney cartoon (*Sabotage*), 189–93 *passim*, 196
Dithyrambic verse (Nietzsche), 102, 104, 118f
Don Roberto. *See* Cunninghame Graham
Dostoevsky, Fyodor, 97
Dream, 90; dream-work, 50, 112, 115; dream-image, 52
Drugs, and culture, 78, 122, 198
Du Maurier, Daphne, 191
Duncan, Ian, 69, 71
Dutch East Indies Company, 221n95

East India Company (British), 65f, 81–84, 206n47, 216, 221n95
Economic determinism, 171, 175
Education, 4, 13, 19, 47f, 57f; and women, 94f, 98–101 *passim*, 117f, 209n93. *See also* Culture; Bildung
Egerton, George (Mary Chavelita Dunne), 101
Eight-hour day, struggle for, 135, 139
Eisenstein, Sergei, 172, 183
Ekphrasis, 80ff, 217n69
Eliot, George, 107
Ellipsis: narrative, 174, 186; of social

agency, 176–77, 181ff; of consciousness, 177, 179

Emerson, Ralph Waldo, 108–11 *passim*, 115

Engels, Friedrich, 127. *See also Communist Manifesto*

England: and question of culture, 20, 58f, 78; country-house setting, 62, 67, 72; significance for Nietzsche and Schreiner, 106ff; and utopian narrative, 129, 135; in Hitchcock films, 190f, 232. *See also* Britain; British Empire; Victoria

"England and its Cortège" (Kupka), 9f, 44

English, James, 178f

English country house. *See* Country estate; Country-house novel

Entertainment, 13, 187, 189, 194, 197f. *See also* Culture; Culture industry

Epic of Kings, The (Zimmern), 103f

Epstein, Jacob, 223n8

Eratosthenes, 29, 31

Erlebnis und die Dichtung, Das (Dilthey), 180, 212n19

Ethnic identity, 12, 155, 161, 197; and working-class consciousness, 170, 172; fantasy of, 190, 193f, 232n74. *See also* Nationality; Race

Ethnography, 142, 155, 158, 180; ethnographic phantasm, 189, 197, 232n74. *See also* Anthropology

Eurocentrism: and culture-hypothesis, 27, 49, 205; and Ratzel, 41; and Reclus, 49f; and Marxism, 49, 128, 210n103

Europe: and world history, 2–5, 24ff, 100, 113ff, 119-23 *passim*, 205; and humanism, 5, 7, 40, 129; and enlightenment, 7, 52, 88; Continental educational models, 78, 208n5; phantasm of, 105f, 109, 113, 119, 123; and revolution, 128, 153, 162, 173. *See also* Cosmopolitanism; Culture-hypothesis; Nihilism

European nihilism. *See under* Nihilism

Family, 60, 62, 69, 187ff

Far Away and Long Ago (Hudson), 159

Fascism, 162. *See also* National socialism

Feminism, 89, 97, 116f

"Ferishtah's Fancies" (Browning), 103

Feuerbach, Ludwig, 107

Fictional form, 7, 59f, 65, 90f; of Nietzsche's Zarathustra persona, 101–6. *See also* Aesthetics; Cinema; Narrative form; Novel form; Perspective

Firdusi, 104

First, Ruth, 106, 108

First Principles (Spencer), 88, 90, 100, 107, 116; Schreiner's reading of, 222n98

Flynn, Elizabeth Gurley, 169

Forrest, Denys, 68, 70

Förster-Nietzsche, Elisabeth, 5; supervision of Nietzsche's work, 88, 94; on Zarathustra, 92–96 *passim*, 101ff; enmity with Salomé, 93–96, 219; *Life of Nietzsche*, 94

Foucault, Michel, 73–76 *passim*

Foundations of Modern Europe, The (Reich), 36

France, 8, 78, 172, 210n98

Free speech, 135, 147

Free spirit, 90, 93–98 *passim*, 101, 109

Freud, Sigmund, 19

Friedrich Nietzsche (Salomé), 94, 101

Fuchs, Eduard, 80

"Future of the Proletariat, The," (*The Secret Agent*), 174f

Galsworthy, John, 160, 167

Garnett, Edward, 135, 141–50, 156f; and the *Over-Seas Library*, 142–46, 156, 224

Gaucho, 130, 133, 135, 150, 153–58 *passim*

Gaumont newsreels, 8

Gaze: geopolitical, 28; male, 189, 196, of the other, 193. *See also* Good looks; Visual image; Visualisation

Geddes, Patrick, 206n47; proposed Scottish-based National Institute of Geography, 211n114

Gender, 74, 91, 112, 118, 191

"Geographer, The" (Kupka), cover illustration, 9f

Geographical Institute (Oxford), 203n13, 211n114
Geography, 1, 3, 17–53 *passim*; imperialist, 1ff, 19–22 *passim*, 27, 46, 50; anarchist, 1ff, 9, 11, 25, 46-53 *passim*, 205n35; "new geography," 3, 19, 22, 27; textbooks, 18, 20, 28, 198; "social geography," 25, 47f; institutes of, 51ff, 203n13, 211n114
Geopolitical Aesthetic, The (Jameson), 13, 18, 160f
Geopolitics: definitions of, 1f, 45; as pseudo-science, 1, 21, 45, 51; discursive formation of, 1ff, 17–53 *passim*, 85, 87, 198; and culture, 1, 4, 13, 19, 23, 40, 43, 58, 79, 85; fiction of, 2, 7, 12f, 51, 85, 120, 123, 162, 194, 197f; geopolitical image, 7–10 *passim*, 17–53 *passim*, 67, 191, 207n57, 216n60; German Geopolitik, 18, 24, 42, 50f, 88, 161; geo-political (hyphenation of term), 35f, 43, 202n9, 207; catchwords of, 42, 162, 186; American, 51, 161; anti-geopolitics, 151; and cinema, 159-62, 186f, 189.
Germany, 18, 22f, 42f, 78; models of education from, 23, 78, 204n19; First Reich, 87, 120; Third Reich, 88; socialism, 172. *See also* National Socialism
Gilroy, Paul, 190
Giovannitti, Arturo, 168, 228f
Glasgow, 130, 132, 141, 151, 160
Globes, 32ff; Reclusian Great Globe, 51ff, 210f
Goethe, Johann Wolfgang von, 8, 19, 27, 107, 120; *Wilhelm Meisters Lehrjahre*, 19, 223n4
"Good looks," 196f
Graham, Cunninghame. *See* Cunninghame Graham
Gramophone, 192f
Gramsci, Antonio, 49, 210n103
Great Exhibition (1851), 52
Great Globe (Reclus), 51ff
Greenwich Bomb Outrage (1894), 173, 177, 179, 182f
Gregory, Derek, 28, 205, 210f

Grundriss zu einem System der Politik (Kjellén), 36
Guaraní, 159
Guha, Ranajit, 213n25
Gwilt, 64f

Halbkultur (semi-culture), 40. *See also* Kultur
Hall, Stuart, 210n104
Handbook of Geography, The (Reich), 36
Hardie, Keir, 130, 132, 135f
Hardy, Thomas, 96–99, 116
Haushofer, Karl, 24, 51
Headingley, A. S., 170
Heartland thesis (Mackinder), 20
Hegel, Georg Wilhelm Friedrich, 27; and culture-hypothesis, 48; and Bildung, 48, 209; and the State, 48, 209. Works: *Phenomenology of Spirit*, 177, 209n92; *Philosophy of History*, 27
Hegemony, 6, 51, 53, 210n104; and Reclus, 49; "hegemonist," 132, 141, 151, 155; definition, 201n8
Heidegger, Martin, 52f, 88f, 99, 211n115
Heller, Tamar, 73f, 215
Herbertson, A. J., 203n13, 206n47
Herder, Johann Gottfried: and Bildung, 19, 26f, 43, 47f, 208; and culture-hypothesis, 26f, 205n33, 223n4; *Ideen zur Philosophie der Geschichte der Menschheit*, 26f, 37, 41f
Herrschaft. *See under* Nietzsche
Hitchcock, Alfred, 3, 6, 11f, 77, 160–70 *passim*, 173f, 182–98 *passim*, 232; MacGuffin, 12, 186; motif of sabotage in, 160, 174, 190, 195, 197, 232; transatlantic crossover, 160f, 190f, 196, 198. Films: *Jamaica Inn*, 191; *North by Northwest*, 190, 232; *Rebecca*, 191; *The Thirty-Nine Steps*, 190, 232
—*Sabotage* 6, 160, 170, 183–98 *passim*; dictionary definition in title sequence, 163–67 *passim*; acts of sabotage in, 163–67 *passim*, 185f, 188; Bijou cinema house, 165, 184–92 *passim*, 197,

231n58; psychologized trauma of Mrs. Verloc, 188; Disney cartoon, 189–93 *passim*, 196; retitled *The Woman Alone*, 190
—*Saboteur*, 160, 194–98; acts of sabotage in, 162, 165, 194f; chase plot, 162, 194f, ambiguity of saboteur motif in, 195; American landscape in, 162, 173, 190f, 194ff; logic of betrayal and loyalty, 173, 190f, 195f; advertising in, 191, 196; filmmaking and sabotage, 194; Hitchcockian blot, 195f; "good looks," 196f
—*Young and Innocent*, 191–98 *passim*; Tey's *A Shilling for Candles* as basis for screenplay, 191ff, 197; innocent motif, 192; cinematic labor process, 192f, 197f; blackface, 193–96 *passim*; Hitchcockian blot, 193, 197
Hitchcockian blot, 11, 77, 193–97 *passim*. See also Anamorphosis; Blot; Cinema; Victorian blot
Hobsbawm, Eric J., 5, 141, 149, 153
Holbein, Hans, (*The Ambassadors*), 74, 77
Hölderlin, Friedrich, 93
Hollywood, 7, 13, 161, 189f, 198; star system, 189. See also Cinema
Homolka, Oskar, 163, 167, 170
Hook, Theodore Edward, 81f
Horace, 37f
Horkheimer, Max, 196, 227f
Horton, Susan, 108, 111, 221n84
How We Shall Bring About the Revolution (Pataud and Pouget), 175
Hudson, W. H., 158f
Humanism, 5, 7, 40, 129
Human sciences, 3, 7, 20, 95, 180
Humboldt, Alexander, 24, 36
Humboldt, Wilhelm von, and Bildung, 4, 19, 96, 99, 204n27; *The Limits of the State*, 47; quoted in *Jude the Obscure*, 96f, 99
Husserl, Edmund, 177

Huxley, Thomas Henry, 89
Hysteria, 62, 67, 71–74, 118, 195, 197

Iconography: of geopolitics, 20; of military victory, 70f, 215n45; of subjectivity, 71, 215n45
Ideen zur Philosophie der Geschichte der Menschheit (Herder), 26f, 37, 41f
Image consécutive. *See* Afterimage
Imperialism: and geography, 2, 18, 22, 25, 27, 43–51 *passim*; British, 9, 12, 43f, 46, 67–71, 81–85; critique of, 9, 43f, 142–45, 151, 153; "new imperialism," 25, 27, 143; complicity with, 67–71; and aesthetics, 119–23. *See also* Colonialism; British Empire
Impressionism, 129, 134, 152, 156f. *See also* Sketch-artistry *under* Cunninghame Graham
Independent Labour Party, 140, 170
India, 35, 67–71, 173, 216; relation to Britain, 59f, 79–85, 144, 213–16 *passim*, 221n95. *See also* Indian Mutiny
Indian Mutiny (1857–8), 58, 67ff, 206n47, 213n26, 215f
Indians (Native Americans), 135, 149f, 158
Industrialization, 57, 160, 180f. *See also* Industry
Industrial Workers of the World (I.W.W. or Wobblies), 164–70 *passim*; and immigrant politics, 170
Industry, 5, nexus of industrial relations, 50, 168, 176, 181–89; film industry, 161, 164, 188–91, 198; industrial conflict, 149, 163–73, 177f, 181f; and war, 163, 165, 172f, 198; and culture, 167, 184–98 *passim*; and afterimage, 180–84, 187–90, 196f; cinematic labor process, 185–93 *passim*. *See also* Cinema; Culture; Consumption; Industrialization; Production; Working class
Institut für Geopolitik, 51
Ireland, 12, 20, 59, 135
Irish Home Rule movement, 135

Iron, Ralph. *See* Schreiner, Olive
Irony, 173ff, 178f
Islam, 84, 134
Italy, 78, 172

Jacobinism, 59, 84, 212n6
Jacobsen, Dan, 113
Jamaica, 58, 67
Jameson, Fredric, 13, 18, 34, 153, 158, 160f; *The Geopolitical Aesthetic*, 13, 18, 160f; *The Political Unconscious*, 13, 34, 153, 161; *Postmodernism*, 13
Jenkins, Edward (*Blot on the Queen's Head*), 57, 59
Jesuit missions, 134
John Company, 65f, 83. *See also* East India Company
Joke-work, 178–81 *passim*, 194
Journalism, 134, 137, 141, 144; "new journalism," 134. *See also* Media; News telling; Newspapers
Joyce, James, 17ff, 28; *A Portrait of the Artist*, 17f, 177; Stephen's "green wothe," 17, 19f, 29, 51, 177
Jude the Obscure (Hardy), 96–99, 116
Justice, 170

Kahane, Claire, 91, 118
Kant, Immanuel, 26f, 43, 47f; "Perpetual Peace," 47
Kantorowicz, Ernst, 83
Kaufmann, Walter, 109
Keltie, J. Scott, 23, 25
Kent, Philip, 108
Kingship. *See* sovereignty
Kipling, Rudyard, 12, 143f, 159
Kittler, Friedrich, 7, 95, 104, 122f, 231n58
Kjellén, Rudolf, 2, 36, 45; on coining term geopolitics, 36; definition of geopolitics, 45; *Grundriss zu einem System der Politik*, 36
Koh-i-noor, 79, 84, 216n60
Krauss, Rosalind, 34
Kropotkin, 205, 218

Kultur: and strategy, 23f, 38, 42f, 50; formulations in Ratzel, 40ff; relation to Bildung, 43, 47f. *See also*, Bildung; Civilization; Culture
Kulturgeographie. *See* Anthropogeography
Kulturkampf (culture war), 6
Kulturwissenschaften (cultural sciences), 22f
Kupka, Frantisek, 8–11, 44, 209n79; *Amorpha, Fugue in Two Colours*, 8–11 *passim*; *Amorpha, Warm Chromatics*, 8; *Disks of Newton*, 8; illustrations for Reclus, 9f, 44, cover, part openers

Label (syndicalist strategy), 168, 228n20
Labor. *See* Industry
Labor movement (Britain), 130, 149; and leadership, 136–9 *passim*; and sabotage, 170
Labour Elector, The, 127, 141
Lacan, Jacques, 11, on anamorphosis, 74f
Laclau, Ernesto, 6, 139ff, 171f, 210n104
Lacoste, Yves, 48
Larousse (dictionary), 169
Laughter. *See* Bergson; Joke-work
Lavery, John, 130ff, 135, 141, 151, 223; full-length portrait of Cunninghame Graham, 130f, 143, 156, 158; portrait with horse Pampa, 130, 133, 154–58 *passim*
Lebensraum (living space), 3, 22, 42, 162
Lefort, Claude, 59
Lenin, V. I., 48, 229n38
Lewes, G. H., 107
Life of Nietzsche (F94rster-Nietzsche), 94
Limits of the State, The (Humboldt), 47
Loder, John, 167, 185
Lombrose, Cesare, 180
London Dockers' Strike (1889), 136f, 170
Looking Backward (Bellamy), 128, 149
Loot, 60, 68ff, 80–85, 152, 214. *See also* Moonstone; Wilkie, *Sir David Baird Discovering the Body of the Sultan*
Lothe, Jakob, 180

Loyalty: territorial, 161, 172f; in Conrad, 179; in Hitchcock, 190f, 195f. *See also* Betrayal
Lukacs, Georg, 111
Luther, Martin, 103, 105, 109
Lutheran (Nietzsche's and Schreiner's fathers), 109
Luxemburg, Rosa, 172
Lyotard, Jean-François, 7, 25, 203n9, 204n27

McClintock, Anne, 106f
MacGuffin (Hitchock), 12, 186
Mackinder, Sir Halford J., 3, 17–37 *passim*, 45–50 *passim*, 53, 203–8 *passim*, 211; and "new geography," 3, 19–22 *passim*, 27f; and visualisation, 7, 28f, 39; use of maps, 17, 20, 29–35 *passim*; Heartland thesis, 20; on the position of Britain, 29–33, 43–46 *passim*, 53; Visual Instruction Committee, 33, 206n47; Mackindergarten, 206n38; and Ratzel, 37–40; and Reclus, 43ff, 205n42; and Reich, 35f, 43. *Works: Britain and the British Seas*, 12, 29–36, 45f, 50, 205; *Democratic Ideals and Reality*, 20, 23; "The Geographical Pivot of History," 20f, 35; *Lands Beyond the Channel*, 17; "Natural Seats of Power" (map), 20f; "On the Scope and Methods of Geography," 20; *Our Own Islands*, 35
Madrid, Bomb of (1907 assassination attempt), 160, 167f, 181
Mandel, Siegfried, 219n30
Mann, Tom, 136, 139
Mansfield Park (Austen), 66
Maps, 17, 20, 29–38 *passim*
Martin, Biddy, 93f, 219
Marx, Karl, 27, 128, 133, 159, 221n95; and culture-hypothesis, 48, 223n4; on the State, 48, 209n93; Conrad parody of, 175. *Works: Capital*, 27, 63, 79; *Communist Manifesto*, 162, 202n9
Marxism, 6, 48, 127ff, 140f, 153, 175, 202n9,

210n99; Second International, 6, 140f, 153, 175; meaning of utopia for, 127ff. *See also* Communism; *Communist Manifesto*
Mass culture. *See* Cinema; Culture; Culture Industry; Media
Mass political movements, 6, 172, 189. *See also* Anarcho-syndicalism; Industry; Labor movement; Working class
Mass Strike, The Political Party, and The Trade Unions, The (Luxemburg), 172
Maugham, Somerset, 201f
"Meaning of Sabotage, The" (Orwell), 162ff, 173
Media, 7f; aesthetic mixing of, 71, 80, 120, 122, 149, 206n47, 215n45, 231n58; news, 149; and propaganda, 161, 183f, 226n64; cinematographic coordination of, 183f, 189, 192f, 196ff; and mass movements, 189. *See also* Aesthetics; Cinema; Culture; Culture Industry; Industry; Journalism; Newspapers
Mediterranean, 27–33 *passim*
Mehta, Jaya, 67–71 *passim*, 212n10
Meller, Helen, 211n114
Melodrama, 62, 66, 68
Memoirs of a Picture (William Collins), 80, 217n65
Memory-image, 179f, 188, 230n45. *See also* Afterimage
Men and Women's Club, 107
Metonymy of stain, 72, 75, 78. *See also* Blot
Metropolitan Radical Federation, 135
Middle class, 4ff, 58, 82–85, 100f, 212; and Bildung, 6, 100f; and world history, 60, 82f; blurred perspective of, 63–66 *passim*, 77; mirage of self-respectability, 73–78 *passim*; female education, 65, 100f; and entitlement, 71, 82–85. *See also* Blot; Culture; Europe; Perspective; Respectability; Victorian blot
Mill, J. S., 4f, 97, 99, 116; *On Liberty*, 99; *Political Economy*, 116
Miller, D. A., 68f, 73

Missionary, 109f, 115f; Jesuit, 134. *See also* Christianity; Colonialism
Mitchell, Timothy, 52f, 203n5, 210f, 222n108
Mitchell, W. J. T., 80
Modern Times (Chaplin), 231f
Modernism, 8, 11, 17ff, 33f, 52, 152; "high" and "low," 129f, 134, 141, 150, 223n12; and anarchism, 173f, 178–81. *See also* Ellipsis; Impressionism; Irony; Montage; Narrative form
Montage, 77, 163, 167, 183–88 *passim*
Morality, 57; and Collins, 62, 64; for Nietzsche, 94, 98f, 102–6 *passim*, 123; Christian, 148; of sabotage, 165
Morant Bay Rising (1865), 58, 67
More, Thomas, 128
Morocco, 127, 134, 141
Morris, William, 104, 128f, 135–37, 149, 153, 226n62; *News from Nowhere*, 128, 135, 137, 149
Moslem. *See* Islam
Mouffe, Chantal, 6, 139ff, 171f, 210n104
Mulvey, Laura, 191

Nadel, Alan, 13
Nancy, Jean-Luc, 86f
Narrative form, 7, 24–27; across media, 71, 77, 80–82, 183–98 *passim*, 217n69; in Schreiner and Nietzsche, 91ff, 102–5, 109, 111–19; of utopian narrative, 128, 134, 149f, 153f, 174f; and *The Secret Agent*, 173–78 *passim*, 183; and cinematography, 183–98 *passim*. *See also* Cinema; Bildungsroman; Ekphrasis; Montage; Novel form; Sketch-artistry
National Institute of Geography, 211n114
Nationality, 12f, 142, 155. *See also* Ethnic identity; Nationalism; Race
Nationalism, 4f, 43, 116; "official nationalism," 4f, 23, 204n19
National security, 6, 160
National Socialism (Nazism), 5, 18f, 50f, 87, 163; and Nietzsche, 5, 87

Nation-state, 4, centrality for geopolitics, 45–48; Hegel and Marx on, 48, 209; and cultural heritage, 57, 85; and hegemony, 151, 155; industrialized, 160, 183; and propaganda, 184
Natural sciences, 20–4 *passim*
"Nature" (Emerson), 108
"New geography," 3, 19, 22, 27
News from Nowhere (Morris), 128, 135–37, 149; role of Bloody Sunday in, 135f; role of newspapers in, 137
Newspapers, 149, 151, 154, 161, 226n62. *See also* Journalism; Media
News telling, 134, 149, 151, 154
New Woman, 89, 94–101 *passim*
New World, 78f, 158. *See also* America
Nietzsche, Friedrich, 4f, 8, 86–114 *passim*, 117–23, 218ff; diagnosis of nihilism, 5, 86ff, 92, 95, 99, 102, 105f, 120f, 123; and Nazis, 5, 87f; rhetoric of world power and war, 87, 113, 120–23; and mental breakdown, 88, 92f, 101, 105, 219; and "sister" figures, 90, 92, 97–101 *passim*, 123; Zarathustra-persona, 91ff, 96, 102, 108f, 120; on women, 95–99 *passim*, 220n49; critique of Bildung, 96, 122; and culture, 100, 220n53, and Emerson, 109. *Works: Beyond Good and Evil*, 95, 104; *The Birth of Tragedy*, 120, 122; *The Case of Wagner*, 120ff; *Ecce Homo*, 87, 101f, 109; *The Gay Science*, 92f, 96–102 *passim*, 107, 109, 122; *Nietzsche contra Wagner*, 120; *On the Genealogy of Morals*, 87, 90, 106, 123
—*Thus Spoke Zarathustra*, 91ff, 101–10 *passim*, 118ff, 123; aesthetic style of, 91, 93, 102–5; Orientalism of, 102–5; problem of European perspective, 105f. *See also* Fürster-Nietzsche; Salomé; Zoroaster
Nihilism, 3ff, and culture, 4f, 90, 99ff, 115; "European nihilism" (Nietzsche), 86ff, 92, 100, 102, 105f, 120ff, 218n4; changing meaning of, 86–90; Heidegger on, 88f; Russian nihilism, 89, 94, 97,

260   INDEX

142, 218n13; and death of God, 91f, 109; and transcendentalism, 109. *See also* Nietzsche; Schreiner; Victoria

Novel form, 6f; and reading-effects, 11, 74f, 78, 123; sensational, 11, 59f, 71, 77, 83; Bildungsroman, 19, 64, 91, 93, 115, 117, 180, 212n19; and Collins, 59f, 64, 66, 74; detective fiction, 59, 63, 67, 69, 79, 197; country-house novel, 63–66 *passim*, 74, 79; formal realism, 65, 213n24; and gender, 74, 117f; and Schreiner, 86, 97, 111–20, 123; historical novel, 111. *See also* Narrative form; Perspective; Plot; Victorian novel; *and under individual novels*

O Tuathail, Gearóid: critical geopolitics, 2, 7; Cartesian perspectivalism, 7, 33; classical geopolitics, 18; on Mackinder, 28, 33; on U.S. reaction to German Geopolitik, 51, 161; on hyphenated form of term "geo-politics," 207

O'Brien, William, 135

Ocularcentric, 7, 51

OEcumene (habitable world), 37–40

On Liberty (Mill), 99

"On the Nature and Use of Sabotage" (Veblen), 164ff

Opera, 120ff, 222n108

Orientalism, 84, 103ff, 120, 214; late-Victorian Orientalism, 103ff, 120

Orwell, George, 143, 162–70 *passim*, 173

Over-Seas Library, 142–46, 156, 224; Garnett's prospectus, 142–45 *passim*, 156, 224; *The Ipané* as first in series, 142, 224n36

Painting, 8–11, 60, 67–74 *passim*, 80, 130–33, 214–17 *passim*; abstract, 8f; realist, 9, 39f; historical, 70, 214n43; genre, 70f; decorative, 72; portrait, 60, 67–74 *passim*, 80, 130–33, 214f. *See also* Anamorphosis; Media; Narrative form; Perspective

Pall Mall Gazette, 138

Pampa (Cunninghame Graham's horse), 130, 133, 158

Pampas, 130, 150, 157f; signifying "space" in Quichua, 158

Parable, 90f, 102, 104

Paraguay, 159

"Paris, Capital of the Nineteenth Century" (Benjamin), 52

Parliament (British), 129, 136–40 *passim*; labor representation in, 136

Pataud, Emile, 175

People's Press, The, 171

Perception-image, 179, 188, 230n45

"Perpetual Peace: A Philosophical Sketch" (Kant), 47

Persian, 92, 102–5

Perspective: optical, 7–11, 39f, 74, 77, 188f, 194ff; Victorian middle-class, 11, 52, 63–67 *passim*, 65, 71, 83; colonial and subaltern, 65f, 77, 83f, 153, 181f, 213n25; Renaissance, 74, 77; Nietzsche and the problem of European perspective, 102–6, 119–23; in Schreiner's narrative, 111–19; Cunninghame Graham's utopian perspective, 135f, 147, 159; obliterated perspective in Conrad, 177–87; phantasmatic ethnic perspective in Hitchcock, 189–98. *See also* Anamorphosis; Blot; Painting; Victorian blot

Phenomenology, 177; and culture-hypothesis, 11, 177. *See also* Subjectivity

Phenomenology of Spirit, The (Hegel), 177, 209n92

Philosophy of History, The (Hegel), 27

Phonograph, 7, 226n64

Photography, 32ff, 52, 93, 142, 183, 226n64

Photomontage, 8, 183

Pilbeam, Nova, 197

Plot: Collins family plot and blot, 11, 57, 60, 66, 69, 75; MacGuffin, 12, 186f; of thrillers, 59, 163; of detective fiction, 59; mid-Victorian turn in, 62; and trope of West Indian estate, 66; marriage plot, 97, 118f; spy plots, 161f;

chase plot, 162, 195: Hitchcock family plot, 187
Police: policing in Collins, 68f, 73; in "Bloody Sunday," 136f, 167; and Conrad, 178, 185ff
Political Economy (Mill), 116
Poovey, Mary, 215n49
Poradowska, Marguerite, 178
Portrait of the Artist as a Young Man, A (Joyce), 17ff, 177; Stephen's "green wothe," 17, 19, 177
Positivism, 88ff, 95f, 99, 109; and nihilism, 88, 90, 99, 109; Nietzsche's critique of, 90, 96; and relation between nihilism and culture, 99
Pouget, Emile, 168–71, 175, 228f; *Le Syndicat*, 168; *Le Sabotage*, 168ff, 228f; and Pataud, *How We Shall Bring About the Revolution*, 175
Power: Nietzsche's rhetoric of, 87, 113, 120; pathology of, 120–3; territorial state, 155; power-complex and culture-complex, 122, 201. *See also* Colonialism, Hegemony, Imperialism, Sovereignty
Production, 13, 50, 187f; and women, 189; split scene of production and consumption, 190, 194. *See also* Consumption; Industry
Proletariat. *See* Working class
Propaganda, 50, 150, 161, 169, 173–77, 182ff, 226n64; by the deed, 174; Conrad's dialogization of, 173f; mode of address turned inside out, 175
Prophet-voice, 92, 101–4, 111, 120f
Proust, Marcel, 17, 51, 181; *A la recherche du temps perdu*, 181
Psychiatry, 180
Psychoanalysis, 11, 74, 77
Ptolemy, 29, 31

Quichua, 158

Race, 12f, 40, 66, 170, 172, 222n97; white racial identity, 13, 112, 155, 189, 193f, 197; and maps, 34f; racist stereotyping, 145, 197. *See also* Ethnic identity; Nationality
Radio, 162ff, 173, 192f
Ramaswami, N. S., 214n39
Ratzel, Friedrich, 3, 17–23 *passim*, 28, 36–48 *passim*, 53, 208n67; and Lebensraum, 3, 22, 42; coinage of anthropogeography, 22; and biogeography, 22, 45; and OEcumene, 37–40; world chart, 38ff; and anthropology, 38–43, 208n67; and the State, 45f. *Works*: "Geographische Bild der Menschheit, Das" [The Geographical Picture/Image of Humankind], 42f; *Der Lebensraum*, 22, 42; *Politische Geographie*, 22, 37, 42; *Völkerkunde*, 41f
—*Anthropogeographie*, 21f; concept of the OEcumene, 37–40; and anthropology, 38, 40f; world chart, 38–40; culture-concept in, 40f, and image of the State, 45
Reading-effects. *See under* Novel form
Reclus, Elisée, 3, 17, 19, 160; and nineteenth-century geography, 24–28 *passim*, 36, 204f; Kupka's illustrations for, 9ff, part openers, cover; "social geography," 25, 47f; liberty in, 25, 204n27; and Mackinder, 43ff, 205n35; and State, 45–48; and Eurocentrism, 49f; rejection by French academy and Marxism, 49, 210n98; projected Great Globe, 51ff, 210f. *Works*: "The Hegemony of Europe," 49f; *L'Homme et la Terre*, 9f, 25, 43f, 47f; *La Nouvelle Géographie Universelle* [*The Universal Geography*], 24f, 49; *La Terre*, 25. *See also* Anarchism; Geography
Rée, Paul, 93f, 107
Reed, John R., 68f, 85
Réflexions sur la violence [*Reflections on Violence*] (Sorel), 171, 181
Reform, 58f, 136, 212n6
Reform Bill (1867), 58f
Reich, Emil, 35–38 *passim*, 43, 207; hy-

phenated coinage of "geo-political," 35f, 43, 207; *Foundations of Modern Europe*, 36; *Handbook of Geography*, 36

Respectability: and middle-class values, 4, 60, 64, 216; and military loot, 69, 83; and scandal, 73–77 *passim*, 83; and marriage, 96ff. *See also* Middle class

Revolution, 84, 136, 162, 172–75, 181, 216n58; and wartime sabotage, 162; 1905 and 1917 Russian revolutions: and colonial discourses, 182. *See also* Jacobinism

Richards, Thomas, 13, 202

Ritter, Carl, 24, 36, 45f; *Erdkunde*, 24; image of the State, 45f

Robinson Crusoe (Defoe), 78

Ross, Kristin, 210n98

Rothenstein, Will, 223n8

Rothman, William, 232n72

Rowell, Margit, 8

Roy, Ashish, 69, 85

Royal Academy Exhibition of 1839, 70, 81, 217n69

Royal Geographical Society, 20, 35, 211n114

Royal Titles Act (1876), 59

Ruskin, John, 104

Russell, Bertrand, 164–67 *passim*; "The Syndicalist Revolt," 164

Russia, 172. *See also under* Nihilism

Sabotage, 3, 6, 160–98 *passim*, 228f; motif in Hitchcock, 160, 174, 190, 195, 197, 232; geopolitical meaning of, 162, 173, 186; wartime appropriation of, 162, 172f, 198; definition and polemic over, 162–70 *passim*, 187, 198, 227n9; syndicalist meaning of, 164–69 *passim*, 186, 190, 198; polemicized foreignness of, 170, 229n30; and ca' canny, 170, 229n30; and General Strike, 172, 181; territorial riddle of, 173; in Conrad's *The Secret Agent*, 176f; and utopia, 227f

Sabotage, Le (Pouget), 168ff, 228f

"Sabotage: The Conscious Withdrawal of Workers' Industrial Efficiency" (Flynn), 169

Saboter, 168

Saboteur, 162, 167, 172f, 190, 194

Sabots, 164f, 168, 228n22

Said, Edward, 4, 57ff, 65f, 120f, 203n5, 222n108; *Culture and Imperialism*, 57f, 66, 120f, 203n5; *Orientalism*, 120

Salomé, Lou Andreas, 92–104 *passim*; on Zarathustra, 92f, 103f, 118, 123, 220; enmity with F94rster-Nietzsche, 93f, 219; 1894 study of Nietzsche, 94, 101

Saturday Review, The, 140

Scandal, 60, 62; of looting, 68, 70; of narrative form, 73f; middle-class self as an effect of, 77; "European scandal" of Nietzsche-Rée-Salomé affair, 93

Schiller, Friedrich, 19, 76

Schreiner, Olive, 4f, 86–92 *passim*, 97, 101, 106–23, 145, 222; as freethinker, 88f; and colonialism, 90, 106–23 *passim*; narrative voice, 92, 109, 111, 116–19; and pseudonym Ralph Iron, 108; on reading *First Principles*, 222n98. Works: *From Man to Man*, 117; *The Story of an African Farm*, 5, 86, 91, 97, 106–23, 221f; *Woman and Labour*, 117

Scorched earth policy, 162

Scotland, 12f, 129, 133f, 150f, 155, 170f, 190

Scott, Ann, 106, 108

Scottish Labour Pary (S.L.P.), 130, 135, 139f

Screenplay, 167, 191f, 196f, 201n8

Second International Working-Men's Association, 141

Self-culture, 76f

Self-Help (Smiles), 76f

Self-incrimination, 73ff, 78, 83

Sensational novels, 11f, 59f, 62. *See also* Novel form

Seringapatam, storming of (1799), 60, 68–81; controversy over looting, 214n39

Sexuality, 62, 73–77 *passim*, 98; sex appeal of Cunninghame Graham photograph, 142; sexual betrayal, 190
Sharpe, Jenny, 216n60
Shaw, George Bernard, 139, 223n8; *Arms and the Man*, 139
Shaw-Sparrow, Walter, 132
Shilling for Candles, A (Tey), 191ff, 197
Showalter, Elaine, 97, 101, 117
Sidney, Sylvia, 167, 188f
Sir David Baird Discovering the Body of the Sultan Tippoo Sahib (Wilkie), 60f, 67–71, 80–84, 214f
Sketch-artistry. *See under* Cunninghame Graham
Smiles, Samuel, 76f, 216n57; *Self-Help*, 76f
Smith, Woodruff, 22, 204n16
Social-Democrat, The, 145
Social-Democratic Federation, 135, 170
Socialism, 4f, 18, 51, 127, 129, 134f, 138f, 150, 159, 171f, 181; utopian, 5, 127; and utopias, 5, 133, 135; Sorelian myth of, 171; German, 172. *See also* Labor movement, Working class
Sorel, Georges, 171f, 181; *Réflexions sur la violence* [*Reflections on Violence*], 171, 181
South Africa, 5, 35, 112ff, 117
South America, 130, 134f, 150–59; Pampas, 130, 135
Sovereignty, 59, 82–85, 209n93, 212n6. *See also* Victoria; Victorian blot
Spanish, 134, 152, 159
Spanish-American war (1898), 156–59
Spencer, Herbert, 88ff, 100, 218n13, 222n98; *First Principles*, 88, 90, 100, 107, 116, 222n98
Sphinx, 149, 169
Spivak, Gayatri, 117, 119
State. *See* Nation-state
Stationery, 184, 231n58
Stepniak, Madame (wife of Sergei Stepniak/Kravchinsky), 142
Strang, William, 223n8

Striker, heroic figure of, 162, 172, 229n38, 232n63
Strike (Eisenstein), 172
Strikes, 135f, 140, 149, 168, 228n20, 229; London Dockers' Strike (1889), 136f, 170; General Strike, 171f, 181
Subaltern, 66, 77, 116
Subjectivity: disciplinary subjectivity, 11, 73; and ego-ideal, 11, 77; and culture-hypothesis, 11, 177; and hysteria, 62, 72, 74; iconography of, 71, 215n45; mirage of respectable middle-class self, 73–78 *passim*; phantom colonial subject, 112–19, 123; and cinema, 193, 196
Suleri, Sara, 84, 217n72
Surveillance: and Victorian novel, 62, 68f, 73; film apparatus, 194. *See also* Police
Symbolic capital. *See* Cultural capital
Syndicalism, 6, 162–72 *passim*, 189, 228; Russell on, 164f; syndicalist meaning of sabotage, 164–69 *passim*, 186, 190, 198. *See also* Anarcho-syndicalism; Criminal syndicalist statutes
Syndicalist, The, 170
"Syndicalist Revolt, The" (Russell), 164f
Syndicat, Le (Pouget), 168

Taussig, Michael, 224f
Television, 190
Tennyson, Alfred, Lord, 108
Tey, Josephine (Elizabeth MacKintosh), 191ff, 197; *A Shilling for Candles*, 191ff, 197
Thackeray, William, 70
Theory of the Leisure Class, The (Veblen), 227
Third World, 79, 153, 158
Thompson, E. P., 136, 212n17, 213n25, 226n62
Thrillers, 59, 161ff
Time Machine, The (Wells), 128, 149f, 153f
Tipu Sultan, 60f, 68–71, 81–84, 214, 217
Tobacco. *See* Drugs
Tolstoy, Leo, 89, 97

Tracking shot, 193. *See also* Hitchcockian blot
Trafalgar Square, 135f, 138, 148, 165, 185
Transcendentalism, 109, 115; and nihilism, 109
Transvaal, 114, 117
Truffaut, François, 12, 186, 190f
Tsuzuki, Chushuchi, 135ff
Turgenev, Ivan, 88, 97
Tylor, E. B., 208
Typewriter, 7

Unions, 135f, 140; "new unionism," 140. *See also* Syndicalism
United States. *See* America
Unwin, T. Fisher, 142, 146
Utopia, 3f, 52f; and nineteenth-century socialism, 4, 127ff, 175, 211, 216n58; and Marxism, 127ff, 133, 159; anti-geopolitics, 151; and America, 127f, 155, 190, 223n4; and cinema, 190f, 196f; and narrative, 128, 134, 149f, 153f, 174f; and sabotage, 227f. *See also* Cunninghame Graham, Utopian narratives
Utopia (More), 128
Utopian narratives, 128, 134, 149f, 153f, 174f. *See also* Cunninghame Graham; Bellamy; Morris; Pouget and Pataud; Wells

Value, 58, 63, 80–85; middle-class Victorian, 58, 63; surplus-value, 63. *See also* Cultural capital
Veblen, Thorstein, 164–67; "On the Nature and Uses of Sabotage," 164; *The Theory of the Leisure Class*, 227; Adorno on, 166, 227f
Verdi, Giuseppe (*Aida*), 120f, 22n108
Victoria, Queen, 59f, 68, 83, 113, 143, 206; Royal Titles Act (1876), 59; Proclamation as Empress (1877), 83f; Golden Jubilee Celebrations (1897), 143
Victorian blot: as problem of narrative and political form, 11f, 59f, 85; as reading-effect, 11f, 77, 123; as convergence of culture-concepts, 57ff, 79, 85, 100; as incoherence of Victorian period, 85. *See also* Blot; Collins; Culture; Hitchcockian blot; Perspective
Victorian novel, 7; and Collins, 59f, 64, 66, 74; and Schreiner, 86, 97, 111f, 117ff. *See also* Novel form
Visual image, 7ff, 33, 39, 71f, 191, 195; pre-Raphaelite, 72; voyeurism, 73; gendered rivalry with literary text, 191; reversibility in narrative, 195. *See also* Aesthetics; Media; Visualisation; Painting; Perspective
Visual Instruction Committee of the Colonial Office, 33, 206n47
Visualisation, 7, 28f, 39, 52, 205n37
Viswanathan, Gauri, 4, 65, 203n9

Wagner, Richard, 120ff
Wallace, Alfred Russel, 180
War machine, 163, 165, 173
Watt, Ian, 65, 179f, 231n46; formal realism, 65, 213n24; delayed decoding, 179f
Watts, Cedric, 136–39 *passim*, 145, 147, 152, 156f, 180
Webbs, Sidney and Beatrice, 229n30
Wellington, Duke of, 113
Wells, H. G., 17, 128f, 134, 149f, 153f, 181, 226n64; *The Time Machine*, 128, 149f, 153f; *When the Sleeper Wakes*, 150, 226n64
West, the, 3, 49, 79, 89
West End Riots (1886), 135
When the Sleeper Wakes (Wells), 150, 226n64
White Atlantic, 190, 194
White man's burden (Kipling), 143, 159
White racial identity. *See* Race
Wilhelm Meisters Lehrjahre (Goethe), 19, 223n4
Wilkie, Sir David, *Sir David Baird Discovering the Body of the Sultan Tippoo Sahib*: as source for *The Moonstone*,

60, 68, 214n31; problem of historical perspective, 67–71; depiction of looted objects, 80–84, 214f; Wilkie's fascination for Tipu's treasures, 217n66

Williams, Raymond: on culture, 4, 20, 57ff, 208; *Culture and Society*, 57f, 63; on country house novel, 63f, 74; *The Country and the City*, 63, 212n17

Wobblies. *See* Industrial Workers of the World

Wollaeger, Mark, 183, 232

Women, and virtue, 62; and hysteria, 62, 67, 71–74, 118, 195, 197; and New Woman, 89, 94–101 *passim*; and feminism, 89, 94, 97, 116f; and education, 94f, 98, 100f, 117f; Nietzsche on, 95–99 *passim*, 220n49; and culture, 117f; and narrative authority, 117ff, 191; as workers and consumers, 189; position of in Hitchcock, 190, 196.

Workers, 127, 173. *See also* Industry; Working class

Working class: consciousness, 5f, 136f, 148, 172, 177, 216n58; and political leadership, 6, 136–41, 151, 172; exclusion of working-class perspectives, 63, 66, 77, 212n17, 216; unity of, 136f, 140f, 148f, 153; origins of sabotage, 164–69 *passim*, 186, 190, 198; and ethnic/racial identity, 170, 172

World-as-exhibition, 52f, 222n108

World Exhibition of 1900 (Paris), 51ff, 211

World history, 2ff, 35, 62f, 69, 83f, 103, 111; and Europe, 2ff, 24ff, 100, 113ff, 119–23 *passim*, 205; and middle-class consciousness, 60, 71. *See also* Cosmopolitanism; Culture-hypothesis

World system, 13f, 18, 79; world-system theories, 13f, 202, 210n95

World war, 6; Second World War, 12, 173; First World War, 163, 166, 172; Nietzsche's rhetoric of, 87, 113, 120f; and class warfare, 162, 172, 198; geopolitical imperative of, 172

Young, Robert J. C., 58, 208n69

Zhang Yimou, 232n73

Zimmern, Helen, 103f; *The Epic of Kings*, 103f; sister-figure and translator of Nietzsche, 104

Žižek, Slavoj, 11, 59, 77; Hitchcockian blot, 11, 193, 195

Zoroaster, 92, 103f

The authorized representative in the EU for product safety and compliance is:
Mare Nostrum Group
B.V Doelen 72
4831 GR Breda
The Netherlands

www.ingramcontent.com/pod-product-compliance
Lightning Source LLC
Chambersburg PA
CBHW021805220426
43662CB00006B/184